SELECTIVE SERVICE: CONFLICT AND COMPROMISE

. . .I do not recommend that we start changing this law. You can do most anything under this law which is more than you can say for a great many laws that are on the books.

General Lewis B. Hershey

Selective Service: Conflict and Compromise

HARRY A. MARMION

JOHN WILEY & SONS, INC.
New York • London • Sydney • Toronto

Library of Congress Catalog Card Number:68-8107 SBN 471 57235 7
Printed in the United States of America

To My Mother and Father

PREFACE

In May of 1966 I joined the American Council on Education to work with its Commission on Federal Relations. Soon after I started Jack Morse, Director of the Commission, asked me to "keep an eye on the draft question." His specific request was that I concern myself particularly with the law as it pertained to students, colleges, and education in general. The first rumbles of the draft controversy were just beginning to be heard. More and more people, including college students and faculty, were becoming restive over the interference in the educational process of the Federal government in the guise of the Selective Service System. Behind this interference was the nation's increased commitment in Vietnam, a conflict unpopular with a great many people. Students were more militant, more involved, and more concerned with the war's consequences to them personally, as well as with the moral position of the nation as it became more and more bogged down in a land war in Asia.

During the next several months I attended meetings in Washington and Chicago to plan national conferences on the draft. As a result of these meetings, the American Veterans Committee were hosts at a conference in Washington on November 11-12, 1966; shortly thereafter, from December 4 to 7, the Chicago Conference—sponsored by the University of Chicago and financed by a Ford Foundation grant—was held. As a participant at both conferences I can attest to their value to me and, aside from that, to the important permanent additions to the literature that both produced.

Over approximately one year of intensive debate on the draft I attended the various Congressional hearings on the subject. In June 1966 the Committee on Armed Services of the House of Representatives held inconclusive hearings on the administration and operation of the Selective Service System. The hearings were closed, in that only members of the legislative and executive branches of the government testified. Public witnesses were not heard. The long-awaited Pentagon study of the draft, ordered by President Johnson in 1964, was also presented at the House hearings, but it proved to be nothing but a résumé of the report. There were many angry comments regarding the brevity and quality of this document, and from that time on various Department of Defense officials were constantly plagued by inquiries about the true nature of the still secret "complete study."

By the early spring of 1967 almost everyone outside the Congress had had an opportunity to speak in an attempt to influence legislative change. Slowly the scene shifted to the national legislature for the serious business of renewing the law. The Congress had available two reports of national commissions appointed to study the issues. The first—a lengthy, literate, persuasive document that advocated significant changes in the draft system—was the work of a Presidential panel headed by Burke Marshall. Not to be outdone by the executive branch, the legislative branch produced its own study of the draft. L. Mendel Rivers, powerful chairman of the Committee on Armed Services of the House of Representatives, named a national panel headed by Mark Clark, a retired General and President Emeritus of The Citadel. The Clark report called for a continuation of the status quo in the operation and administration of the draft.

The first hearings in 1967 were conducted by the Senate Subcommittee on Employment Manpower and Poverty, chaired by Senator Edward Kennedy. At these wide open hearings both government and nongovernment experts on various aspects of the issues were called to testify, but, of course, legislative authority rested with the Armed Services Committees. The main effect of the Kennedy hearings was to attract national publicity. Only the later testimony of Senator Kennedy in which he summarized his own hearings before both parent committees, became a part of the legislative history.

Since time was growing short (important provisions of the legislation expired on June 30, 1967), the Senate hearings began on April 12 and those in the House on May 2. I watched with fascination the cool, unreceptive hearing that Burke Marshall received before both committees. On the other hand, the reception accorded to Mark Clark was effusive. In the process one learned a great deal about Congressional prerogative—one group studying the problem having been appointed by Congress and the other by the President of the United States.

The appearance of General Hershey before both committees was, as always, colorful. This crusty old man, head of the draft system for more than 27 years, answered questions, avoided questions, and just plain filibustered, depending, of course, on the questions.

At the very end I was present in the Senate Gallery when Senator Edward Kennedy tried to awaken his colleagues to the fact that the prospective legislation which had emerged from a House-Senate Conference contained serious defects, as well as some totally new language that had not been the subject of hearings or previous debate. Two factors controlled the outcome. First, many congressmen and senators felt that a vote against the draft legislation, or even serious questioning of its provisions, would be construed by their constituents as being against the best interests of the men fighting and dying in Vietnam. Certainly this was a powerful emotional argument. Even more important was the second factor, the seniority system of the Congress. There was little hope that a relatively junior senator would be able to overturn a Conference Report in which fellow senators had participated and approved. Further, one of the most respected senior senators, Richard Russell of Georgia, Chairman of the Senate Committee on Armed Services, was the floor leader of the report. Senator Kennedy received a respectful hearing of some two hours' duration during a break in the Dodd censure debate. When the vote finally came, Kennedy lost, but 23 of his colleagues voted with him against accepting the Report. Soon thereafter the Conference Report was accepted by the House. (It is interesting to note that many of the points raised by Senator Kennedy concerning the shortcomings of the proposed draft law were quite accurate. In mid 1968 there is still great uncertainty, for example, about the method of selecting draftees, the status of college graduates and graduate students, and other matters.)

Several books were written during this period by persons attempting to bring about change in the draft. Initially, I wanted to write a book, not to influence opinion or promote a point of view but rather to take a look at the whole controversy as it developed and to place various arguments into some perspective. It proved to be impossible to investigate the problems of the draft without developing definite views. At first my main interest had been with the relation of higher education to the draft. As I researched the subject, my concerns broadened to include the problems of the Selective Service System itself, the effects of manpower decisions made by the System, alternatives to the draft, and the legislative process surrounding the subject. Simply stated, my biases are as follows. First, I see no viable alternative to a system of selective service; in fact, one of the alternatives, the voluntary army, has, in my judgment, serious shortcomings. Second, the present system, with all its weaknesses, appears to me to be the only logical basis on which to conscript young men. It could be modified significantly enough to make it responsive to the needs of the nation and the well-being of a majority of our young men. Third, I feel an argument can be made for student deferments, particularly on the undergraduate level, if deferment does not mean exemption. This argument is a difficult one to present because it can be construed as favoring an elitist group within our democratic society, but there are nonetheless good reasons for taking that position. Fourth, because of the numbers of eligible registrants, there seems to be no other way to select those who must serve than with some type of random selection system. Finally, although I have stated that the present system should be maintained, I think its administrative form should be changed. I feel that a Federal manpower agency should be established. This agency should inherit the present duties of Selective Service as well as the manpower functions of various other government agencies. If this solution is too drastic, then Selective Service should become a part of a governmental agency, very probably the Department of Labor. In this way manpower decisions would be made after consideration of all their possible effects. The Selective Service System would also be freed from the present narrow military personnel controls established by General Hershey.

To be sure, some issues have been left out or not treated in detail. For this I take full responsibility. In my judgment the System itself was the issue, and the prime reason for closely scrutinizing it was the question of student deferments. The treatment of conscientious objectors, the calling of reserves, and the use of the national guard as a haven for professional athletes and others were ancillary to the deferment question.

Basically, the book is divided into three parts. First, Chapters 1 to 5 sketch the background, including the organization and operation of the System and the various problems facing Selective Service. The second section, Chapters 6 to 8, is devoted to the legislative hearings and a transition Chapter that deals with the public dialogue. The third section of the book, Chapters 9 to 1, is concerned with an analysis of the new law, a discussion of its more recent controversial aspects, and conclusions.

My intention is to convey the excitement surrounding the draft debate as well as some of the frustration that results when one realizes that well-thought-out reforms are not being accepted. This book is about an issue, people, pressures, and personal power. Essentially, it is a book about political compromise.

In any undertaking of this kind there are numerous people who deserve to be mentioned because of their help and cooperation. My thanks go to: Dr. Logan Wilson, President of the American Council on Education, for providing the encouragement to write this book; Mr. Jack Morse, Director of the Commission on Federal Relations of the American Council on Education, for allowing me the latitude to pursue the topic in detail; Dr. Stephen L. Wasby, Assistant Professor of Government, Southern Illinois University, for commenting on the first rough outline of the manuscript; Mrs. June Willenz of the American Veterans Committee, who called relevant materials to my attention and who made available the files of the American Veterans Committee; Mrs. Mary E. Snyder, Librarian at Selective Service Headquarters, Washington, D.C., for her help and patience in providing me with the basic source materials; Miss Laura Kent, without whose editorial assistance I would have been just another unpublished author; Miss Chris Thompson, who came from England just in time to type, retype, and type again and who also provided so many helpful suggestions, all beyond the scope of her responsibility; Mr. John Sullivan of John Wiley and Sons, whose help and advice were essential during the entire project; and Patricia, my wife, and my three daughters, Elizabeth, Sarah, and Sheila, who were patient and understanding when, more than occasionally, I could not spend time with them because of my work.

HARRY A. MARMION

Washington, D.C.
June 1968

CONTENTS

SELECTIVE SERVICE: CONFLICT AND COMPROMISE

1 | ALL IS QUIET

On Friday, March 1, 1963, at 10 a.m., the Committee on Armed Services of the House of Representatives, under the chairmanship of Carl Vinson, held hearings on H.R. 2438, a bill to extend the induction provisions of the Universal Military Training and Service Act and related matters. The Honorable Norman S. Paul, Assistant Secretary of Defense for Manpower, was the first witness. He testified for about 10 minutes. There were no questions. General Hershey, the next witness, read a prepared statement of approximately one minute's duration. There followed the usual laudatory comments about General Hershey and his long career in the service of his country and a few questions. General Hershey was through also in about 10 minutes. For the balance of the day 13 witnesses, primarily from peace groups that urged an end to the draft, were heard. No member of the Committee, including the chairman, asked questions other than to seek clarification of particular points. The Committee adjourned at 3:50 p.m. On Monday, March 4, 1963, the Committee met again and heard five witnesses. It adjourned at 11:23 a.m. Finally, on March 5, 1963, the Committee met at 10 a.m. and by a vote of 37 to 0 recommended that the legislation be passed by the House. The time of adjournment was 10:32 a.m. The hearings on H.R. 2438 took a little more than five hours. On Monday, March 11, 1963, the House passed the bill, after perfunctory debate, 388 to 3, with Representatives Abele (R. Ohio), Gross (R. Iowa), and Brown, Jr. (D. Calif.) voting against it. Two amendments to limit the extension of the legislation to two years and to limit the induction provisions of the bill to those young men between the ages of 18½ and 22 were soundly defeated.[1]

On Tuesday, March 12, 1963, at 10 a.m., the Special Subcommittee of the Committee on Armed Services of the Senate met under the chairmanship of Senator Richard Russell (D. Georgia) to consider the Senate equivalent of the draft-extension legislation. The pattern of testimony was the same as in the House. Roughly 30 witnesses were heard in approximately four hours of

[1] *Congressional Record,* March 11, 1963, pp. 3917-3938.

testimony, all on the same day. The full Senate passed the bill on Friday, March 15, by a voice vote. The entire procedure on the floor of the Senate took less than 10 minutes. Senator Russell explained the bill for part of the time, and Senator Yarborough (D. Texas) made a pitch for the cold-war G.I. bill he was sponsoring. Senator Morse (D. Oregon), who was in Costa Rica with President Kennedy, had inserted in the *Record* a statement that explained his position against the bill[2] This was the full extent of the Senate consideration.

President Kennedy signed the bill into law on March 28, 1963. From start to finish, the whole process took less than one month to accomplish. No amendments to the legislation were accepted. Editorial comment at the time was sparse, though Hanson Baldwin, the *New York Times* military expert, did discuss "new attitudes on peacetime draft" in a March 8, 1963, column. The thrust of his article was that with nuclear power and other technological advances the need for the draft as presently constituted was no longer present. One might say that things were quiet in 1963.

OTHER EVENTS

The next significant development took place on September 10, 1963, when President Kennedy issued an executive order that had the effect of exempting married men from being drafted by placing them in a call of lower priority. At the time this order was signed more than 1.7 million men were available in the 1A pool, and this action affected 20 percent of them, or 340,000 men. There were more than enough men left to meet the draft requirements, which averaged about 7500 men a month. The President's action also had the effect of lowering the average age of men being drafted, for married men were usually called up at an older age.

At the end of September President Kennedy set up a special task force on manpower conservation to study and report on the alarmingly high draft rejection rate for physical and mental reasons among young men of draft age. Early in 1964, the task force reported to President Johnson, who ordered rehabilitation programs set up to handle those who failed the examinations. This order was coupled by a request from the President to the Selective Service System for early classification and examination of men in order that those who were found qualified could better plan their military and personal activities; moreover, this action would provide an early means of identifying those men in need of rehabilitation. Therefore, beginning July 1, 1964, Selective Service implemented the President's request so that each registrant was classified as soon

---

[2] *Congressional Record,* March 15, 1963, pp. 4327-4329.

as possible.[3] Those men found unqualified were *offered,* but not required to obtain, assistance from various manpower programs such as the Job Corps.

THE 1964 NATIONAL ELECTION

The advantage of having legislation that extends the draft act coming up in odd-numbered years has been mentioned frequently: this timing keeps the issue out of the politics of a national election. Early in 1964 President Johnson did even more to prevent the draft from becoming an issue. On April 18 he announced approval of Pentagon plans for "a very comprehensive study of the Selective Service System." The President also indicated that the study would contain other alternatives for meeting military requirements, including a voluntary army. In September Barry Goldwater, the Republican candidate for president, said in an early campaign speech that if elected the Republicans would end the draft as soon as possible. Subsequent evidence indicates that Goldwater favored the voluntary army as the primary means of providing the necessary military manpower for the national defense. The draft-study proposal of the President did much to blunt the Republican campaign oratory. The answer given by vice-presidential candidate Hubert Humphrey and others to Goldwater's speech was that it would be premature to talk about ending the present system without first studying all possible alternatives. The Democrats tried to make it obvious to the American public that the appropriate stand to take on this issue was to await the results of the Pentagon study. It was all made part of the Democrats' main theme of the campaign: namely, that Goldwater was toying with the security of the nation and that he was an extremist and could not be trusted. The election results proved beyond a doubt that the strategy was effective. Again, as far as the draft was concerned, 1964 was a quiet year.

ESCALATION

After the sweeping Democratic victory in November there was a period of about six months of increased Vietcong activity in South Vietnam. On June 28 the President announced a decision of great import to the nation: the war effort was to be accelerated:

"We intend to convince the Communists that we cannot be defeated by force of arms or by superior power. . . .I have asked General Westmoreland what more he needs. . .he has told me. We will meet his needs."

[3] *Annual Report of the Director of Selective Service, 1965,* U.S. Government Printing Office, Washington, D.C., p. 16.

Draft calls were increased to the highest level (35,000 per month) since the Korean war. An air mobile division was sent to Vietnam, which increased our forces from 75,000 to more than 100,000 men. The summer and fall of 1965 marked the end of the quiet period. The escalation of the war prompted protests throughout the country: teach-ins and draft-card burnings and even one case of self-immolation. To be sure, the antiwar group was a small minority of the American public, but it was a vocal and militant minority. As positions quickly polarized, Congress passed an amendment to the draft law making it a Federal crime to destroy or mutilate draft cards knowingly. By April of 1966 *Newsweek* magazine was able to state that for the first time in history while America was at war avoidance of military service had become socially acceptable.[4]

---

[4] "The Draft: The Unjust vs. The Unwilling," *Newsweek*, April 11, 1966, pp. 30-34.

2 | THE SELECTIVE SERVICE SYSTEM

To begin to understand what happened between 1963 and the beginning of the protest period in the latter part of 1965, aside from the escalation of the war in Vietnam, one must look at the long-range development of the Selective Service System in America.

The introduction of modern draft legislation in America followed the sad experience of both North and South during the Civil War. The conscription laws of that era contained serious defects. There were bounties, exemptions, substitutions, and occupational deferments. Those who could afford it could evade the law entirely with relative ease. Terms of service were for stated periods of time, unrelated to how long the war might last.

Shortly after the end of the Civil War Brigadier General James V. Fry, Provost Marshal General of the Army, asked Brevit Brigadier General James Oates to report on the administration and effectiveness of the Civil War draft law in the North. General Oates had been Assistant Provost Marshal General and was responsible for the administration of the law in the state of Illinois. After the report was completed it was "filed" for a 50-year period somewhere in Washington. Before World War I General Enoch H. Crowder, Judge Advocate General of the Army, utilized the report to a significant degree in preparing the draft legislation requested by President Wilson. It is fair to say that it was the basis for much of the reform contained in the World War I legislation and indeed that Oates is more responsible for draft reform than anyone in the history of the country.

Among the Oates report recommendations accepted in the national draft law of World War I were the following:

That a system of local boards be set up to administer the law:

"As soon as an emergency requiring a conscription can be foreseen, let the acting. . .provost marshals. . .give general and emphatic public notice. . .that a draft is impending. . .and that all persons between the prescribed ages must appear before the board of enrolment of their district. . . .Let the several boards be required to hold meetings for that purpose in a sufficient number of places in each county, for the proper and speedy accommodation of all liable to enrolment, and let a sufficient time be allowed for the purpose at each point." [1]

That the primary administrative unit be the state rather than the voting district:

"That in case operations should ever be resumed the action of the government should be kept with states only. . .and the management of all details of the draft for each state be entrusted with the respective acting assistant provost marshal general." [2]

That each citizen be required to report to a designated center rather than relying on house-to-house canvass to accomplish registration:

"I think the government should impose its supreme demands directly upon the people themselves, and require them under the sternest penalties, to report themselves for enrolment. If the government has a right to the military service of its citizens. . .it has the right to secure such services in the simplest, cheapest and most direct manner." [3]

That the term of service be for the duration of the conflict or emergency rather than for a fixed period of time:

"Knowing long enlistments to be the true policy of the government in time of war, and. . .believing. . .such policy could be practically carried out, it should by all means be the settled rule of enlistments in the future wars." [4]

That all bounties, substitutes, and computations of service be eliminated:

"I am of the opinion that a still better policy would be. . .to dispense with government bounties altogether as a means of promoting volunteering, and, instead, to increase the regular pay of the soldier. . .as to enable him. . .to support his family." [5]

The day after war was declared on April 7, 1917, the draft legislation was introduced into Congress. A bitter six-week debate — centered around the question of raising a voluntary army, as opposed to employing the cumbersome mechanism of a selection system — followed.

On May 18, 1917, "An Act to Authorize the President to Increase

[1] *Report of the Provost Marshal General, Document No. 11 Historical Report of the Operations of the Office of Acting Assistant Provost Marshal General, Illinois* (Oates Report), p. 25.
[2] *Ibid.* p. 23.
[3] *Ibid.* p. 25.
[4] *Ibid.* p. 31.
[5] *Ibid.* p. 31.

Temporarily the Military Establishment of the United States," known as the Selective Service Act of 1917, was passed. Four days later President Wilson named General Crowder as director of the system with the title of Provost Marshal General.

The new law can be characterized in one phrase: "supervised decentralization." The degree of planning was so high that no less than a month after President Wilson signed the bill into law, on June 5, 1917, 10 million men were registered, peacefully and with great dispatch. One need only reflect on the analogous situation in July of 1863, when some of the great cities were wracked by disorders and riots and the situation bordered on anarchy. On July 20, 1917, the greatest lottery in history was held in Washington, D.C. It established the order of selection for the original registrants. Ultimately more than 24 million Americans were registered and more than three million selected and inducted. The law was so well received that it required only minor revisions on three occasions during its application. [6] It was general in nature and left the operational details to the chief executive of the nation who was ultimately responsible even though he had appointed General Crowder to head the day-to-day operation of the System.

The 1917 legislation gave the President authority to set up local boards. "One of these local boards was to be established for every 30,000 of the population. The boards were empowered to hear and determine, subject to review, all claims of exemption and all questions of, or claims for, including or discharging persons from the selective draft." [7] The President was also authorized to establish appropriate appeal boards but to retain final appellate review to himself. The effect of this legislation cannot be overemphasized. First, it did away with the notion theretofore popular that the nation could rely on volunteers in time of war. Second, it introduced the concept of selectivity into the military manpower lexicon. Finally, and probably most important, it recognized that in a national emergency the nation must control the agricultural-industrial complex by means of selective draft and in some cases must utilize deferment. In this way it was possible for the government to pull together all facets of the economy in order to bring the war to a successful conclusion.

In 1920, after the war had ended, the draft legislation was amended to allow a national selective service planning organization to operate in peacetime. Part of the amendments provided for a War Department general staff whose duties were to prepare plans for national defense and for the utilization of military forces for

---

[6] *Backgrounds of Selective Service, Special Monograph No. 1,* Vol. I, U.S. Government Printing Office, Washington, D.C., 1949, p. 266 contains the language of the Act.

[7] *The Selective Service Act, Special Monograph No. 2,* Vol. I, U.S. Government Printing Office, Washington, D.C., 1954, pp. 53-55. This volume has a good analysis of the 1917 legislation.

that purpose. The amendments also provided for planning in the area of manpower mobilization and military preparedness. At the request of the service secretaries, a Joint Army-Navy Selective Service Committee was formed for the purpose of submitting appropriate law and regulations to apply if the country again faced a military crisis. In the ensuing years various studies were undertaken, reports were written, and, in general, the staff work necessary in any long-term planning agency was discussed, modified, and refined. Many of the recommendations made by the Joint Committee were adopted by Congress in the Selective Service Act of 1940; for example, in World War I the day-to-day operation of the draft was the responsibility of the Provost Marshal General of the Army. He reported to the Secretary of War, who in turn reported to the President. The Committee recommended that the President appoint a Director of Selective Service (either civilian or military) and that he report directly to the President. The Committee also recommended that a national headquarters be set up, which was done by the summer of 1940. State offices also were opened during this period.

As the war raged in Europe, the War Department became deeply concerned about how (and when) legislation necessary to activate the draft could be passed by Congress. President Roosevelt and his War Department advisers wanted to move cautiously with the peacetime draft concept lest unfavorable reactions from the public became translated into negative votes in the Congress. After all, such legislation would clearly mean that the nation was preparing to fight another war. An interesting point is that leadership in this matter came from a group of civilians outside the government.

During a similar period before World War I the "Plattsburg idea" was born. This idea involved the establishment of a system of voluntary training programs at army camps, primarily in the Plattsburg, New York, area. The volunteers served one month, during which time they were given rudimentary military indoctrination. When they returned to their communities, they were disciples of national defense and served as catalysts for support of the war, which was to come in the near future.[8] The 1940 version of the same concept, now called the Military Training Camp Association,[9] was advocated chiefly by Grenville Clark, an influential New York attorney. Clark is one of those people who play critical roles in important matters pertaining to the national interest, yet are virtually unknown to most of the public. When the group decided to fight for peacetime draft legislation, they initially met strong resistance. General George Marshall,

---

[8] Frederick Palmer, *Newton D. Baker: America at War,* Vol. I, Dodd Mead & Co., New York, 1931. This volume provides details of the Plattsburg program.

[9] Albert A. Blum, *Drafted or Deferred — Practices Past and Present,* University of Michigan, 1968, pp. 1-17. An excellent account of the pre-World War II draft problems. Much of the information included in this portion of the chapter comes from Blum's book.

Army Chief of Staff at the time, was opposed to pushing for the legislation because he felt that the timing was wrong and, more important, that such a move might hinder the passage of adequate appropriations by alienating the Congress. Harry Woodring, Secretary of War at that time, was also unenthusiastic about the proposal, particularly because he had strong isolationist attitudes. Although rebuffed, Clark was not discouraged. In discussions with Justice Frankfurter, a confidant of President Roosevelt, he suggested the need for a new Secretary of War, naming Henry L. Simpson as the best candidate. In June 1940 Simpson, who, not surprisingly, was a member of the Military Training Camp Association, was appointed to the position. Democratic Senator Edward Burke of Nebraska and Republican Representative James Wadsworth of New York introduced into Congress a bipartisan Selective Service bill. Public reaction to the proposed legislation was, as one would expect, mixed. The nation was sharply divided on the issue of military commitments in Europe. Forums and debates were held, pamphlets were issued, and articles were written around the theme "Should America Adopt Compulsory Military Service – Now?" After much debate an act "To Provide for the Common Defense by Increasing the Personnel of the Armed Forces of the United States and Providing for Its Training," commonly known as the Burke-Wadsworth bill, was passed on September 16, 1940. The legislation called for the registration of all men between the ages of 21 and 35, inclusive. Since this was a peacetime draft and since the Congress was aware of the public attitude toward military compulsion, the period of training was for only one year. Only 900,000 men a year were to be trained and service was limited to the confines of the United States and its territories and possessions.

The true climate of the nation in 1940 is difficult to describe. People were apprehensive about involvement in another world war, and many felt strongly that isolationism was the general foreign-policy theme that the nation should follow. America still reflected the immigrant background of a large number of its citizens, and there were pockets of support for Germany, but a strong majority recognized the predicament of England and France and the other nations of Europe. Roosevelt was faced with a critical national election for an unprecedented third term as president. In June, when France fell to the Nazi legions, Roosevelt came out with his "short of war" policy. The America First Committee, the Hearst papers, and public figures like Charles Lindbergh kept up a constant barrage against the policy of F.D.R.

With this background in mind, President Roosevelt had to select a Director of Selective Service to administer the new law. On October 8, 1940, Dr. Clarence A. Dykstra, President of the University of Wisconsin, was summoned to Washington for a meeting with the President. Dr. Dykstra was a Phi Beta Kappa from the State University of Iowa, had taught history and government at the

University of Chicago and at Ohio State, and had been head of the Department of Political Science at the University of Kansas. Later he also taught at U.C.L.A., which he left to become the city manager of Cincinnati, Ohio. During his tenure in the city on the Ohio River he received national prominence for his handling of the terrible Ohio floods. He was named President of the University of Wisconsin in 1937. During his meeting with President Roosevelt Dr. Dykstra was offered the position as Director of Selective Service. On October 12 he accepted, after talking to the Regents of the University by telephone and obtaining their permission. On October 14 the nature of the appointment was explained by Dr. Dykstra in a statement in the *Daily Cardinal*, the University of Wisconsin newspaper:

"I shall continue to be President of the University. . .the Regents are merely loaning me to the Federal government, and the business of the University will be conducted through the President's office as usual."

It is probable that President Roosevelt's intention in appointing a civilian director was to ensure public confidence in a system that drafted American men into the armed forces during peacetime. The appointment also indicates the nature of President Roosevelt's concept of Selective Service, namely that it be considered a civilian rather than a military agency.

Granting the editorial bias of any news magazine, it is noteworthy that the October 21, 1940, issue of *Time* said of Dykstra's appointment:

"It was the addition of one more big name to President Roosevelt's impressive defense corps. . .in keeping with the U.S. tradition and that of a basic conscription principle: to keep the army from civilian draftees until actually inducted into service."

The Senate confirmed the appointment of Dr. Dykstra on October 14, two days before the registration of almost 17 million men.

Dr. Dykstra commuted to Washington from October 1940 until March 21, 1941, when he resigned, effective April 1. The reasons for his resignation, although obscure, seem to be personal: primarily his health and some unrest at Madison, where the Board of Trustees at the University of Wisconsin were increasingly concerned over his absence. President Roosevelt waited from March until the end of July before appointing General Hershey as Director of Selective Service. General Hershey assumed the post on August 8, 1941, and has held it during the ensuing 27 years.

PEARL HARBOR AND 1941 AMENDMENTS
TO THE SELECTIVE SERVICE ACT

Within a week after the attack on Pearl Harbor Congress amended the Selective Service Act to remove restrictions on where men in the armed forces could be stationed and to extend the period of service for the duration of the war plus six months. Another important change in the World War II Selective Service Act should be mentioned at this point. The legislation ensured re-employment of a veteran in the job he had left to enter the armed forces. During the war the legislation fulfilled a twofold task: it had the duty of furnishing men (more than 10 million of whom were inducted between November 1940 and October 1946) for the armed forces, and it had the collateral responsibility of keeping adequate manpower resources available to operate the nation's wartime economy.

POSTWAR ACTIVITY

Throughout American history some method of military manpower procurement — either voluntary, compulsory, or in combination — has been a principle of American wartime policy. In early 1947 President Truman recommended to the Congress that the Selective Service Act be allowed to expire at the end of March. Congress acceded and passed a law that established an office of Selective Service Records whose job it was to maintain files, data, and records concerning the entire Selective Service process. Once again General Hershey was named Director of the agency. He served along with a small nucleus of Selective Service personnel who were retained to provide continuity in case of a national emergency that might necessitate almost instantaneous manpower mobilization. At this time in the nation there was much discussion about a peacetime draft as well as about the possibility of inaugurating a system of universal military training. For almost four years President Truman fought to have Congress pass a universal military training bill which would require one year of military training of all American men. The national debate on this issue engendered bitter arguments from proponents of both sides of the question. Church groups and educational organizations in general spoke out against any such system; for example, the National Education Association in 1946 issued a statement opposing compulsory military training in peacetime.[10] Some of the objections to universal military training were that the danger of a military elite would be greatly enhanced if a large professional army were maintained during a peacetime period, that the concept of compulsory military training is undemocratic, and that the power of the Federal government would be greatly increased.

The issue was finally resolved by the adoption of a policy of national defense that depends on air-nuclear deterrents; this policy cost the universal military

10 *Journal of the National Education Association,* Vol. 35, April 1946, Washington, D.C., p. 191.

training concept most of its Congressional support.[11] Universal military training was a dead issue.

The modern national selection system devised to meet the military manpower requirements of the nation was first made operational in World War I. The changes between World War I and World War II were important but not basic to the system. The original Oates recommendations concerning local boards and the like were still followed. The Joint Army-Navy Selective Service Committee did recommend plans for a national headquarters and a staff to be made up of reserve officers specially trained as Selective Service specialists. It showed great foresight not only in recommending these changes but also in implementing the training of a staff for any emergency.[12] A group of Selective Service specialists made up primarily of reserve officers from the army, but with all services represented, was selected and trained by means of correspondence courses, periodic on-the-job training, and conferences on organizational problems, usually held in Washington, the first of which was in November 1929.[13] After this group of specialists was formed, both the Joint Committee and the Selective Service specialists worked together to make further studies and recommendations.

The national Selective Service System, as envisioned at that time, would consist of a director, and executive officer who had general supervision of the system, and a headquarters of eight divisions.[14] Every state would have a headquarters under the governor, who would appoint an officer to head it. The rest of the system would consist of local boards, appeals boards, appeals agents, a medical board, and a registrants advisory board to help registrants with the applications.

By 1938 the planning had reached the stage in which both the Joint Committee and the Selective Service specialists were concentrating on the details of implementation and on the perfection of regulations regarding industrial mobilization, recruitments, physical requirements, and the like. Until this point the proceedings had been conducted on a confidential basis, but by 1938-1939 it was decided to inaugurate a broad informational program that would involve more people. A monthly bulletin, which brought the activities of both groups to the attention of the public, was issued.[15]

---

[11] Congress and the Nation 1945-1964, pp. 266-272. Contains a good synopsis of Congressional action on the draft and universal military training.
[12] Organization and Administration of the System, Special Monograph No. 3, Vol. I, Text, U.S. Government Printing Office, Washington, D.C., 1951, p. 36.
[13] Ibid. p. 36.
[14] Administration, Finance and Supply, Inspection, Legal, Medical, Mobilization, Public Relations, and Registration and Classification.
[15] Organization and Administration of the System, op. cit. p. 40.

The organization of Selective Service in 1967 is still basically the same as that initiated by the 1940 legislation. Local board members are appointed by the President on the recommendation of the governor in each state. Local boards are assisted by civil-service clerks. The government appeal agent, who is independent of the board, is also appointed by the President on the recommendation of the governor. The appeal agent usually represents the interests of the government, particularly with reference to the classification given a registrant. State directors, who are appointed in the same manner, represent the governor in all matters pertaining to Selective Service and are responsible to the Director of Selective Service for the functioning of the system within each state. Their staffs contain both civilian and military personnel, and the size and population of the state determine their size. Each state director has an appeal board within each Federal judicial district in the state. These five-member boards, also recommended by the governor and appointed by the President, reflect the widest possible range of economic activities; those usually selected are a doctor, a lawyer, and representatives from labor, agriculture, and industry. These boards have jurisdiction over any decision referred to them by local boards. Each state also has several advisory committees to assist the state director, primarily in developing occupational deferment policies. There are advisory boards for science, medicine, and dentistry and a board of doctors concerned with medical problems of registrants. The medical advisers are appointed by the President on the recommendation of the governor. The Scientific Advisory Committee is appointed by the governor, and the Committee of Physicians and Dentists is appointed by a National Advisory Committee of the same name which assists the national director.

SUMMARY OF OPERATIONS[16]

The Selective Service System celebrated its twenty-fifth anniversary in 1965. As of June 30, 1966, the System had registered more than 32 million men during its quarter century of existence. More than 4000 boards operate with about 40,000 uncompensated personnel, 16,000 of whom are local board members, and about 6000 full- and part-time paid workers. The 4000 local boards range in size from one in Hinsdale County, Colorado, which has a total registration of 28, to the largest board in the country in North Hollywood, California, which has more than 50,000 registrants. There are 95 state appeal boards, one in each Federal judicial district, with 23 extra panels in most heavily

[16] The material in this section comes from the *Annual Report of the Director of Selective Service, 1966*, U.S. Government Printing Office, Washington, D.C., pp. 1-4.

populated districts which have more than 500 unpaid board members. There are 56 state headquarters. All of these, plus the national office, make up the Selective Service System.

THE PURPOSES OF SELECTIVE SERVICE

The basic purpose of the Selective Service System, which is to procure the necessary military manpower for the armed forces of the nation, particularly the Army, is accomplished primarily by registering, classifying, and inducting men between the ages of 18½ and 26. Monthly calls are levied on the System by the Department of Defense. Monthly draft calls vary, depending on the needs of the military as determined by world conditions, and have ranged in recent years from a low of zero calls in May and June of 1961 to a high of 80,000 a month from January through March of 1951, a result of the Korean war. Obviously calls and inductions were much higher during World War II. The fact that the monthly calls vary widely places a premium on the ability of the System to react quickly once a call has been levied.

The direct induction of men into the armed forces represents only one way in which the System achieves its primary purpose. The System traditionally has inducted a number of "voluntary enlistments." As draft calls fluctuate, so do enlistments in the various services. When calls are low, enlistments are generally low – the exception being during the period following high school commencement, when young men who have recently graduated drive the enlistment figures upward. Conversely, when draft calls increase, enlistments increase. Young men who know they may soon be drafted often prefer to enlist in order to be assured of particular training, schooling, membership in an elite service, or other benefits. This method of procuring military manpower, though indirect, has proved effective. The System itself has been most liberal in allowing men about to be drafted to make their own arrangements for service almost up to the moment of actual induction.

Channeling

The second, and more controversial, purpose is the channeling of registrants into critical activities and occupations. Many critics feel that Selective Service became involved in this purpose by administrative action, not by legislative intent of the Congress. (The controversial aspects of channeling are discussed in Chapter 4.) Channeling, as viewed by Selective Service, is accomplished primarily by the process of deferment, which may prompt a young man to stay in college or to obtain a job in the national interest. By holding over a man's head the threat of induction the System is able to offset shortages in a variety of important industries and occupations.

Inventory

The third broad purpose of the System is to maintain a current inventory of the manpower resources of the nation in order to ensure the availability of resources, particularly to the military, in times of national emergency. Thus, as of June 30, 1965, the System registered and classified more than 30 million men. In its classification system a broad inventory of the status of available manpower is readily at hand.

The next purpose that places heavy responsibility on the Selective Service System is to determine the availability for active duty of individual standby reservists. The Reserve Forces Act of 1955 amended the operational draft act (Universal Military Training and Service Act) by providing that standby reservists can be ordered to active duty in the event of a national emergency declared by the Congress but only after the Director of the Selective Service System has determined their availability for recall.

Because of the complexities of the reserve problem, I will not dwell on this particular phase of Selective Service activities in any great detail. It is necessary at this point, however, to explain reserve activities as they affect the functioning of Selective Service.

The Reserve Forces Act provides that, without quotas, a man may enlist in a Ready Reserve Unit before reaching age 18½ for a period of eight years' total service: six months on active duty and the remaining seven and one-half years on duty with the Ready Reserve Unit. This provision would give all services adequate reserve forces, which could be called to active duty if the Congress declared a national emergency. According to the law, if a man did not satisfactorily perform his reserve duty, he could be inducted ahead of other categories of draft-eligible men. Thus Selective Service was given an enforcement role in this particular plan.

The Act also provided for a reserve made up of men with "critical skills." Local boards were assigned the responsibility of selecting men within their own areas who would be eligible to enlist. Once selected, a man would spend six months on active duty and the remainder of his eight-year obligation with the standby or the ready reserve. The general practice of Selective Service was to allow these men to revert to the standby reserve; they would not be required to participate in the activities of the ready reserve unless they ceased to be employed in a critical activity. This program was discontinued in August 1963.

The 1955 Reserve Forces Act also required that Selective Service determine the status of standby reserves for potential call to active duty. As one can imagine, there is tremendous traffic into and out of the standby reserve category. By 1960 more than 1.6 million files were in active status within the local board system.

The System also has the function of classifying men as soon as possible after registration in order to eliminate the uncertainty surrounding military service. The System cooperates with the antipoverty program of the Federal government. Those men not qualified are referred to various rehabilitation programs, including the Job Corps or other existing Federal programs.

SELECTIVE SERVICE PROFESSIONAL STAFF

The national headquarters of the System consists of 62 commissioned officers and 174 civilians; the key positions are held by the officers. There are 12 regional field officers, two in six regions, each coinciding with an army area. The System conducts a constant training program for reserve and National Guard officers who have been designated for training and potential duty. This program was authorized by law in 1947 and implemented with the cooperation of all the armed forces. The selection process for assignment to the Selective Service System is the responsibility of the Director. On the state level the state adjutant general is responsible for training these officers. The state directors and the state offices are staffed primarily by men holding military rank; for example, 49 of the 56 state directors are military officers.

SELECTIVE SERVICE AND THE PUBLIC

The Vietnam buildup and the unpopularity of the war has made the whole draft system the center of much recent attention. As a result of unfavorable comment, an office of Public Information was established in December 1965. Much of the public information, however, comes from the Director himself, who is always eager to explain the draft in light of current conditions. During the first six months of 1966 more than 75 interviews were given by the Director or the Public Information Officer.

SUMMARY

Selective Service, as it is presently constituted, was largely planned during the interim between World Wars I and II. The System devised enabled the nation to meet the extensive military requirements of World War II. It operates independently, though it cooperates closely with the Department of Defense. It is staffed at all decision-making levels by men with military service, many of whom still hold reserve commissions in the armed services. The primary purpose of the System is to provide military manpower to the armed forces.

3 | THE CURRENT OUTMODED SYSTEM

It has been necessary to renew Selective Service legislation every few years since 1951. The Congress has not been willing to try new approaches to manpower procurement, primarily because of cold-war pressures during this period. Also, widespread criticism of the draft did not take place until quite recently. The procedures in effect during the two world wars (quite similar in basics to the system today) functioned relatively efficiently and the public was not overly aroused, probably because of the dangers facing the nation. After World War II there was much discussion about the necessity of a peacetime draft and also about the possibility of an alternative means of providing military manpower in some form of universal military training.

As a result of the Korean conflict, coming soon after World War II, the American public began to learn to live with the draft, even in less than all-out war situations. It was not until the tempo of the struggle in Vietnam accelerated in the late spring of 1965 that public opinion began to mobilize. All at once the war's escalation, its unpopularity, and the relatively recent student militancy in the country all converged to bring the whole Selective Service System under close and critical scrutiny. The draft has become uppermost in the mind of every American man between the ages of 18 and 26 and, in some cases, 35. The new inductee stands a good chance of being sent to Vietnam, for "the army sends one out of three of its draftees to Vietnam." [1]

In the 20 years since World War II America has undergone startling changes in its economy as well as in its educational system. Despite these changes the basic draft law has remained virtually unchanged since 1951. Much of the controversy about it centers around the policies described in this chapter.

[1] Joseph A. Loftus, *New York Times,* August 10, 1966, p. 7.

18

THE MISNAMED UNIVERSAL MILITARY TRAINING AND SERVICE ACT

In testimony before the Subcommittee on Employment and Manpower of the U.S. Senate Committee on Labor and Public Welfare in November 1963 Mr. John C. Esty, Jr., Headmaster of the Taft School, stated the problem clearly:

"Present practice makes a mockery of the original intent that every able-bodied man serve his country. Our present difficulties arise from the strain of maintaining a semblance of universality while armed service needs dictate greater and greater selectivity. The time has come when we can no longer reconcile these opposites and must choose between them."

The principle behind the legislation in question has caused confusion, and many voices, particularly in higher education, have called for a re-examination; for example, Kingman Brewster in his baccalaureate address to the 1966 Yale graduating class said:

"I realize that service to the nation has been mocked by a policy which offers no reason to justify the imposition of involuntary military service primarily upon those who cannot hide in the endless catacombs of formal education. The carryover of a manpower policy designed a generation ago seems heedless of the differences in both need and capability which have been brought about by change in population and military technique. The result has been to encourage a cynical avoidance of service, a corruption of the aims of education, and a tarnishing of the national spirit.

"You have been deprived of such pride as you might have had either in response to honest need or in response to the luck of the draw. Selective Service in order to staff a two million man force from a two hundred million population has invited a cops and robbers view of national obligation. National morality has been left exposed to collective self-corruption by the persistent refusal of the national administration to take the lead in the design of a national manpower policy which would rationally relate individual privilege and national duty."

How did this confusion over principle happen? As mentioned earlier, universal military training in any form was dead; all that remained of it was the misleading title of the 1951 legislation introduced in an attempt to bring about some type of universality in military service. When that failed, draft legislation entered a state of ambiguity. The basic law had been intended to meet the needs of all-out war. It was continued because of world tensions. Now the legislation is amended here, patched there, in an *ad hoc* manner to meet changing manpower needs. Again, there are differences between a world war and our problems in Vietnam. Any law passed by the Congress must have a clear and unambiguous purpose, especially a law that forcibly takes certain of our young men into the military.

DECENTRALIZATION OF THE SELECTIVE SERVICE SYSTEM AND THE ABSENCE OF NATIONAL STANDARDS

During the 1940 hearings and many times thereafter General Hershey has hailed the fairness and democracy of the local boards which form the basis of the supervised decentralization of the System. Yet this "supervised decentralization" has been criticized because it creates apparently undemocratic situations by permitting a lack of uniformity in interpretation. During the first two days (June 22-23, 1966) of General Hershey's testimony before the House Armed Services Committee which was looking into the administration of the System, the questioning by members of the Committee made it abundantly clear that many of the complaints of their constituents concerned this lack of uniformity. Draft boards throughout the nation have a wide latitude of action which in some cases may be used arbitrarily; for example, one local board may induct part-time students before married men; another board may have the opposite policy.

It should be made clear that agency guidelines, presidential executive orders, test scores, and rank in class are only advisory in nature. Section 6(h) of the Act says in part:

"Notwithstanding any provisions of this Act, no local board, appeal board, or other agency of appeal of the Selective Service System shall be required to postpone or defer any person by reason of his activity in study, research, or medical, dental, veterinary, optometric, osteopathic, scientific, pharmaceutical, chiropractic, chiropodial, or other endeavors found to be necessary to the maintenance of the national health, safety or interest solely on the basis of any test, examination, selection system, class standing, or any other means conducted, sponsored, administered, or prepared by any agency or department of the Federal Government or any private institution, corporation, association, partnership, or individual employed by an agency or department of the Federal Government."

The rules governing the draft shift in emphasis from one section of the country to another, from one state to another, from one town to another, and from one board to another. Local autonomy is not limited to deferments. The *1965 Annual Report of the Director of Selective Service* reveals that 4F rates differ widely from state to state. In Michigan, for example, it is 1.7 percent, whereas in Massachusetts it is 8.9 percent. As the author of a recent book on the draft asks, Does anyone believe that the youth of Massachusetts are five times as likely to be in poor health and have lower intelligence than those in Michigan?[2]

---

[2] Bruce K. Chapman, *The Wrong Man in Uniform,* Trident Press, New York, 1967, p. 52.

It should be remembered that the local-board concept, which was originated by General Oates in his report issued just after the Civil War (see Chapter 2) and instituted as a part of the legislation enacted just before World War I, was an ingenious innovation. It placed the responsibility for deciding "who goes" in the hands of the neighbors of potential inductees. This procedure worked well in America before the increase in urbanization, but today there are, for example, in New York City, 68 local boards, each with more than 20,000 registrants. Selective Service has categorized the boards as "the grass roots units of the system where its fundamental operations are performed."[3] The President's Advisory Commission on the Draft, however, after investigating local boards carefully, said: "Very little evidence exists to suggest that the fact of drafting by local boards has more than symbolic significance, if that, in urban settings."[4]

The man who probably knows more about the operation of local draft boards than anyone else is sociologist Roger Little of the Chicago Circle Branch of the University of Illinois, who had this to say about the Illinois draft boards:

"In Illinois in 1965, the over-all rejection rate was 34 percent, well below the national average for inductees. But in rural down-state Illinois the rate was 28 percent, in metropolitan Chicago the rate was 43 percent. . . .These [rates] are significant in affecting a registrant's chance of service because the quota is allocated on the basis of the rejection experience of each jurisdiction."[5]

Thus a man's future can depend on the accident of birth or place of registration.

These weaknesses, plus the problem of student deferments, constitute the major criticisms of the draft during this period. As the velocity of the dissent increased, Congress passed its amendment to the draft law concerning the destruction or mutilation of a draft card. During the House debate on the amendment, L. Mendel Rivers (D. South Carolina) said that passing this law was "the least we can do for our men in South Vietnam fighting to preserve freedom, while a political minority in this country thumb their noses at their own government." Some of the Southern conservatives felt that the student protests were outgrowths of the successful methods of civil disobedience utilized in the Civil Rights Movement of the early 1960's. The theory was that because civil disobedience was literally countenanced by Federal authorities — especially in the various civil rights marches, summer programs, and the like — the same

---

[3] *Annual Report of the Director of Selective Service, 1966,* U.S. Government Printing Office, Washington, D.C., p. 3.
[4] *In Pursuit of Equity: Who Serves When Not All Serve? Report of the National Advisory Commission on Selective Service,* U.S. Government Printing Office, Washington, D.C., February, 1967, p. 20.
[5] *Dialogue on the Draft: Report of the National Conference on the Draft,* edited by June A. Willenz, American Veterans Committee, Washington, D.C., 1967, pp. 26-27.

tactics were now being used with far more dangerous results to the nation. It is important to note that there were actually two separate campaigns being conducted by the dissidents, one against the war in Vietnam and the other against the draft.

When class-rank and draft-deferment test scores were resumed as criteria for deferment in May 1966, primarily on the advice of the American Council on Education, many in the academic community began to focus their activity on this phase of the Selective Service operation. A number of colleges appointed faculty and student committees to study the problem and advise the college administration of a course of action to follow. Early in June two national conferences on the draft were planned for the late fall, one to be held in Washington under the sponsorship of the American Veterans Committee and the other in Chicago under the sponsorship of the University of Chicago with a Ford Foundation grant. There were other conferences in various colleges throughout the country. One, for example, was held at Antioch in Ohio. From all sides came requests for Congressional hearings, not only from students and faculty but also from the press and even from the floor of the United States Congress itself. Finally L. Mendel Rivers, Chairman of the House Armed Services Committee, announced that hearings would be held in June to review the administration and operation of the Selective Service System. The hearings started on June 22, 1966, and continued for six days, ending June 30. Rivers, in his letter to General Hershey on May 18, said in part:

"It is my intention to make the hearings public, and. . .I will request you to answer the questions of the members of the Committee. It is also my intention to ask other members of Congress to present their views to the Committee. . .I am receiving complaints from various members of the Congress concerning the inconsistent application of regulations in different parts of the country. . . .There seems to be no national regulation with respect to part-time students. As you know, many persons have expressed the belief that a lottery would be preferable to the present system. . . I mention these items just to give you an idea of the range of complaints. . .I hope that you will be prepared to make the proper recommendations."

Rivers had highlighted a few of the issues raised by many, including the proposal to use a lottery to select those who must be drafted. The proponents of a lottery argued that because there are more potential draftees than the armed forces need at any particular time and the present mechanism for selection apparently does not function equitably why not rely on chance?

The stage was set and the ground rules established. The hearings would be public, but only members of the legislative and executive branches of the government would be heard. No one outside the government was asked to testify. The Director of Selective Service could expect to be questioned about the inequities of the System, the lack of uniformity in applying standards, deferments, and the lottery. Another ground rule that the chairman set was that all members of the Committee would be allowed to ask questions, beginning with the most junior member. This procedure was a far cry from the days under Chairman Vinson, who liked to do most of the talking.

General Hershey was the first witness, and he made a strong plea for a continuation of deferments. "If the nation needs those who are trained, it should be prepared to defer them when the needs of the armed forces permit, and the individual continues to serve the national interest." He concluded his prepared statement with his own views on equity and a strong statement against a lottery.

"At the same time, there is concern over 'inequity.' Equality of ability, equality of service do not exist. Selective Service in issuing orders for induction, can approach equality only to the extent of the numbers that the Armed Forces requisition. Even so-called universal military training asks nothing of those disqualified, a segment of our registration too often ignored in calls for 'equity.'

"Through these and related criticisms, those bold enough to suggest improvements eventually fall back on suggestions of a lottery. The idea that a lottery solves any of our problems is an illusion. For the most part, those urging a lottery recognize that you can't apply it to the disqualified, and hesitate to apply it in disregard of all the other circumstances of the individual whose number is drawn. You return to a selective system, the lottery replacing nothing but the process used now of considering registrants in the order of date of birth. This date of birth process, by the way, was turned to in World War II when the lottery idea was proved unworkable. And lottery advocates pay too little attention to the effect on recruiting, the inability of any government by lot or otherwise to guarantee one he need not serve – and finally to the gravest weakness, the substitution of chance for judgment in an area where we need much more wisdom that we have – that is the proper utilization of our manpower."[6]

At the end of his statement the questioning began, restrained at first but soon a little sticky. The members of the Committee were obviously loath to engage the General in an exchange of opinions because the General is a master at creating embarrassment. At one point Congressman Otis Pike (D. New York) imprudently became involved in just such a situation while discussing local board members:

[6] *Review of the Administration and Operation of the Selective Service System, Hearings before the Committee on Armed Services, House of Representatives,* U.S. Government Printing Office, Washington, D.C., 1966, p. 9627.

Mr. Pike.	General, we are going to the wisdom of the local board now.
General Hershey.	Right.
Mr. Pike.	A member of a local board must be a male, he must be 30 years old, and he must reside in the country. Does he have to be a college graduate?
General Hershey.	No, sir; he doesn't.
Mr. Pike.	Does he have to be a high school graduate?
General Hershey.	No, sir.
Mr. Pike.	Does he have to be a grade school graduate?
General Hershey.	No, and not only that, there are many other occupations that we have in Government for which people are chosen that do not have to be *(laughter)*. [7]

Congressman Schweiker, (R. Pennsylvania) discussing the need for national standards and, in their absence, the need for a lottery, described one situation in his district in which three pilots, all working for the same airline, with Department of Defense cargo commitments, were treated differently by local boards. Two were deferred, but the third (with more experience) was declared eligible for the draft by his board. This, Schweiker felt, was a good example of the need for national guidelines. General Hershey first suggested that the draft-eligible pilot should appeal, with the possibility of overturning the decision of a local board and thus establishing some sort of uniform policy, at least on a state-wide basis. In this case, however, the Congressman informed General Hershey that the pilot in question had appealed and his appeal was denied. Schweiker added that although Hershey talked about judgment as a basis for selection it is actually a matter of chance — the chance being which local board a person happens to be registered under. Hershey's answer, though not responsive, amounted to a defense of local boards.

Finally, Schweiker suggested that modern computers could handle the classification process more efficiently. General Hershey's answer indicates clearly his position on the operation of the System:

"I have had about four or five surveys made,[8] and it is very plain, they say to me, 'If you want to run a decentralized system we can't do much for you with the computer. If you will let us have a centralized system, we will let the computers make the mistakes rather than the human beings.'

"I personally am still sticking with people." [9]

---

[7] *Ibid.* p. 9667.

[8] The surveys were done by reservists on active duty for two-week periods. There is no indication of any in-depth study of this problem.

[9] *Review of the Administration and Operation of the Selective Service System, op. cit.* p. 9635.

The next significant exchange took place between Chairman Rivers and General Hershey. It shows the General's views on local board autonomy, the use of computers, the lottery, and states' rights (a subject close to the heart of the conservative Mr. Rivers), and it illustrates concisely his unique way of handling Congressional committees.

Chairman.	Now, do you think we should have some kind of regulation making it a uniform policy that all boards follow the same policy in this student deferment?
General Hershey.	I think the board is entitled to the best information available. I think they are in a place where they have to meet the calls and we do have some laws which permit the induction of all kinds of health specialists by direct call. Therefore, they are not – they not only have the jeopardy that comes with the ordinary citizen, but we use that jeopardy to take them at a time when we need specialists. But, on the other hand, I am not one of those who believe that you can guide a thing successfully in too much detail from a central headquarters.
Chairman.	In other words, you are for states rights, are you?
General Hershey.	I have more confidence in the people down in Charleston – of course, they have proved that several times, I guess, by the fact that we have seniority from some of the people who come from there,– but, anyway –
Chairman.	You sure know how to get along before this committee all right.
General Hershey.	I have more confidence in them solving these problems. There is another thing a lot of people forget. We took in 16 and a half million people in World War II. Of course, it is a long time ago. We have taken in about a million in this past year. If we would have had each person come before a specialist up here before we got him into the forces we wouldn't have had him. If you want to act quick, you have got to let them act down where the action is.
Chairman.	Well, now, I think you have also touched on another question that came in my mind. I don't ask you about why one board in close proximity to another selects somebody and the other one doesn't. You said you would have to look at that I believe on an

individual basis. This is the way you answered the question. I think that was a satisfactory answer, because you said the people down on the level knew more of what that board's requirements were than a board which might have been a few miles away. That was the answer in substance, wasn't it?

General Hershey.

Well, I still think that if each community does its share, they ought to be allowed to do it in a way that they want to do it, because I think people will fight longer when they participate in the decisions than they will when somebody furnishes them ready-made. I don't mean to say that I believe in mutiny or democratic voting down in the company when you are going to decide to attack, but to the limit I can make my boys in a company feel that I am looking out for their interest and I am doing what they want done if I possibly can, I think it will make them stay longer than any other way I know.

Chairman.

Well, now, General, this committee has no reason to have any peculiar affinity for or love for computers, we don't have any reason to recommend them. But do you think you could use any of these things, these data gadgets in your organization?

General Hershey.

Yes; I don't think there is any question, because most, a lot of the policy that I have carried out has originated in this committee and if I get quoted in the paper I want to include that once in a while we also heard from the committee of the other body — you see I want to stay in some sort of arrangements with both. But I am an individual who tries to carry out what the Congress has thought the people wanted carried out. I am not an originator of policies. I am an administrator and obviously I think there are many things that you suggested we can very well take. I am sorry sometimes I can't take all of them and I do not recommend that we start changing this law. You can do most anything under this law which is more than you can say for a great many laws that are on the books.

Chairman.

I was asking you the specific question. Now, you don't need any computers or data gadgets down there?

General Hershey.   Well, I have had three studies made by some of the Reserve officers who are attached to us and I think their desires to make a sale would be greater than their fear of me, and they recommended that unless we wanted to change our decentralized system there wouldn't be much they could do for us.

Chairman.   I just wanted to be certain, because you see we got 200 million people in this country and I was just throwing that out as a suggestion of improving the efficiency of the organization by taking advantage of modern technology from the headquarters down to the local boards. This is what I had in mind.

General Hershey.   Well, I believe that we ought to use everything we can, but when we get into the sort of machinery that starts using us and that we begin to restrict what we can do because it won't go in the machine, then it bothers me not a little. You know we have a saying about the machine, that it is GIGO, garbage in-garbage out and you will get out of it just what you put in.

Chairman.   That is exactly right, precisely. A computer is no better than the stuff you put in. It is like a deep freeze, if you want a good steak, put a good steak in it. I would like to have one. You are as right as you can be on that. Now, have you said all you want to say about this lottery proposition? Is there anything else. . .?

General Hershey.   Well, I am a little bit like one of our Presidents who was asked about the church service one time. He said the preacher preached on sin, and he was asked, "What did he say?" and he said, "He is agin it." I think it is a backward step. I know it is very — now there was an editorial in the paper yesterday, and I was very amused by it. . . . [10]

To summarize the testimony and responses of General Hershey during this phase of the 1966 hearings is an easy matter: the General is against change. Specifically, he is against any restrictions on local board autonomy, against a lottery, against alterations in the method of selection, and against modifications in the deferment policies currently in force.

[10] *Ibid.* pp. 9697-9699.

As Congressional witnesses were heard, it became apparent that each one interested enough to testify had his own solutions to the problem. Congressman Curtis (R. Missouri) made a strong statement in favor of a voluntary army. Senator Edward Kennedy (D. Massachusetts) advocated national guidelines, national quotas, modernization of local boards, and raises in military salaries; he also strongly advocated taking the youngest men first by lottery. Congressman Morse, (R. Massachusetts) representing 25 Republican members of the House, stressed lack of uniformity in local board practices and advocated use of data-processing equipment to facilitate efficiency; he too advocated a lottery. Congressman Ryan (D. New York), although praising the hearings to review the draft, chided the Committee for not inviting nongovernmental witnesses to testify.

It was left to Congressman Schweiker, himself a member of the Armed Services Committee, to come up with detailed suggestions, the most important of which was a proposal for a national pool.

Mr. Schweiker.

A national manpower pool should be established to replace the 4061 separate local manpower pools now existing. Under the present system in which each local board is told how many men to draft monthly, one local board conceivably may have more volunteers than it can use while another is drafting married men exclusively.

A national manpower pool would eliminate these inequities so that all "singles," "marrieds," and "students" throughout the nation would receive exactly the same judgment, with the draft call being issued by Selective Service headquarters rather than by each of the 4061 local boards.

Creation of a national manpower pool would make feasible the use of centralized computers and other automated equipment to increase the efficiency of the Selective Service System. As an example, after a local board had registered and classified a boy, a record of his file would be placed in a computer at Selective Service System headquarters. Any subsequent changes by the local board in the man's file would also be entered in the computer to update the records. General Hershey mentioned to the committee last week some studies that have been made of the possible advantageous application of computers to the Selective Service System. Mr.

Chairman, I would like to suggest that the committee might find these studies helpful in its review of the draft and that perhaps General Hershey could supply us with copies. . . .[11]

On June 30 the final witness, Thomas D. Morris, Assistant Secretary of Defense (Manpower), testified. He began by saying: "I would like to present a summary of the Department of Defense study of the draft." The crowded hearing room fell quiet except for people moving to the press table to pick up the few extra copies of "the study" that were available. At first glance – and after subsequent scrutiny – it does not appear to be much of a summary or much of a study. The whole document is very short: double spaced and with wide margins, it runs just over 20 pages. No tables, data, or questionnaires are included.[12] The following is a synopsis of the material presented by Secretary Morris:

1. *What has been our experience with Selective Service?*

The study indicates strong support for the draft system and heralds its success in meeting manpower requirements. It cites the need for the draft during the present Vietnam period.

The problem of the growing supply of draft-age men in relation to military requirements is recognized. The study indicates that in 1958 70 percent of men reaching age 26 had served; today the figure is about 46 percent; and by 1974 (at pre-Vietnam levels) the figure will dip to 34 percent. Assuming a continuation of Vietnam strength levels, the proportion of draft-age men serving in 1974 would still be only 42 percent.

Finally, the report defends the decentralized operating system of the Selective Service System. On this point the Department of Defense agrees with General Hershey that the system is responsive to local conditions and minimizes processing time.

2. *What are the problems in the Selective Service process?*

(a) The most undesirable feature of the present selection system procedure is that the oldest men are called first. During the last five years the median age of

---

[11] *Ibid.* p. 9769.
[12] The Department of Defense did provide many data for the official record of the hearings. At various times representatives of the Department of Defense, when asked about the completeness of the draft study, indicated that most of the pertinent material from which the summary of the draft study was taken was contained in the appendix to the record of the House hearings, pp. 9999-10052. After a careful reading of this information I came to the conclusion that the material contained therein is an adequate basis for the draft study.

draftees ranged from a high of 23.7 in 1963 to today's low of 20.3. Because of the growing supply of draft-age men, the outlook is again toward an upward trend in the median age.

(b) Past deferment rules have favored college men. As of June 1964 only 40 percent of college graduates had served in the armed forces, compared with 60 percent of college dropouts, 57 percent of high school graduates, and 50 percent of non-high school graduates. Although there are compelling reasons for continuing student deferments, the study cites only one: namely, that the military departments look to civilian colleges for 90 percent of their new officers.

(c) Past deferment rules have favored married men without children. Registrants married after August 26, 1965, should no longer be deferred.

(d) Department of Defense standards in recent years have disqualified more men for lack of adequate mental ability and education attainment.

The study indicates that the principal opportunity for revising standards lies in reassessing mental standards, which have been raised substantially since 1958. Legally, a man must pass the Armed Forces Qualification Test (AFQT) with a score in the tenth percentile or above (i.e., in the upper 90 percent of the population tested); but the law permits the Secretary of Defense to raise these standards in peacetime. Between 1958 and 1963 standards were raised by adding the requirement that those with low AFQT scores be required to make passing scores in three out of seven areas of an aptitude test battery.

Acceptable levels for high school graduates differ from those for non-high school graduates. The report indicates that the raising of the standards has eliminated "many of the problems of discipline and marginal performance which were experienced during and after Korea."

3.   *Can foreseeable manpower requirements be met without the draft under present manpower policies?*

Although the draft has produced less than one-third of new enlisted entrants into the armed forces since 1950, it has had a decided influence on the decision of many of the remaining two-thirds to volunteer, according to a Defense Department survey. The survey also indicated that an all-volunteer force would fall far short of any force level required since 1950.

4.   *Would improvements in pay and other manpower practices enable us to sustain an all-volunteer force?*

The study, having concluded that elimination of the draft would make it impossible to sustain force levels of the size required, next examined the possibility of attracting more volunteers by (a) increasing pay, (b) offering liberal educational and fringe benefits, and (c) replacing military with civilian employees in certain noncombat jobs. Consequently the Bureau of the Census was asked to conduct a survey of nonveterans, ages 16 to 34, to determine their attitudes toward military as opposed to civilian employment and toward the factors they considered important in choosing a job or career.

Cost of Sustaining Volunteer Force

The responses revealed that "equal pay" with civilian jobs and "considerably higher" pay than in civilian life were considered the most important factor by 21 percent of those surveyed (4 percent and 17 percent, respectively). The study also found that the amounts of increased pay required to establish and maintain an all-volunteer active force varied, depending on current unemployment rates.

Unemployment Rate	Range of Increased Payroll Costs
4.0 percent	$6-17 billion
5.5 percent	$4-10 billion

These estimates represent the cost required to sustain force levels at pre-Vietnam requirements. To obtain volunteers at requirements above the level would, in the words of the study, "necessitate greater-than-proportionate increases for each increment added to the force."

Improvement in Fringe Benefits

The Census Bureau survey indicated that improved fringe benefits would have a limited effect as an inducement to enlistment. Fewer than 3 percent of those surveyed indicated that fringe benefits were the most important consideration, and they placed eighth out of nine factors considered by survey participants.

Replacement of Military with Civilian Personnel

Early in the Department of Defense study analyses were made of opportunities for greater substitution of civilians in support jobs now performed by military personnel. As a result, in the fall of 1965 plans were implemented to release 74,300 military personnel for combat assignments by substituting 60,500 civilians. This program is being watched carefully, and additional support jobs that might permit substitution are being sought. Several limitations exist in the extent to which civilian substitution can be utilized.

1. The need to provide training billets in all important categories.
2. The development of military personnel in specialist billets.
3. The rotational problem of the military at home and overseas.

In summary, the study finds it possible to "buy" an all-volunteer force in theory, but the implication is that, practically speaking, this is not a reasonable alternative.

5. *Are there ways of improving the process of choosing those who must serve?*

In this study the factor considered to be the "key criterion" for future improvements is the need for concentrating military service among the country's youngest male citizens. This conclusion is based on several lines of evidence: a nationwide poll in 1964 indicated that an overwhelming number of people polled (72 percent) indicated that military service between the ages of 16 and 20 was desirable; military commanders feel that younger men make better soldiers; there is obviously less disruption of personal plans concerning education, marriage, and career.

The study suggests the following approach as a means of concentrating the major requirements for military service among a young age group (age 19 or 20):

1. All men would be classified, as at present, by local boards. Present deferment rules would be continued in respect to student status, occupational status, dependency status, ROTC, and Reserve status.

2. Inductions of men from the Class 1A available pool in any one year would be made from a priority category consisting in large part of the current 19- or 20-year-olds.

3. For those men preferring to complete their college education before serving, deferments could be granted until the student completed or terminated his education. At that time he would have equal exposure along with the 19- or 20-year-olds of that year.

4. The priority category, called after draft delinquents and volunteers for induction, would thus consist of (a) available 19- or 20-year-olds; and (b) older men, up to age 35, who become available for service in the current year after expiration of their student or other temporary deferments.

5. Men not reached for induction by the end of the year would be placed at the bottom of next year's draft list, after men in the new class of 19- or 20-year-olds and the newly available exstudents.

6. The principal feature of the system described is that it reverses the present policy of calling the oldest men first to one of calling young men either at age 19 or 20 or on completion of school (if later).

COMMENT ON THE DRAFT STUDY

As a study of the draft, the Defense Department document is obviously inadequate. Representative Curtis said of it, "the so-called Defense Department study of the draft is one of the greatest travesties ever perpetrated on the Congress or the American people." Yet Congress accepted the study with little adverse comment. The same is true of the general public. Only those working closely with the subject showed any real concern.

Some persons feel the full report is still classified. My own impression is that when the decision was made to escalate the war in Vietnam many of the bases for the original study were no longer tenable, and so at least part of the study was not released because it simply did not apply any more. From 1965 to 1966 a new study, or portions of one, was made, but whether it will ever be released is not known. In any event, I can say at least that the summary, and the data supplied for the record, will give an interested person a good background into the problem as it is viewed by the Department of Defense.

Among the objections that have been raised to the study are the following:

1. It contains no discussion of the lottery or other reasonable alternatives, with the exception of a completely voluntary system, to the present draft process.

2. It contains no real discussion of manpower problems such as the impact of the draft on skilled manpower resources.

3. The study does not meaningfully discuss deferment for college students in connection with manpower needs or future national needs. It merely states that fewer college graduates than noncollege graduates serve, a fact disputed by General Hershey in his own testimony before the Committee. The prime reason for deferment, according to the study, is that the military depends on college graduates for a significant portion of its officer corps. Again, this sharply conflicts with the opinions of General Hershey, as well as those of a significant segment of the educational community, who feels that deferments are valid only in the national interest.

4. The study contains little information not already known to those interested and involved in the topic.

(a) The experience of the Selective Service System since 1948 is well known from the Selective Service System's Annual Reports and testimony before Congress.

(b) The problems of the Selective Service System are discussed, but with little emphasis on possible changes, with the exception of drafting younger men first.

(c) The conclusions that the draft is needed because of the current world situation and that a completely voluntary force is not realistic are scarcely original thoughts.

5. The conclusion that improved pay, better fringe benefits, and the

replacement of military personnel with civilians in some categories would not enable us to sustain an all-volunteer force may be true, but how this conclusion was reached is not spelled out. To answer their questions the Bureau of the Census surveyed nonveterans between ages 16 and 34, but no copy of the questionnaire was attached to the resume, no hint was given of the type of questions asked, or the numbers of people queried, and no information about the pretesting of questions was given. In view of these shortcomings it is impossible to judge the scientific competence of the survey. Further, why were only nonveterans surveyed? Many men in this group probably never made a conscious decision concerning military service; they simply were not drafted. Also, if veterans had been included in the sample, they would obviously have had some reasonable basis for answering questions concerning careers in the service.

6. Finally, a way of improving the process of choosing those who must serve was discussed. Basically, the improvement would come from drafting young men first. Failure to do so has been the main criticism of the present draft for some time. Further, the military departments obtained information from 102,000 men on active duty and 46,000 ready reservists in order to determine their reasons, including the influence of the draft, for entering service. Since no copy of this questionnaire was attached, it is again difficult to assess its adequacy.

To summarize, the study's failure to include certain items is a prime target for criticism. What was included did not significantly add to the information already available on the topic. In the words of the Interim Report of the Committee on Armed Services of the House of Representatives (released August 5, 1966) the statement of Assistant Secretary Morris "revealed that the Department of Defense study had failed to consider the basic question of 'equities' in the application of the Universal Military Training and Service Act."

During the questioning that followed Secretary Morris' reading of a prepared statement it was interesting (but not surprising) that this Department of Defense spokesman seemed reluctant to become involved in making critical comments of the Selective Service System. An exchange at the very end of the hearings indicates clearly the extent of this withdrawal from the issues.

Mr. Hébert.	I am going to ask you this question, and I readily tell you you do not have to answer, but I would like your personal opinion, if you feel free to give it in this connection. Do you believe that there should be more definitive instructions to the draft boards as related to educational deferment than the broad aspect of it now, where 4000 draft boards can come up with 4000 deferment decisions.
Mr. Morris.	Sir, I do not have a judgment on that question.

Mr. Hébert.   You answered the question. After the hearings I would like to
                    talk to you and find out what you think.[13]

The hearings were important, though initially critics of the draft felt that
they would be a sham, especially since nongovernmental witnesses were not to
be heard. General Hershey defended the Selective Service System vigorously, and
he was not an easy witness to question. His answers to questions propounded to
him depended on his assessment of the impact the question had on the
organization he was defending; for example, if the question were difficult or if it
attempted to put Selective Service in a bad light, he would ramble on at length,
never really giving an adequate answer. At first he was accepted by the
Committee as an old soldier whose career had been in the service of his country.
By the end of the hearings, however, it was apparent that his obstinate refusal to
accept any reasonable criticism and to offer to institute meaningful reforms was
highly annoying to some members of the Committee. More important,
Hershey – and through him the whole Selective Service System – was slowly
alienating himself from most groups who could accept the present system with
some changes. Of course, his relationship with Congressmen Rivers, Hébert, and
several other senior members of the Committee was in no way affected and the
alienation was far from complete. The other major testimony, given by the
Department of Defense, was significant in that the Committee felt that the
Department had left many questions unanswered. The highly touted study was
rather a bust and left some members of the Committee feeling considerable
doubt about the Department's ability to provide adequate answers to manpower
questions.

SUMMARY

In 1963 everything about the extension of the draft legislation was
perfunctory. The decision in 1965 to raise the level of the nation's commitment
in Vietnam was decisive in bringing about public protest to the draft and the war
in Vietnam. The antidraft campaign reached such a peak that many people
demanded that hearings be held. Although the hearings were rather restrictive,
they provided much information concerning the inadequacies of the present
system and set before the public the dimensions of the problem. From June
1966 to early in 1967 the arena changed from the Congress to the public sector,
particularly the national press and the colleges.

---

[13] *Ibid.* p. 9974.

4 | DEFERMENTS—WITH EMPHASIS ON STUDENTS

Deferments are as old as the country itself. In the War of Independence some colonists in critical occupations were excused from service. In the Civil War the South made extensive use of occupational deferments when, under the law, the Secretary of State was given the right to exempt men in certain occupations: presidents and professors of colleges and academies, farmers and superintendents, and operators in wool and cotton factories. As the Civil War continued, the South was forced to do away with most occupational deferments because of military manpower needs.[1] Until World War I deferments were given to men in particular occupations, and during that struggle men were drafted or deferred on the basis of individual contribution to the war effort.

Until World War I no serious thought had ever been given to deferring students in the United States, except that they were often regarded as too young to serve. The possibility of some type of educational deferment was considered in 1917 and a program devised that would allow students under 21 to be relieved of military service in order to attend college for three years. It should be remembered that at no time during this period were local boards close to the bottom of the available manpower pool. More than 500 college units were established in the country to handle approximately 145,000 young men in the Student Army Training Corps. Before the first students began their course of instruction, however, the draft age was reduced to 18 years by Congress and the period of instruction for students to nine months. The armistice was signed in November 1918, less than one month after the first students had been activated. Although the program was of short duration and its value was never assessed, the principle of student deferment had been established.[2]

As World War II approached, those planning for such an eventuality were

---

[1] Samuel Eliot Morison, *The Oxford History of the American People,* Oxford University Press, New York, 1965, pp. 666-667. Contains a short discussion of conscription.

[2] The material in this section comes from *A Working Paper: The Student Deferment Program in Selective Service,* prepared in the Planning Office, Office of the Director, National Headquarters, Selective Service System, Washington, D.C., February 1952.

once again faced with the problem of individual or group deferments for men in essential occupations. Throughout the conflict first one industry and then another attempted to obtain total deferments, but only the farmers came close to success.[3] In late 1944 even they were considered draftable, and James Byrnes, Director of the Office of War Mobilization, advised General Hershey to draft them. The Selective Training and Service Act of 1940 provided for the deferment of men whose employment or activity was essential to the welfare of the nation. College students were in this category, and by the end of 1941 more than 100,000 students had been deferred. As the manpower situation grew more critical, however, student deferment was restricted to those preparing for critical occupations and essential industries, such as engineering, science, and medicine. By mid-1944 the male college population in the country declined to approximately 30 percent of the 1939-1940 base. Since students were not considered a distinct group within the Selective Service System, there are no statistics to indicate the total number of student deferments granted during the war. As deferments tightened, the Office of Production Manpower provided the national Selective Service headquarters with lists of those occupations that were in dangerously short supply.[4] An indication of how dangerously low the supply of men in critical occupations really became is given by Dr. M. H. Trytten, Director of the Office of Scientific Personnel, National Research Council, in his testimony before the House Armed Services Committee on April 28, 1967. It was Dr. Trytten's responsibility to provide men for the Manhattan Project. The difficulty that he faced is exemplified in the following statement:

"The narrowness of the gap between success or failure is, I believe, attested by what occurred in the Manhattan District project. When the decision to go ahead with the atomic bomb was taken, it was immediately evident that a greatly stepped up effort would call for hundreds of additional scientists and engineers. But by that time most personnel were either deferred for essential activities and heavily engaged in projects with their own priorities or were already inducted. There was a prime recourse and one only, to comb the armed services for persons of the required capabilities and to reassign them. I was personally involved in this exercise, and as I recall some eight or nine hundred scientists and engineers were thus made available. No less an authority than General Groves stated, as I recall, in a Senate Hearing, that without this resource the Manhattan District project could not have been finished in time. Historians may wish to speculate on what then might have happened."

[3] For details of this situation see *Agricultural Deferment Selective Service, Special Monograph No. 7,* U.S. Government Printing Office, Washington, D.C., 1947, 335 pp.
[4] *The Problems of Selective Service, Special Monograph No. 16, Vol. 1,* U.S. Government Printing Office, Washington, D.C., 1952, pp. 133-156 discusses education and Selective Service during World War II.

The armed services had large numbers of students in uniform throughout the war. Both the Army and Navy operated educational programs at colleges and universities, and more than 200,000 men were maintained as military students for various periods.[5] The Navy V-12 program, for example, was set up to train prospective naval officers in the shortest possible time. The Army had a similar program. Many felt that these programs were undemocratic in that the student enlisted in the service but could remain in school until the service called him up. Thus enlistment in the armed services was in this case a device for staying in college.

After the war, for the short period from March 1947 to June 1948, there was no draft law, though Congress did pass a law establishing an Office of Selective Service Records with General Hershey as Director. In 1948, however, cold-war tensions forced Congress to reinstitute the draft.

For the first time serious study was given to the total concept of student deferments.

After the passage of the 1948 legislation General Hershey appointed a committee of scientists, educators, and others to look into the problem of maintaining an adequate supply of military manpower, but at the same time providing for a pool of educated men in a variety of fields essential to the national interest. Dr. Trytten was named head of the committee.[6] General Hershey called its attention to the fact

". . .that Congress declared that the national security requires maximum effort in the fields of scientific research and development and the fullest possible utilization of the nation's technological and scientific manpower resources, and that the Act authorizes the President to provide for the deferment from training and service of those whose activity in study, research or medical, scientific or other endeavors is found to be 'necessary to the maintenance of the national health, safety or interest.' "[7]

The full committee had six subcommittees representing the agricultural and biological sciences, engineering sciences, humanities, healing arts, physical sciences, and social sciences. After considerable study, the reports of these subcommittees were consolidated, and the "Trytten plan" was presented to the Selective Service System in 1950. The plan called for an uninterrupted flow of

[5] *Student Deferment and National Manpower Policy*, Columbia University Press, New York, 1952. See pp. 23-38 for a full discussion of this situation.

[6] M. H. Trytten, *Student Deferment in Selective Service*, University of Minnesota Press, 1952. This book carefully analyzes the need for considering college deferments during the 1950's, a period of less than all-out national emergency.

[7] *Outline of Historical Background of Selective Service and Chronology*, U.S. Government Printing Office, Washington, D.C., 1965, p. 31.

students through college, who would be chosen for deferment on an either/or basis: either their performace on a nationwide aptitude test or their performance in class based on a system of class rank. Although both criteria would be helpful to local boards, they were to be considered as advisory in nature. The value of having two criteria was that a high score on the test would offset low grades in college and vice versa. A second purpose, though not one clearly spelled out in any official document, is that these criteria also served the purpose of protecting students who ranked low in their classes at competitive colleges but could pass the deferment examination. On the other hand, given the diversity of American higher education, a significant proportion of the student body of less competitive institutions might fail the nationwide examination but receive deferment through class standing. The concensus was that deferment was not to mean exemption, merely postponement of service in the national interest.

The rationale behind student deferments was the recognition of a national need for educated people to support the economy with essential skills. In this context deferments are construed to be in the national interest, not in the interests of students' particular fields of endeavor or even particular industries.

During the Korean war, from 1951 to the spring of 1963, more than 600,000 students took the draft deferment examination. From the spring of 1963 until the spring of 1966 nearly all draft boards in the country deferred students who were making satisfactory progress toward a degree, and the test was discontinued because the manpower needs of the nation were relatively modest in this pre-Vietnam build-up period. With recent developments in Vietnam and the accelerated rate of American military commitments to that country, however, the deferment situation has changed. The Selective Service test was reinstituted and offered again during May 1966. The reinstatement of this test, along with class rank, at this time caused significant reaction throughout the country. In fact, much of the serious criticism of the Selective Service System during 1966-1967 was directed at the policy of deferments for college students. The *1966 Annual Report of the Director of Selective Service* shows that there are 11 deferment categories which by July 30, 1966, had been used to classify more than 12 million men out of a total available pool of more than 32 million. More than 80 percent of the total deferment population is classified in four major deferment categories, which are as follows:[8]

Class 3A, Fatherhood and Dependency Hardships. Most fathers are in this, the largest single deferment group. The more than three million men in this classification constitute 29.4% of all deferred registrants.

[8] Material in this section is taken from the *Annual Report of the Director of Selective Service, 1966,* U.S. Government Printing Office, Washington, D.C., pp. 16-17.

Class 4F, Not Qualified for Service. This is the classification of those men rejected primarily for physical and mental reasons. It is the second largest deferment classification and includes the more than 2.5 million men who make up about one-fifth of all deferred registrants.

Class 1Y, Qualified for Service Only in Time of War or National Emergency. This relatively new classification, in effect only since 1962, has grown in size by constant screening of the 4F Class and also by current preinduction and induction examinations. There are more than 2.3 million men currently in this classification or about one-fifth of all deferred registrants.

Note. Deferred for physical and mental reasons, the 4F and 1Y classifications *combined* account for 4.8 million men, almost 40 percent of all those who have deferred status.

Class 2S, Active in Study. This group experienced significant growth during fiscal 1965 by increasing by nearly a half million to more than 1.6 million. From 1965 to 1966 the figure increased again to 1,782,416, or almost 14 percent of the deferred registrants, though less than 5 percent of the total number of registrants.

Today there is a conflict between two demonstrated needs; the first for an uninterrupted flow of military manpower because of unsettled world conditions in general and Vietnam in particular, the second for a continuous flow of educated citizenry to operate our economy. Both needs must be met by young men between the ages of 18½ and 26. Dr. Trytten made an important point along these lines in a paper presented at the American Veterans Committee Conference on the Draft in November 1966:

"In World War II there was a general acceptance of the thought that we were totally committed to a struggle in which the interests of the nation were basic and its total resources dedicated to the national effort. The result was that policies and practices. . .relating to the disposition of individuals were made on the simple criteria of whether the particular action was in the national interest, meaning. . .the war effort."

It is clear that today in America no such well-understood criteria exist. The national interest in manpower, other than military, has not been evaluated nor made a factor in establishing policy. There is no clear definition of manpower policies as they affect the country's interest today. This lack of clarity has created a vacuum into which those who are antiwar, antidraft, and antideferment have moved.

The leading proponent of deferments is General Hershey himself. It has been one relatively clear position that the old soldier has held for more than 15 years, and it has formed the basis of the Selective Service function of "channeling" (which is discussed later in this chapter). Almost none of the leaders of American higher education has spoken out in favor of deferments, though some have spoken out vigorously against them, particularly Kingman Brewster, President of Yale, and Richard Keast, President of Wayne State University in Detroit. Brewster's famous 1966 baccalaureate address, quoted in Chapter 3, received national publicity; his phrase about students hiding in "the endless catacombs of formal education" is frequently cited with approval. It was essentially a critical speech with no alternatives proposed. In 1966 Wayne State, with the complete backing of President Keast, ceased to classify students by rank in class. There are many reasons why prominent members of the American higher educational establishment, particularly presidents, have failed to speak out in favor of deferments. Undoubtedly many more are silent because of the strong feelings of faculty and students against the draft. College presidents are about as secure as Middle Eastern dictators, and although one may not like their silence one can at least understand it.

On the other hand, the American Council on Education, which purports to be the voice of higher education in America, has supported the principle of deferments on a number of occasions, though it believes that deferment should not mean exemption. As the velocity of the debate increased, the Council reiterated its position in a statement filed for the record of the House Armed Services Committee hearings in the spring of 1967, but this time it had to qualify its remarks. The statement did not attempt to speak for the entire membership of the organization. Instead it came from the 19-member Commission on Federal Relations of the Council, and even so only a majority of this Commission could agree on it. During the crucial debate on educational deferments American higher education was hopelessly divided.

With all the emotional wrangling stripped away, the main argument against deferments is a simple one. Deferment gives people who can afford to go to college and who are bright enough to remain in good standing the opportunity to postpone going into service in time of war. The point is that they have a choice, whereas the person who for whatever reasons does not go to college has none. The argument continues that a student can pyramid deferments by graduate study, occupational deferments, and the acquisition of dependents and reach the age of 26 without serving at all.

As mentioned earlier, the use of the college deferment test and rank in class as a basis for granting deferments has also been severely criticized in recent years, though the same procedures were used during the Korean war without causing extensive controversy. The combination of the two indices was thought to provide local boards, which ultimately make the decisions, with the best available information on a student's status.[9] General Hershey admits that the test has only the appearance of being fair, since it tends to stress ability in mathematics.[10] Recent research also indicates that high grades on tests of this kind are valid only in showing that students will do well on tests and that there is no necessary correlation between the test scores and later productivity or success.[11] Further, it is readily admitted that these indices assume that a student's mastery of college courses is a reasonable indication of his potential value to the nation – a questionable assumption, though one traditionally relied on by institutions of higher education for retaining or failing students, awarding fellowships, scholarships, and teaching assistantships, and admitting applicants to graduate school.

One may ask just how many college men are drafted? The answer is, not many. Although more than 1.7 million students were deferred in 1966, the number inducted is almost miniscule. During the 1966 hearings on the draft the Department of Defense supplied data on the educational level of a 5 percent sample of army inductees who were on active duty as of February 28, 1966: only 1.8 percent were college graduates. The percentage of draftees with some college education was higher – about 13 percent in the same sample. The study was done during a period when the Vietnam buildup had started and draft calls had increased. It should be noted that college graduates serve in far larger numbers in a variety of officer categories. (This point is discussed in more detail later.)

There are other factors to be considered in connection with college deferments. First, a large group of young men is deferred for other reasons. The national rejection rate of men is almost half the total available pool each year. "The pre-induction examination was given to 581,716 registrants nineteen years of age and over during fiscal 1965. Among those 287,582, or 49.5%, were found qualified while the *remaining 50.5% were not*"[12] [emphasis added]. During fiscal 1966 examinations were given to 1,725,084 registrants, of whom 59.1 percent were found qualified and 40.9 percent were not.[13]

---

[9] Undergraduate score of 70 on national test – Rank: end of freshmen year – upper 50% of class; end of sophomore year – upper 66% of class; end of junior year – upper 75% of class. Graduate score of 80 on national test or rank in upper 25% of male students in senior year of undergraduate school. After first year of graduate school making normal progress toward degree.

[10] "General Hershey Interview," *U.S. News and World Report,* January 10, 1966, p. 40.

[11] Philip Price, Calvin Taylor, James Richards, and Tony Jacobsen, "Measurement of Physician Performance," *The Journal of Medical Education,* Vol. 39, No. 2, February 1964, pp. 39, 203-211.

[12] *Annual Report of the Director of Selective Service, 1965,* U.S. Government Printing Office, Washington, D.C., p. 22.

[13] *Annual Report of the Director of Selective Service, 1966, op. cit.* p. 22.

This sharp drop in the number of those rejected undoubtedly stems from the increased needs of the military because of the war. These figures are not misleading, for roughly the same percentages apply over an 18-year period from 1948 to 1966, when 42.1 percent of those examined (4,429,161) were found to be unqualified. This period includes the Korean war and part of the Vietnam buildup, when it can be assumed the standards would be less rigorous. The important point is that roughly half those who registered were found unqualified for physical or mental reasons. Essentially this group comes from the lower socioeconomic strata of our society and so does not contain many students. Thus one type of deferment – initial rejection – is given to almost half the available population.

Second, the accessibility of higher education today calls into question the contention that student deferments are undemocratic because they favor the more affluent. The junior college movement, low tuition rates at most public institutions, work-study programs, Federal loans, and money from other sources make college available to many, if not all, qualified students. This is the main argument that the Office of Education makes for increased Federal expenditure for higher education, namely, that higher education should be available to all, regardless of financial ability.

Third, college graduates do serve in the armed forces after graduation. New officer acquisitions vary in all the armed forces, but they approximate 40,000 per year, about 90 percent of whom come from the college graduate population. The exact number or percentage of graduates who serve is difficult to ascertain, however. Statistics are misleading and can be utilized to justify almost any position taken; for example, on June 22, 1966, when General Hershey testified before the House Armed Services Committee hearings on the administration and operation of the System, he was asked by Congressman Evans (D. Colorado) about the percentage of college men who serve. General Hershey replied:

"At the present time the best information we have is that of the people we defer for college about 56 percent of them get into service, and only about 43-44 percent of those who do not go into college get into service, and it is quite easily understandable, because we have over two million that have been rejected for educational reasons, obviously they didn't go to college and they didn't get into the service."

The General went on to say, "the percentage of college people who have served is ten points higher than the percentage of people who didn't go to college."[14]

[14] *Review of the Administration and Operation of the Selective Service System,* Hearings before the Committee on Armed Services, House of Representatives, U.S. Government Printing Office, Washington, D.C., 1966, p. 9642.

This statement, which appears to be a clear one, should have silenced the charge that college men hide from the draft. Yet eight days later it was directly contradicted by Assistant Secretary of Defense Thomas D. Morris in his testimony before the same Committee. He said:

"Our analysis of Selective Service records of men reaching age 26 as of June 1964 reveals that only 40 percent of college graduates had served compared to 60 percent of college drop outs, 57 percent of high school graduates and 50 percent of non-high school graduates. . . ."[15]

The apparent contradiction between the two statements is explained by the fact that General Hershey talked about "people who are deferred for college" and Secretary Morris distinguished between college dropouts and college graduates. When Congressman Samuel S. Stratton (D. New York) asked for clarification, General Hershey agreed that his figures were based on men who had been to college and not on college graduates.

In the report of the National Advisory Commission on Selective Service a chart entitled "Percentage of Men Who Served by Educational Level (men aged 27-34 in 1964)" indicated that 70 percent of those with college degrees serve as opposed to 68 percent of college dropouts and 74 percent of high school graduates.[16] The chart utilized by the Commission is somewhat misleading because it goes back as far as the Korean war, when obviously more college graduates served.

One of the misleading features is the key phrase "men aged 27-34 in 1964," who would have been in the 18-26 age group in 1950 to 1958. During that period also fewer men were in the pool; for example, in 1955 the pool contained about a million men, whereas in 1967 the pool contained almost two million men, an increase of more than 60 percent in 12 years.

The Clark Report, accomplished at the behest of the House Armed Services Committee, states:

"The deferment of students has not meant that they have been protected from the draft or received favored treatment compared to non-students. In recent years sixty percent of the college student group has served in the armed forces either as volunteers or inductees, whereas fifty-seven percent of the non college students were called to or entered military service."[17]

---

[15] Ibid. p. 9930.

[16] In Pursuit of Equity: Who Serves When Not All Serve? Report of the National Advisory Commission on Selective Service, U.S. Government Printing Office, Washington, D.C., February, 1967, p. 23.

[17] Civilian Advisory Panel on Military Manpower Procurement Report to the Committee on Armed Services, House of Representatives, U.S. Government Printing Office, Washington, D.C., February 28, 1967, p. 11.

Percentage of Men Who Served by Educational Level
(men aged 27-34 in 1964)

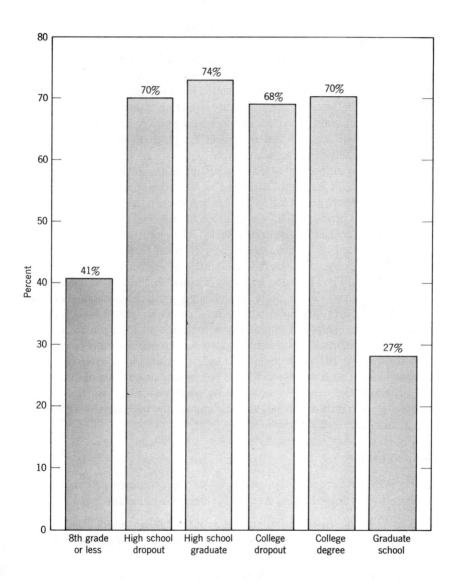

Source. Military Service in American Life Since WWII: An Overview, National
Opinion Research Center, 1966

It is difficult to ascertain the exact percentage of students or college graduates who actually serve. One can take whatever statistics one wishes to bolster the position being promoted. I would judge that *in time of war* college graduates do serve in the armed forces in numbers roughly proportionate to their percentage of the population. They serve, however, not as draftees but rather as volunteers in officer programs.

Graduate student deferments present different problems. In the past men going to graduate school were virtually immune from service. The pyramiding of deferments for educational reasons, bolstered by being deferred for dependency, occupation, or by reaching age 26, clearly shows up in several sets of statistics that indicate that only 27 percent of those with graduate degrees serve. There is no question about the fact that deferment for graduate study leads to virtual exemption from service in the armed forces.

The following points can be made in summary. Inequities will be present in any draft system, at least until such time as all, rather than just some, men are needed. Any attempt to correct or change one inequity could well create others or could lead to problems that would affect the national economy. The armed forces look to civilian colleges for roughly 90 percent of their new officers. Moreover, the need for an educated citizenry is clearly essential to the future of our nation. Finally, and most important, the decision made concerning deferments should not be made with only Vietnam in mind. It must provide the flexibility necessary in a more complicated wartime situation. Certainly deferments are necessary to permit trained people to function in a postwar situation. In my judgment any decision to abandon deferments completely would be shortsighted. The argument against student deferments is not so strong as it might appear to be. On the other hand, it is difficult to defend a position that would seem to favor establishing in our nation an intellectual or economic elite. The situation could be remedied by some system of random selection, which, after a transition period, would eliminate the necessity for deferments. This point is discussed in Chapter 5.

CHANNELING [18]

The Selective Service System as a part of the deferment process has for a number of years assumed what it calls "the channeling function."

"The term *channeling* refers to that process through which registrants are influenced to enter and remain in study in critical occupations, and in other

---

[18] The material on channeling is taken from my article "Selective Service: Are There Any Alternatives?" *Educational Record,* American Council on Education, Washington, D.C., Spring 1967, pp. 116-125.

essential activities in the national health, safety, and interest by deferment or prospect for deferment from military service." [19]

"Selective Service channels thousands of young men through its deferment procedures into those fields of endeavor where there are shortages of adequately trained personal. . . . Many younger engineers, scientists, technicians, and other skilled workers have been kept in their jobs through occupational deferments. Young male teachers are induced to remain in the teaching profession through deferment and additional students are attracted into the profession. The fields of medicine and dentistry also have benefited from student and occupational deferment channeling." [20]

The System bases. its channeling function on the very general language in Section 1(e) of the law (Policy and Intent of Congress of the Universal Military Training and Service Act).

"(e) Congress further declares that adequate provision for national security requires maximum effort in the fields of scientific research and development, and the fullest possible utilization of the nation's technological, scientific and other critical manpower resources."

The most recent analysis of the Universal Military Training Act, released on March 1, 1966, by the Committee on Armed Services, House of Representatives, contains no reference to channeling or to Section 1(e) of the Act to indicate that this is intended to be a function of the Selective Service System.

On the one hand, the System talks about blanket channeling into fields of endeavor in which there are shortages of trained personnel. The language used in the 1965 Report of the Selective Service System is that persons will be "induced to remain. . .in certain occupations," etc. On the other hand, the disposition of each case of individual deferment is the responsibility of the local draft board.

Some authorities are of the opinion that explicit authority for the channeling activity is not contained in the basic law and, further, that even though administrative interpretation over the years has created this function the Selective Service System's position on channeling and the language it uses to describe the function are inconsistent with the decentralized decision-making authority of local boards. If channeling is to be accomplished, Selective Service should provide definitive guidelines. More important, there is some question that the System is. the proper agency for establishing and carrying out manpower policies.

[19] *Annual Report of the Director of Selective Service, 1966, op. cit.* p. 16.
[20] *Annual Report of the Director of Selective Service, 1965, op. cit.* p. 18.

Those who questioned the purported success of channeling pointed out that although the manpower pool was expanding current draft calls were minimal, fewer men were affected, and the capacity of the System to channel effectively was diminished. Finally, and most important, to use the deferment-channeling device as an incentive for men to enter certain fields is highly questionable, for it may provide false motivation and reward evasive behavior.

THE CURRENT PROBLEM

The basic elements of the Selective Service law in effect in 1967 were derived from the Oates Report, completed after the Civil War. The organization of the Selective Service System itself is basically the same as that initiated by the 1940 legislation. This is the crux of the problem. In the period since World War II the nation has undergone startling economic changes. The educational system, especially higher education, also has changed. The predominantly rural society of the early twentieth century has all but disappeared, and urbanization is the keynote of life in America today. Finally, the wars we have fought since the end of World War II, those we are currently fighting, and those we will probably fight in the future seem not to be all-out, worldwide struggles. No one can say the Selective Service System has not been successful in the past. As of June 30, 1966, the System had registered more than 32 million men in its quarter century of existence, but the point is that we are not concerned with the past, but with the present and the future. The remaining discussion of deferments takes place in the context of the debate on the proposed 1967 legislation.

5 | RANDOM SELECTION AND OTHER ALTERNATIVES TO THE DRAFT

Those advocating change in the current draft system suffer from one near fatal weakness – they cannot agree on a practical alternative. A system of random selection appears to many to be the solution, but others see randomness or chance as a bad way to select people to send to war. A voluntary army would please many, but it would be expensive, inflexible, and considered by some to be undemocratic. Universal military training has the merit of utilizing everyone, but there is no need for everyone to serve in the kind of war we are now fighting and will fight in the foreseeable future. Finally, National Service or alternative service has its youthful protagonists. Yet others see it as a colossal waste of time. The question seems to be, is there a viable alternative? If not, should we just continue to patch the current system?

RANDOM SELECTION

The idea of using some random system to select men for the armed forces, or, more precisely, to arrange the list of eligibles into an order of call, is not a new one. A form of lottery was used by the North during the Civil War and by the nation during the early part of World Wars I and II. West Germany, Australia, the Philippines, and several South American countries are currently relying on this system. Why has it been suggested that the United States return to such a system? Of the many reasons given, one is paramount: the dramatic increase in the number of eligible young men reaching age 18. According to many people, this reason, coupled with the fact that only a portion of these young men are needed by the armed forces, dictates the necessity of instituting some type of random selection system as the only equitable way to determine who will go and who will not.

The numbers problem cannot be emphasized too strongly. The low point in the number of 18-year-old men occurred in the early 1950's as a result of the low birth rate during the depression. At that time slightly more than one million eligible men reached age 18 each year. The well-known "baby boom" after World War II changed the pattern completely. In 1967 there were almost two million eligible men, and this number will increase in the 1970's. The Department of Defense figures, released in June 1966, which base their estimate on the 1955 figure of 1.15 million, predicted an 84 percent increase (1.2 million) in the number of young men reaching age 18 by 1974, but these figures have already proved to be conservative. Granting the size of the pool and its steady increase, we may turn to the next question. What are the annual requirements of the military? The requirements fluctuate, of course, with world conditions. In fiscal 1966, because of Vietnam requirements, the Department of Defense requested, and received, 335,000 men from the draft. To give the figures perspective it should be noted that at the height of the Korean war 587,000 men were drafted during a one-year period. It should not be forgotten that draftees make up only about one-third of those entering the armed forces; the other two-thirds volunteer. Admittedly many volunteer reluctantly to avoid the draft and to obtain a choice of service, technical training, and various service schools. The following graph derived from the Department of Defense testimony before the House Armed Services Committee on May 2, 1967, clearly illustrates what the problem would be in a *post*-Vietnam situation. As the graph indicates, roughly one of every seven men available for the draft would be utilized. The military force level is 2.65 million men.

Finally, there is evidence that under the present system of more than 4000 local draft boards the burden cannot be distributed fairly throughout the nation. Whatever the honesty and devotion of local draft-board members, the various areas of the country differ too greatly in their demographic characteristics for local boards to deal effectively with the manpower problem. Too often the decision whether a man is to be drafted may be based on where he was born, where he lives, where he registers, what level of affluence he or his family enjoys, and possibly even the color of his skin.

Proponents of a lottery system see it as being fair in a way that the present Selective Service process cannot be. At least everyone not selected would have had an equal chance with those who were selected to serve, and both groups would be able to plan their careers with some degree of certainty.

There are several ways in which a lottery system could be set up. The system proposed by Congressman Reuss (D. Wisconsin) in 1966 constitutes a complete program for armed forces recruitment. Reuss calls for greater benefits for servicemen in order to increase enlistments and to spur re-enlistments. He advocates that the military be reduced by the employment of civilians to perform a variety of support functions and that the Department of Defense do away with arbitrary physical requirements. Once all possible reductions had been realized and enlistments increased, the dips into the manpower pool for draftees

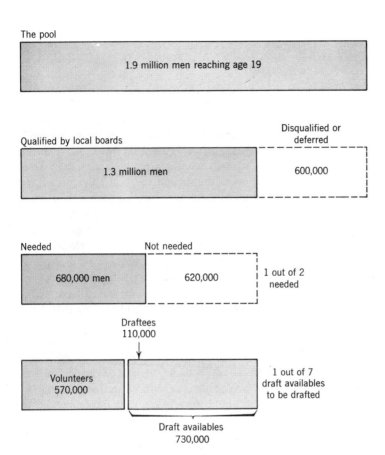

The pool

1.9 million men reaching age 19

Qualified by local boards

Disqualified or deferred

1.3 million men

600,000

Needed

Not needed

680,000 men

620,000

1 out of 2 needed

Draftees
110,000

Volunteers
570,000

1 out of 7
draft availables
to be drafted

Draft availables
730,000

Force level of 2.65 millions used for illustration

would become smaller (even in a Vietnam situation), and with an ever-expanding pool of manpower available the present complex draft system for determining "who goes" would become totally unworkable. At this point, Reuss says, Selective Service should be abolished and replaced by a lottery as a fairer way to distribute the military obligation.

Reuss, who would also abolish student deferment, explains that such a step would not determine *whether* a young man would go to college but merely *when* he would go. To take this reasoning one step further, more men would eventually attend college, for educational benefits would be a part of the rewards for military service. Deferments would be continued only for hardship cases and for certain extremely vital civilian jobs.

Finally, Reuss would like to work toward the concept of universal service in domestic and foreign Peace Corps types of organization. This part of his plan, however, is not given in detail.

Another system has been proposed by Senator Edward Kennedy. At age 18 all men would be examined. At age 19 all physically and mentally qualified men would stand an equal chance of being selected. After all qualified registrants had been assigned numbers by their local draft boards, the Selective Service System would conduct a national drawing, probably once or twice each year. Into the "fishbowl" would be placed as many numbers as the largest draft board had registrants. After each number was drawn and its position recorded, the local board would receive a list of the numbers, and those highest on the list would be drafted first. If the first number selected were 1000, for instance, every draft board with more than 1000 registrants would have some registrant with that number who would be drafted first. It would then be a simple matter for the Department of Defense to ask for the required number of draftees and for Selective Service, using the same kind of formula currently employed, to put the numbers in order and compute how many should be called from each board. Thus registrants at the bottom of the list, knowing immediately that they would be called only during an emergency, could plan their futures with more confidence. At the end of the year the men not called would go to the bottom of the list, and the new 19-year-olds would be listed ahead of them.

Under the Kennedy plan no deferments would be made for marriage, fatherhood, dependents, or occupation, except in extreme hardship cases, although local boards would still hold the responsibility for deferments in order that individual problems might be dealt with compassionately. Educational deferments would be granted but limited to four years. (Since Senator Kennedy proposed this plan he has changed his mind regarding undergraduate student deferments. He opposes such deferments and his plan now approximates that of Mr. Reuss in this respect.) Once undergraduate school had been completed, the students would take their chances with the 19-year-olds in that year's lottery. Because no deferments for graduate school would be granted, it would no longer be possible to pyramid deferments in order to escape the draft altogether. Students going to medical school would not take part in the lottery; rather they would be subject to a "doctor draft" after completing their medical studies. In a statement made on June 29, 1966, before the House Armed Services Committee Senator Kennedy explained the flexibility of the proposed system: "An increase in the draft necessitated by world problems would simply mean local boards would reach further down to those men whose numbers appear lower on this list."

Kennedy's proposal contains an interesting counterargument to the assertion that under a lottery system the rate of enlistments would decline because those men not drafted could be more certain that they would not be called later. Kennedy answers by pointing out that since those who do not serve would in most cases not yet have civilian careers to return to it is likely that the rate of re-enlistment would rise and thus compensate for the decline in enlistments. Re-enlistments could be further encouraged by increasing military pay.

The Selective Service System – meaning General Hershey – opposes any suggestion of a lottery. Most of the General's arguments against the lottery have been disputed, however; for example, he says that under a lottery a man whose number does not come up when he is age 19 is lost forever. Further, he states, the loss of these men would severely limit our flexibility in time of major crisis. These are not persuasive arguments because those not drafted during their prime year would revert to the bottom of the list for the next year at least and could be retained on the Selective Service rolls to be called on in a national emergency.

In Hershey's words, the difference between the present Selective Service System and a lottery is "at bottom the difference between a human being and a machine. The people on local boards have more compassion than a machine. . .the machine cannot tell whether a man is more valuable as a father or student or scientist or doctor than a soldier." By implication Hershey is defending the deferment system and the local autonomy of the boards, but both the Kennedy and Reuss proposals meet this objection. Both would give physical and mental examinations before the lottery, thus eliminating all unqualified applicants. Reuss would make no deferments except for extremely vital occupations. Kennedy would defer students for four years only, with the exception of those in medicine, who would face the doctors' draft later. (See p. 52 for Senator Kennedy's present position on this point.) Questions of hardship could be handled before or subsequent to the lottery, depending on the administrative machinery.

Hershey's antithesis of men and machines, however, is emotional rather than rational. A lottery would, in effect, create a national manpower pool and make feasible the use of centralized computers and other automated equipment to increase the efficiency of the Selective Service System; for example, after a young man had been registered and classified by a local board, his file would be sent to Selective Service headquarters and fed into a computer. Any subsequent change in his status would be updated in the computer records. If he were to move from his local board area, his record could easily be transferred, thus eliminating the possibility that geography would determine his status.

In addition to its fairness, the lottery has, according to its proponents, other advantages. First, the element of uncertainty would be lessened. Those with numbers at the top of the list would be drafted, those with numbers at the bottom would not and could plan for the future. Only those whose numbers fell in the middle zone would suffer uncertainty and then only for one year. Second, after one year a man would be relieved of responsibility to serve in all but extreme circumstances and could make his plans with far more certainty than exists at present. Third, the system could be flexible enough to meet military manpower needs.

These two illustrations of a random selection system are not meant to be exhaustive. Randomness could be achieved by scrambling birth dates or by any number of other means. The point is that the numbers of men available are far greater than those the nation will need in any situation but an all-out war. The main arguments against this method of selection have come from General Hershey and some influential members of Congress. Aside from his sheer suspicion of automatic data-processing equipment, Hershey is against the random selection system primarily because it would be the beginning of an intrusion into the local-board process. Consequently, everyone proposing a random selection system has been careful to state explicitly that local boards would maintain their classification function and would keep the autonomy that has been theirs by law since World War I. It is true, however, that the mechanical process would be centralized and that eventually a national manpower pool would probably be suggested as the logical next step. Finally, local boards might be looked at critically and at some time in the future changed to some degree. So the General is undoubtedly justified in his anxieties — though that, of course, does not cancel out the question whether the status quo is worth defending.

In my judgment some type of random selection system is an absolute necessity, given the needs of the nation, the numbers of young men involved, and the weaknesses of the present system.

THE VOLUNTARY ARMY

The Johnson Administration has been accused of not facing the issue of the feasibility of an all-volunteer armed force. According to critics, the American public has not been told the whole truth about the advantages that this change in military manpower procurement would have for a democratic society; in its study of military manpower procurement policies, released in 1966 (which was merely a "summary" anyway), the Defense Department used only a highly selected portion of its working papers and of the facts and figures.[1] The critics take to task both the President's Commission on Selective Service and the Clark

---

[1] Robert T. Stafford, Frank J. Horton, Richard Schweiker, Garner E. Shriver, and Charles W. Whalen, Jr., *How to End the Draft*, The National Press, Washington, D.C., 1967, p. viii.

Panel Report for their perfunctory treatment of this issue.

Because the question of the type of system to be used to raise the necessary military manpower has been an issue throughout our history, a brief sketch of the historical background is necessary to place the current allegations in perspective.

America has experimented with several distinct methods of raising the military manpower necessary to defend the nation. Before the Revolutionary War the colonies used the militia system with which they had been familiar in England. In Virginia in 1628, for example, the General Assembly adopted legislation which stated that "inhabitants" were required to "go under arms." In Massachusetts the Puritans' enforcement of militia service was second only to their enforcement of observance of the Sabbath. In Connecticut, during the 150-year span of colonialism, more than 100 military laws were passed, 54 of which asserted the doctrine of military compulsion.[2]

All the early colonies had examples of militia enactments. Originally no exemptions were countenanced, but as the frontiers moved farther West and as the number of large population centers increased certain exceptions were allowed. These exemptions, which took the form of bounties, substitutes, and the like, reflect the increased security of the colonies, the changing economy, and, generally, the easier life.

The strengths of the militia system were its immediate availability, its relative democracy, and its flexibility in adjusting to local needs. The weaknesses of the system were made manifestly clear during the Revolutionary War, when none of the colonies was able to formulate a workable law for raising an army. Each of the colonies guarded its right to act independently, and for obvious reasons they were reluctant to give a strong central government the authority to raise a national army. All the Continental Congress could do in 1775 was to "recommend" to the colonies that militia be formed for the defense of the colonies. Washington was never able to procure more than a fraction of the potential army available to him. In 1776 the total force was about 90,000 men, about one-eighth of the available men of fighting age, and in 1779-1780 the army dwindled to half of that figure. Washington had no use for the militia, who ". . .leave you at last at a critical moment."[3]

After the war Washington, as the first President of the new republic, recognized the need for a small standing army. Yet he also realized that the former colonists were highly suspicious of a strong central government and that

---

[2] *Backgrounds of Selective Service, Special Monograph No. 1*, Vol. 1, U.S. Government Printing Office, Washington, D.C., 1949, p. 40. This monograph contains details of all aspects of the early colonial militia and also later developments of Selective Service.

[3] Gottschalk and Lock, "Europe and the Modern World," Vol. 1, *The Rise of Modern Europe*, Scott, Foresman, and Co., New York, 1951, p. 577.

they would regard a standing army as one manifestation of such a government. After debate, amendment, revision, concession, and political maneuvering the Congress passed the Uniform Militia Act of 1792. The Act called for what was actually the opposite of the standing army envisioned by Washington, since it provided for 13 separate state military organizations and made no specific provision for Federal involvement. Two years later Congress gave the President authority, with the approval of the state governors, to raise a militia of 80,000 men. These men were not required to serve more than three months in any one tour, and the life of the legislation was set for one year. The point to be emphasized here is that the President was required to go to the governors for an army — so, again, there were actually 13 separate and distinct armies.

As time passed, the position of Washington and of President Adams on military preparedness, grounded in the concept of a small citizen army, found less and less favor. The legislation of the period favored volunteerism. Bounties and land were offered to those who would volunteer and complete their enlistment. When the war of 1812 started, the manpower crisis worsened, but Congressional response remained inadequate: among other things, the Congress shortened the period of military service and continued to vest final authority in the states. The attempt to pass a conscription act ended in failure. The result of this policy was evident in the battle of Bladensburg, when a British expeditionary force, under General Robert Ross, walked into Washington unopposed by the militia (who turned and ran), sacked the city, and burned the Capitol. The 7000 militia — all that heeded the summons out of the 95,000 called — suffered only 66 casualties before leaving the field.[4] But the opponents of military compulsion learned nothing from this lesson. Daniel Webster warned Congress in 1814 that Massachusetts would not accept a conscription law. Several governors were of the opinion that the Constitution gave neither the legislative nor the executive branch of the Federal government authority to raise a national army for the good of the nation. The turning point came in 1824, when the Supreme Court decided in the case of *Martin v. Mott* that a state did not have the right to withhold militia from national service. Nine years earlier, the Court — which, under Chief Justice Marshall, was never deterred by public opinion or sectionalist feeling — had opened the door to this discussion by its definition of national sovereignty in the McCulloch case. This weakened the position of the states and ushered in the era of nationalism.

By the time of the war with Mexico, however, all the states had ceased to make militia service compulsory. Typical was the action of the New York legislature, which in 1846 reduced the fine for nonattendance at militia drills to

4 Samuel Eliot Morison, *The Oxford History of the American People*, Oxford University Press, New York, 1965, pp. 392-393.

a nominal fee. The ineffectiveness of the voluntary militia system, with its short-term enlistments, was brought home to the nation during the war with Mexico: General Winfield Scott, halfway to Mexico City and sweeping the forces of Santa Ana in front of him, lost half his army when his soldiers quit and returned home because their term of enlistment was over

The inadequacy of the volunteer system was underscored by the experience of both North and South during the Civil War. At the start both sides depended on volunteers — the number of short-term enlistees was large enough to fill easily the calls issued by the leaders of both sides. Soon, however, it became obvious to both sides that voluntary enlistment was neither a sufficient nor a satisfactory way to conduct a war.

The South used conscription as early as 1862 (for a one-year period) but allowed a wide range of occupational exemptions that increased as time went on. The law was easily abused and led to some discontent in the Confederacy. The Union passed its first conscription act on March 3, 1863. It required all men between the ages of 20 and 45 to register. Draft calls were based on the populations of the various states. Enrollment districts, patterned after voting districts, were established, with provost marshal offices to handle the administration of the act. An exemption could be purchased for 300 dollars — not a small sum to most men, but easily within the reach of the wealthy. Bounties were also provided under certain conditions.

On July 11, 1863, a week after the battle of Gettysburg, the names of the first enrollees were drawn by lot. It was a hot sultry Saturday in New York City. Provost Marshal Charles Jenkins drew the first name and announced: "William Jones, 46th Street, Corner 10th Avenue."[5] Shortly after that the rioting started, abetted by an undetermined number of Confederate troops who had filtered into the city. "Copperheads" (Southern sympathizers) and immigrants, in competition with the recently freed Negroes for unskilled work, incited riots with cries of "Kill the niggers!" and "A rich man's war, but a poor man's fight!" That Negroes were not eligible for the draft compounded the hostility against them. The riots spread, and for five days the city was in turmoil. Hundreds were killed and property damage totaled more than 1 million dollars. General Mead was forced to detach troops to New York and other cities, thereby weakening his army to such an extent that he was unable to follow up the Union victory at Gettysburg. Riots also occurred in Boston, Massachusetts, Worcester, Ohio, Portsmouth, New Hampshire, and Rutland, Vermont.[6] The South carried the concept of occupational deferment, which it originated, to a ridiculous extreme, exempting presidents and professors of colleges and academies, operators in

---

[5] Irving Werstien, *July 1863*, John Messner and Co. Inc., New York, ¡ p. 252. A most compelling chronicle of the New York City draft riots.

wool and cotton factories, and, eventually, farmers. Both North and South required involuntary enrollment of citizens by officers and officials and allowed bounties and substitutes. The law in the North was viewed with open disfavor. The South, more resigned to her fate, was not openly contemptuous of the law; as the war went on, however, it had to be amended in order to tighten up, and in some cases do away with, occupational deferments because of the need for more soldiers.

To all intents and purposes the Civil War was the last major conflict that this nation attempted to fight with voluntary armed forces. To be sure, there were Congressional debates before each of the two world wars over the method to be used to raise the necessary manpower, but the draft law passed during World War I, which established the basic system still being utilized today, generally received acceptance. In recent years, however, proponents of the voluntary army concept have once again become active.

Congressmen Curtis and Ellsworth (R. Kansas), for instance, have favored a voluntary approach to the recruitment of military manpower. Curtis feels that a voluntary force, initiated after all possible manpower savings have been made, would raise the quality of our defense and in the long run save the Government money. He advocates hiring civilians for noncombat jobs, attracting volunteers by increasing salaries, and lowering physical and mental standards to enable high school dropouts to enlist. Ellsworth does not advocate that the draft be abolished immediately, but that this be the ultimate objective of Congress and the Administration. In testimony before the House Armed Services Committee Ellsworth said:

"We never will get rid of the draft until the Government accepts the goal of building a purely volunteer military establishment. This means increased military pay. It means increased career opportunities. It means a radical departure from the existing practice of using uniformed personnel in administrative and supply jobs in the United States which could just as easily be filled by civilians. It means attention to the creation of a more adequate volunteer reserve force which can be activated in crisis time. It means a system of bonuses for enlistment by the reserves for active duty in crises. But most of all it means a determination by the Administration and the Congress to make every effort to undertake the necessary reform to allow the draft to be ended.

"Building a purely volunteer service will cost money. But it is testimony to

---

[6] For a good description of the draft riots see William B. Hesseltine, *Lincoln and the War Governors,* Knopf and Co., New York, 1948, pp. 273-307. For a discussion of the system in a particular state see Eugene C. Murdock, *Ohio's Bounty System in the Civil War,* Ohio University Press for the Ohio Historical Service, Columbus, Ohio, 1963, 58 pp. It should be understood that the evils and corruption in Ohio were not peculiar to that state alone.

the inattention which the Defense Department has given this subject that Secretary McNamara has estimated the annual cost at $4 billion on one occasion and at $20 billion ten months later. What the costs are is unknown. It is conceivable that it may be expensive, but we will never know until we thoroughly explore the steps which must be taken to permit abolition of the draft. I am confident that the American people would be willing to endure a meaningful dollar sacrifice to end a Government policy which drafts the youth of our nation to risk human sacrifice in combat." [7]

The forces arrayed against the voluntary army concept, especially early in 1966, were formidable. Emphatic in his opposition, Secretary McNamara told a Senate subcommittee that to scrap the draft entirely would

"...make it difficult, if not impossible, to guarantee that the necessary manpower would be available in time to meet the kinds of rapid changes in military requirements which we have encountered in recent years. . . . We cannot look forward to discontinuance of the draft in the coming decades. . . ."

In his testimony before the House Armed Services Committee in June 1966 Assistant Secretary of Defense (Manpower) Thomas D. Morris echoed the negative attitude of his chief. Basing his arguments on the Department of Defense study of the draft (reported more fully in Chapter 3), Morris stated that although voluntary enlistments into the army currently exceed inductions by about two to one many of the volunteers are influenced by the possibility of being drafted and would no longer have that motivation for joining if a voluntary army were established. Nor, according to the Defense Department study, could such incentives as higher pay and more fringe benefits induce enough volunteers to join up to offset losses. Moreover, the possibilities of substituting civilian for military personnel in certain noncombat jobs are limited. Were the draft (or some other coercive system of procuring military manpower) to be abandoned, the force level would fall far short of military requirements. The costs of a volunteer army, too, would be prohibitive, particularly in times when military requirements for men were above peacetime conditions. In short, the Defense Department establishment turned thumbs down on the whole concept of the voluntary army.

As Ellsworth pointed out, there has been a great deal of confusion about the approximate cost of a voluntary system. In the June 1966 issue of *The Reporter* Bruce Chapman writes:

"On the question of costs the Defense Department has been more confusing

7 Review of the Administration and Operation of the Selective Service System, Hearings Before the Committee on Armed Services, House of Representatives, U.S. Government Printing Office, Washington, D.C., 1966, pp. 9759-9760.

than direct. Last year Secretary McNamara gave two estimates of the additional cost of an all-volunteer army that were so divergent – $4 billion in a February Congressional budget hearing and $20 billion in a December interview – as to suggest that the Department has either found the computation of cost of this alternative to the draft inordinately complicated or has not given it serious consideration."

At this point in 1966 the voluntary army had relatively few advocates. At the American Veterans Committee (AVC) Conference in Washington, Joseph P. McMurray, President of Queen's College, New York City, delivered a major speech in favor of an all-volunteer system. Stressing the coercive nature of the present draft, he said:

"Men should not be deprived of their liberties, their choices of careers or their choices of action in order to satisfy the Joint Chiefs of Staff, the Admirals, the Congress, or even the President of the United States, unless clearly there is no other way. . .to ensure the security of the nation."

There was little support for this position at the Conference, but the inability of the Department of Defense to answer effectively the arguments raised by adherents created a situation in which the voluntary-army concept gained additional support. At this time the war in Vietnam was being escalated perceptibly, and more and more college and university students and faculty were becoming concerned with the inequities of the draft. The establishment of a voluntary army would soothe the consciences of those who are against the Vietnam war and the draft as it is presently constituted because they would not have to serve in such an army.

Beginning with the Chicago Conference on the draft held early in December 1966, the movement in favor of a voluntary army picked up steam. Although the Conference did not intend to vote on proposals of any kind, an informal survey of the 100 delegates, conducted by voluntary army adherents, indicated that 64, who probably represent a fairly good cross section of those in the country currently studying the problems of the draft, preferred this alternative to the present system. Many of those who did not vote were government employees. New adherents among the delegates came from both sides of the political aisle: Congressman Donald Rumsfeld (R. Illinois), Congressman Robert Kastenmeier (D. Wisconsin), Bruce Chapman, the moderate Republican Ripon Society member, and Milton Friedman, the Goldwater economic theorist of the 1964 campaign. Chapman's book *The Wrong Man in Uniform* is essentially an argument for the voluntary army. To the news reporters covering the Chicago Conference this support emerged as its most surprising development.

Why did the concept find favor at the Chicago Conference? The participants were clearly impressed with the arguments presented by two economists, Milton Friedman of the University of Chicago and Walter Oi of the University of Washington. Friedman's position was that the draft is inconsistent with a free society because it exacts compulsory service from some and limits the freedom of others in a variety of ways. As long as the element of compulsion is retained, the defects are inevitable. Friedman went on to say that a lottery would just make the arbitrary element overt, whereas universal national service would compound the evil, regimenting all youth to camouflage the need to regiment only some.

Friedman's economic argument for a voluntary army is an interesting one: first, the assertion that a voluntary army would cost more is simply a confusion of apparent cost with real cost. The real cost of drafting a man who does not serve voluntarily is not his pay and upkeep costs but rather the amount for which he would be willing to serve. The man himself is actually paying the difference, and this extra cost to him must be added to the cost borne by the rest of society. Friedman illustrates his point by comparing the costs of military service to an unemployed worker and those to a star professional football player like Joe Namath. Both might conceivably have the same liking or dislike for a military career, but since the football player has a far more palatable alternative it would take far more money to attract him to the military. Thus conscription results in concealed taxation, a type of forced labor exacted from men who are compelled to serve against their will. The tax is equal to the difference between the salary it would take to attract the man to the military and the salary he actually receives. This type of tax, implicit though it is, must be added to the direct taxes that citizens pay if we are to arrive at a just estimate of the total cost of maintaining our armed forces.

Friedman continues to build his argument as follows: the real cost of maintaining the armed forces at the present time, including this concealed tax, is greater than the cost of having a voluntary army of the same size because the volunteers would be the men who find military service the most attractive alternative and thus less money would be required to induce them to serve. Moreover, there would be less wasted manpower, less turnover, less training and retraining, and less exploitation of servicemen in the performance of menial tasks such as washing officers' cars and bartending at officers' clubs.

The nonmonetary advantages that would result from abolishing conscription are, in Friedman's opinion, even greater than the monetary savings. The need for draft boards would end, young men could plan their careers with much more freedom, questions regarding college deferments and conscientious objectors would no longer arise, and business, industry, and government could hire young men without concern for their draft status.

The writings of Walter Oi bolster the arguments presented by Friedman with hard data and with the authority of personal experience. Oi worked for a year as a consultant to the Department of Defense, and between June 1964 and March 1965 he was a member of the Military Manpower Study Group. In papers presented at the 1966 national meeting of the American Economic Association and at the Chicago Conference Oi concluded that, from an economist's point of view, a voluntary army is financially feasible, even at the present levels of manpower procurement, namely, 2.7 million men. In his studies he uses the same government figures that Assistant Secretary of Defense (Manpower) Thomas Morris used to conclude that such a system of military manpower procurement is not financially feasible.

Oi feels that the two crucial ingredients in determining the cost estimates of such a force are, first, the supply of voluntary enlistments in the absence of a compulsory draft and, second, the projected demand for new men which is determined by personnel turnover. Oi admits that the cost of a voluntary army climbs rapidly as the force strength increases and that the same increase, if applied to a draftee army, would be much lower. He feels, however, that the *full* economic cost of the draft will climb as rapidly as the cost of a voluntary army. Like Friedman, Oi sees the costs of military service in a far wider frame of reference than do most others who have studied the question; for instance, the narrow view of the Department of Defense leads it to conclude "it is theoretically possible to buy an all-volunteer force, at a cost ranging up to $17 billion a year, depending upon the unemployment conditions in the nation." Oi, on the other hand, sees the full economic cost of the draft as including the cost of acquiring military personnel as well as the cost to the American economy itself. Because Oi sees a wider range of possibilities, he is able to draw different conclusions from the figures supplied by the Department of Defense; for example, Oi would match off his proposed budgetary increases to raise military salaries against what it costs each individual serviceman to serve. In other words, he uses the Namath example to show what the real costs of compulsory service are to any person who gives up a salary of more than he would earn in the military.

In summary, Oi's analysis suggests that a voluntary force of 2.7 million men is entirely feasible. The budgetary increases would amount to about 4 billion dollars a year (as opposed to the Department of Defense figure of approximately 17 billion). It should be pointed out that both figures are estimates and that no one can establish with complete accuracy the monetary costs of such a program. According to Oi, the advantages of implementing this program would be several. First, the increases in military pay necessary to attract volunteers would be offset by the abolition of the implicit tax on individuals previously described. Second, the turnover would be smaller and fewer men from each age category would be called. An obvious implication is that more young people could plan their lives without having to worry about the possibility of serving. Oi concludes by saying that if the force necessary to keep the country secure goes as high as 3.3 million men, a national emergency would exist. Under such emergency conditions the costs of the voluntary army would be accelerated but so also would the costs of a draft.

Aside from its possible economic advantages, the voluntary army holds many attractions for civil libertarians, who see it as an alternative to compulsion and abridgement of individual freedom of choice. A Council for a Voluntary Military, made up of both liberals and conservatives, has recently been formed to continue to push the voluntary system. The American Civil Liberties Union has come out in favor of the system. Bruce Chapman supports the thesis of a voluntary army in his book by pointing out the severe inequities that exist under the present system, which he feels, can be done away with only by a voluntary army. His plan would call for higher pay and better housing, which would include community planning of army bases to avoid the dreariness associated with such places. The epitome of his argument is that the present system is wrong, wasteful, and downright discriminatory. He views the government as the villain in this piece, pointing out that all studies of the voluntary army have been conducted in secret and that the Congress has never been informed truthfully by the Department of Defense of the feasibility of such a service.

The Department of Defense has not done a creditable job in answering the arguments of those who favor the voluntary army approach. In particular, it has failed to spell out clearly the costs of such a proposal at various strength levels. Another shortcoming, and one that has caused many people to question the veracity of its claims, is that the Department failed to give evidence for the conclusions reached in its study of the draft, thus making it impossible to judge their validity. The methodology of the Bureau of the Census survey on which it relied heavily is either obscure or suspect: why, for example, were only nonveterans between the ages of 16 and 34 surveyed to learn what inducements might lead them to enlist? Were pretests made? How many people were surveyed?

In *How to End the Draft* (1967) several Congressmen interested in the voluntary-army concept specifically challenge the methodology of the study, citing as their evidence a section of the questionnaire (released for the record some time after Secretary Morris's testimony before the hearing) addressed to young men between the ages of 16 and 25. One question read:

If there were no draft now, and you had no military obligation at all, which condition would be most likely to get you to volunteer?

The answers from which the respondent was asked to choose only one were the following:

If military pay were the same as you could make in civilian life?

If military pay were considerably higher than you could make in civilian life?

If you were given a $1000 enlistment bonus?

If the minimum tour of duty for the service you prefer were one year shorter than it is now?

If you were guaranteed training in a job or skill useful in civilian life?

If you were sent to civilian school or college at Government expense before or during active service?

If you were given an opportunity to go to civilian school or college at Government expense after active service?

If you could qualify for officer's training or an officer's commission?

None of the above? [8]

The Congressmen conclude:

"The question is patently absurd. . . . It is ridiculous to ask a potential enlistee whether he would be influenced more by pay scales he could match in civilian life or by pay scales considerably higher than he could attain in civilian life. It is not surprising that five times as many chose the latter as the former." [9]

Granted that the Defense Department was evasive and its survey method suspect, it does not follow that a voluntary army is a workable alternative. There are arguments against a voluntary army that need not be couched in statistical or monetary terms. First, to substitute a new method of military manpower procurement during a wartime situation would be ridiculous. Not even the staunchest advocates of a voluntary army deny this fact. For the present, then, the establishment of an all-volunteer army cannot be seriously considered. Even if the Vietnam war should end, proponents of such a system would have difficulty proving the military draft unnecessary in light of unsettled conditions in other parts of the world. In the long run, even given a settled peacetime situation, the proposal for a voluntary army has serious shortcomings. A voluntary army in our nation could easily become an army of minority groups, particularly Negroes. Although Negroes serve at about their proportion of the total population (roughly 11 percent), about 50 percent of them re-enlist. For Negroes and other minority groups the military is a real opportunity for advancement. It is almost universally felt that the military in Vietnam is currently the most truly integrated of all American institutions. If we instituted

[8] Robert T. Stafford, Frank J. Horton, Richard Schweiker, Garner E. Shriver, and Charles W. Whalen, Jr., *op. cit.,* pp. 34-35.

[9] *Ibid.* p. 35.

a voluntary army, we might create a class army made up of minorities looking for upward social mobility. Moreover, because of their educational advantages, whites would probably dominate the officer component of such a service. In a recent *New York Times* article Professor Friedman, though he has undoubtedly heard this argument before, does not completely meet the black-white question when he says:

"The danger to liberty comes from the officers, who are now and always have been a professional corps of volunteers. However we recruit enlisted men, it is essential that we adopt practices that will guard against the political danger of creating a military officer corps with loyalties of its own and out of contact with the broader body politic."[10]

Professor Friedman has avoided the primary questions that must be faced long before the method of officer recruitment is discussed: does America, at this point in time, wish to have its enlisted forces made up primarily of disadvantaged minority groups? Where will the officers come from? At present, the armed forces look to the colleges for 80 to 90 percent of their new junior-officer acquisitions each year. With a voluntary army there would be no pressure on a student to join an officer program in order to meet his service obligation. It is doubtful, in my judgment, whether the necessary numbers could be provided. Even if the quantity were sufficient, I seriously question that they would be of the quality needed to staff our armed forces today.

A voluntary army would be an inflexible military force. The nation would be unable to meet expanding military commitments on a short-term basis with a voluntary army. Of course, those Americans opposed to the war in Vietnam and to the extensive use of American armed forces to maintain peace throughout the world would call this an advantage.

I question whether the United States wants to build a military establishment that is a permanent part of our society, yet at the same time is isolated from it. In his last major address before he left the White House former President Eisenhower warned against the dangers of the military-industrial colossus that was developing and would grow even more formidable with a more professionalized army. More recently Senator Fulbright exposed the far-right infiltration of the armed forces.

In my opinion the military procurement of manpower primarily through the draft has been and should continue to be the greatest single force for democratizing the armed forces. The constant movement in and out of ordinary citizen soldiers guarantees that the military will not become isolated from

[10] Milton Friedman, "An All Voluntary Army," *New York Times Magazine,* May 14, 1967, pp. 23, 114-119.

ordinary American society.

Moreover, the question of cost is at least ambiguous. There are those like Walter Oi who say that a voluntary army is economically feasible. Yet his figures were calculated for a peacetime situation. There are others, primarily within the defense establishment, who, after careful research, submit that such an army would be far more costly in dollars than the nation would be willing to accept.

Finally, I am of the opinion that the strongest democracy in the world should raise the necessary manpower to maintain its national security in such a way that everyone is called on to share the burden. There will, of course, always be room in our military services for volunteers, but calling for volunteers should not be considered now, or in the future, as the sole basis for raising military manpower. An all-volunteer system would create an isolated elite, socially and economically – certainly not a good foundation for a democratic society. The concept is, in fact, morally repugnant.

NATIONAL SERVICE

National Service is not an alternative to the draft in the strict military sense but rather an alternative means of mobilizing the nation's youth in a variety of worthwhile endeavors, both civilian and military. It is difficult to pinpoint the beginnings of the recent National Service movement. Certainly the late President John F. Kennedy instilled in the young people of America a desire to serve society. William Josephson, when he was General Counsel for the Peace Corps, proposed compulsory service for all young men through military or humanitarian service. In New York City, on May 7, 1966, the Overseas Educational Service held a meeting attended by people from higher education, government, and other areas of national life to discuss the concept of National Service. Several weeks later, on May 18, the concept was given new life when Secretary of Defense Robert McNamara, in his famous Montreal speech, said:

"It seems to me that we should move toward remedying [the draft] inequities by asking every young person in the United States to give two years of service to his country – whether in one of the military services, in the Peace Corps, or in some other voluntary developmental work at home or abroad. . .it would make meaningful the central concept of security: a world of decency and development – where every man can feel that his personal horizon is rimmed with hope."[11]

Later McNamara almost qualified his speech out of existence in the face

[11] Secretary McNamara's speech to the American Society of Newspaper Editors, Montreal, Canada, as reported in the *New York Times*, May 19, 1966, p. 11.

of questions from a number of sources. One of his qualifications was to indicate that the obligation to serve was a moral not a legal one. But the movement gained momentum. Late in 1966 the proponents of such a program formed the National Service Secretariat, with private foundation support, and Donald J. Eberly, formerly of the Overseas Educational Service, was named Secretary. National Service as a viable concept capable of being fulfilled by various means reached its zenith of popularity at the Chicago Conference on the draft in December 1966, at which a number of the participants favored the concept and debated it fully to the exclusion of many other important items on the agenda. Also during the early part of 1967 rumors abounded in Washington that the President's Commission on Selective Service would recommend some form of alternative National Service program. A Plan for National Service was submitted to the Commission by Eberly, who also acted as an adviser during the entire period of its study of Selective Service. Although the Commission seemed to have some sentiment for such a program, the practical problems proved to be such that the rumored recommendation never materialized. Once Congress became the arena, all such altruistic considerations died quickly, but the adherents of National Service linger on. The National Secretariat is continuing to work. Senator Brewster of Maryland, for example, introduced a bill that would establish a National Service Foundation to undertake a two-year study of the feasibility of such a program, but there has been no action on this legislation.

What exactly is National Service? Most proponents would agree that it implies the citizen's acceptance of the responsibility to serve the nation in some capacity. A whole range of possibilities for service are at present available, from military to community service, from international Peace Corps work to the domestic VISTA program. The first National Service Conference, mentioned earlier, attempted to put into one sentence the viewpoint of all conferees on a definition of National Service:

"National Service as a concept embraces the belief that an opportunity should be given each young person to serve his country in a manner consistent with the needs of the nation—recognizing national defense as the first priority— and consistent with the education and interests of those participating, without infringing on the personal or economic welfare of others but contributing to the liberty and well-being of all."[12]

The rationale for National Service developed at the first meeting covered several underlying purposes: reduction of draft inequities; provision for cross-cultural experience; alleviation of manpower shortages; instillation of a sense of self-worth and civic pride; fulfillment of service owed to the total

---

[12] *A Profile of National Service,* edited by Donald J. Eberly, New York Overseas Educational Service, 1966, p. 3.

community; and opportunity for education in its fullest sense. Consensus was reached on several other issues relating to National Service.

1. National Service would extend the scope of the private sector's participation in welfare activities.

2. It should not be a crash program but rather a carefully thought out and slowly implemented program.

3. It is not intended as a draft-dodging device nor as a program of direct political action.

4. It should be open to a cross section of young people with varied backgrounds, interests, and abilities; it should not be an elitist organization, of the Peace Corps type, which utilized college people primarily.

Dr. Margaret Mead feels the program developed should be universal in application in that it should give a second chance to those young people who have suffered the disadvantages of poor schools, inadequate health facilities, and poverty. Such a program would uncover their heretofore hidden talents. It would engender self-respect, establish identity, and give young adults an opportunity to experience the satisfaction of service performed for others. To Dr. Mead's way of thinking the inclusion of women in this program is absolutely essential for accomplishing the goals set by the program. Many people agree about its advantages but raise serious questions about the compulsory aspect of the Mead plan. The thought of central control in the national interest is unacceptable to many, including myself; for example, Paul Lauter, of the American Friends Service Committee in Chicago, asks: are we ready to give any government the right to rehabilitate everyone?

Don Eberly has the most concrete proposal: at age 18, when all young men must register for the draft, they would be presented with three choices. First, they would be able to volunteer for the armed forces. Second, they could opt for a period of National Service, their specific alternative service to be proposed in detail and submitted for approval to a National Advisory Board set up for such a purpose. Young men choosing this alternative might serve for a longer period of time than would those choosing the military. Third, the young man could choose to do nothing in the service of his country. Should the armed forces need more men than the system could furnish, the needed manpower would be raised by lottery from among those who at age 18 opted to do nothing. At the end of a year those not selected in the lottery for service would be placed at the bottom of the list and their chances of being called would be lessened.

The advantages of such a system are easy to enumerate. Many young men would receive the training and experience necessary in our highly industrialized society. They would be absorbed into a program that would take them out of the job market at the point at which their unemployment rate is 2½ times the national average. Moreover, they would receive great benefit from the cross-cultural exchange.

Advocates of National Service are in complete agreement in their emphasis on the existing need for such a program. Swarthmore's sociologist Leon Bramson speaks for all when he argues that two societies are being developed in the 18 to 26 age group. One segment of youth fails the draft examination, does not serve, and slips back into the half-world remaining open to them. The other half may serve in the armed forces or may be exempted for many reasons, but in any event they have the ability—the upward mobility, if you will—to move into the complete society. Some of this group achieve mobility through service in the armed forces; others achieve it more conventionally through education. In short, Bramson is saying that only half the youth are participating in the economic promise of the nation, yet the future should belong to the whole of the younger generation. National Service is the vehicle that will enable more young people to take their proper part in this future. Senator Javits (R. New York) sees the rehabilitation of service rejectees as one of the prime justifications for the existence of such a program.

Harris Wofford, former Associate Director of the Peace Corps and currently president of the new and highly experimental Old Westbury College, part of the State University of New York, feels strongly that voluntary National Service should be accepted as an important part of our system of higher education and is implementing this concept at Old Westbury, where voluntary service is built in as part of the curriculum. Moreover, he sees the draft as discouraging nonmilitary service — an obviously valid point to the young man who realizes he will receive no credit for such service from his draft board.

A variation on the theme of National Service is sounded by Bayard Rustin, Executive Director of the Philip Randolph Institute and well-known Negro intellectual, who suggests that a human resources act be passed to require the disadvantaged young to undertake projects that would be fundamentally in their interests in preparing themselves for productive future lives. Such a program, though voluntary, would offer the same basic salaries as the military and would be an alternative to military service.

Not everyone, however, is starry-eyed about the possibilities of National Service. President Nathan Pusey of Harvard expressed his views succinctly, "It could only lead to a colossal waste of time." He went on to say:

"I cannot believe our government could possibly provide a demanding and meaningful experience. . .for the millions of young people who would be involved. Nor can I think of anything worse for young people eager to get on in the world than to stand by marking time."

Other opponents point to the weaknesses apparent in the present Poverty Program. Are they not symptomatic of what might happen under a program of National Service? The cost would be high and the problems of coordination between various government agencies, colossal.

Because of the vagueness of the proposals suggested so far and because of current Federal budgetary problems, it seems doubtful whether such programs will achieve reality in present circumstances. Of course, if rioting and unrest continue to trouble our urban centers, it is possible that a program of National Service might come to be viewed as one approach to a solution to the problems of the inner city. The formation of the President's Council on Youth Opportunity after the riots in the summer of 1967 represents an effort on the part of the government to tackle these problems by providing jobs and educational opportunities for young people between the ages of 16 and 21. If the domestic situation worsens, we may find the National Service concept catching its second wind.

UNIVERSAL MILITARY TRAINING (UMT)

Proposals that everyone be required to share the military responsibility are made whenever young men are involved in a war. The closest the United States has come to accepting the concept f compulsory service for all was during the two world wars, especially World War II, when more than 10 million men were inducted into the armed forces. After the war President Truman tried unsuccessfully to have Congress pass a Universal Military Training act. He was aided in this effort by retired General George Marshall, who, when he became Secretary of Defense, attempted to persuade Congress that all men should serve in the armed forces for one year. Most observers of that period feel that the adoption of a policy of national defense that depended on an air-nuclear deterrent cost the UMT proposal most of its Congressional support. Moreover, except in time of war, the concept has historically been repugnant to the American people.

In 1951 Congress did pass the so-called Universal Military Training and Service Act, which provided for an increase in the sources of manpower available for induction, but by no stretch of the imagination could it be said that this legislation provided for universal military training. From time to time, as the legislation came up for review every four years, people pointed out to Congress the inappropriateness of its title, but until the 1967 bill nothing was done about changing it.

During the period from 1963 to the present the escalation of the war in Vietnam has given added impetus to the discussion of UMT as an alternative to the draft, but support for the idea is fragmented and unorganized. Its most visible proponents are General Hershey and former President Dwight D. Eisenhower, along with a small group of academicians, typified by Dr. Roger Little of the Department of Sociology of the University of Illinois at Chicago.

Whenever General Hershey is asked what his recommendations are for improving the present law, he answers: "Take everyone." He believes that all should bear the responsibility for service in maintaining our democratic system and that universal service is the essence of democracy. In a *Reader's Digest* article (September 1966) entitled "This Country Needs Universal Military Training," former President Eisenhower outlines a complete plan for UMT in which all young Americans, with the exception of those exempted for obvious physical or mental defects, would receive 49 weeks of military training at age 18. Under Mr. Eisenhower's proposal those serving would receive only a small subsistence allowance. At the start of the 49-week training period each man would be offered the option of enlisting immediately for a two-year term in the armed forces, with all the pay and benefits, including the G.I. bill, which accrue to members of the military at the present time. Those who do not enlist would then go on to receive military training for 49 weeks. In conjunction with receiving military training, these men would be available in time of emergency to help fight floods, fires, and other natural disasters. At the end of the 49-week period they would be free to begin their civilian careers without further interruption except in the case of major war. If the inducements of full pay and other benefits did not produce the number of men necessary to meet our present military commitments, the balance of men would be procured, under Eisenhower's plan, through a lottery. At first, it would be necessary to include in the lottery the large pool of young men past the UMT age of 18 but still liable for military service. After this pool of over-age young men was exhausted, the lottery would apply only to those within the UMT program.

The benefits of such a program are, in Eisenhower's opinion,

"First. . .long-term military advantages. After a few years of UMT we would always have a huge reserve of young men with sound basic military training in case of great emergency. . . . A disciplined body of young men in every community would be a priceless asset. Second. . .UMT would. . .do much to stem the growing tide of irresponsible behavior and outright crime in the United States. But above all these advantages of UMT is the matter of attitude towards country. If a UMT system were to become a factor of our national life. . .every young man would take pride and satisfaction in giving a year of his life to the United States of America."

Dr. Roger Little feels that in the draft controversy not enough attention has been paid to the shortcomings of the military and their outmoded personnel policies. Why should there not be a variable enlistment term, he asks, to depend on the number of available men? Men could serve for less than two years, and thus all initial entrants to military service would come in for a shorter period. Voluntary enlistments could be for two years only to reduce the manpower surplus. Those who were motivated toward a career could enlist for longer periods. Under these conditions the military would be forced to focus on more efficient utilization of its personnel.

Little goes on to argue that if the term of compulsory service were reduced even by three to six months another 200,000 men could be utilized. The more people inducted, the more universal the system becomes. The Department of Defense should promote policies to attract volunteers, since the more people who volunteer the less demand there is on Selective Service, which as a result of the present system is discriminatory in that it excludes many people from serving.

Little feels Eisenhower's plan for UMT is motivated by the wrong considerations: to inculcate patriotism, make young men cut their hair, and so forth. UMT is practicable, he says, if the Department of Defense will institute the proper policies. The more appropriate point to be considered, in Little's judgment, is that a system of UMT, brought about by reform in military personnel functioning, would eliminate the need for the draft.

The President's Commission on the draft also looked at UMT as a possible alternative to the present system. Veteran and other prominent organizations, several governors, and other political leaders expressed approval of the concept to the Commission, and there was also some support within the Commission itself for this alternative method of procuring military manpower. One specific reason for considering the program was the fact that in the fiscal year ending July 1, 1966, more than 700,000 men between 18½ and 34 were found unqualified for military service. As the Commission report commented, these statistics "bear the seeds of the destruction of our society."

Nevertheless UMT has been rejected by almost all those studying the problem and for essentially the same reason: there is no military requirement for the numbers of men that UMT would provide. From the Department of Defense estimates included in the Draft Study we can see that such a program of UMT would mean that for the foreseeable future approximately two million men per year would serve in the military, a figure almost three times the capacity of present military training installations. An expansion of this magnitude would turn the armed forces into huge training establishments and, in peacetime situations, the task of utilizing the manpower would be almost insuperable. The costs of such a program have never been adequately estimated, but they would undoubtedly be high and of a continuing nature. An allied reason for not adopting such a program is the problem of officer procurement. At present the military obtains between 80 and 90 percent of its officer corps from a pool of college graduates. If a system of UMT were inaugurated, many of these young men would be reluctant to serve a second time. Of course, it would be possible to allow young men entering college to contract to serve as officers after graduation, but the basic question remains: should the military be used as a rehabilitation agency – a kind of social welfare organization – for those who, under normal conditions, are not eligible to serve because of physical or mental limitations?

Another reason for opposition to UMT is its compulsory aspect. There is no question that many people do not like to be told they must serve and that many feel that compulsion is anathema in a democratic society. Certainly the present mood of our young people over the war in Vietnam would make UMT an even more explosive issue than the draft.

SUMMARY

"Lottery" is a loaded word, with its connotations of winning and losing, lucky and unlucky. These connotations mask the true worth of this type of selection system at a point in time when our nation has many more men eligible for the draft than are needed by the military, even in a limited war situation. The voluntary army as an alternative to the draft is receiving increased support, though during the Vietnam war there is no possibility that such an alternative will be instituted. Universal Military Training as a viable alternative has little chance of success, primarily because of the cost and because the number of young men reaching the eligible age far exceeds our military requirements. The time is unpropitious for National Service, however great its appeal to the enlarged social conscience of today's youth.

6 | THE PUBLIC DIALOGUE

Now that the various alternatives have been discussed, we move to the areas of national discussion and action. Many people, although dissatisfied with the House Armed Services Committee hearings on the draft, were inclined to await Congressional action in the next year. Another group, primarily college students and faculty, were making plans to attempt to influence legislative change.

THE STUDY GROUPS

Two days after the House Armed Services Committee ended its hearings, on July 2, 1966, President Johnson appointed a 20-member Commission to study the Selective Service System. As Chairman, the President named Burke Marshall, Vice President and General Counsel of International Business Machines and former Assistant Attorney General for Civil Rights in both the Kennedy and Johnson administrations.[1] The mandate given to the Commission was to consider the following factors: fairness to all citizens, the nation's military manpower

---

[1] The members of the Commission were as follows: Kingman Brewster, Jr., President, Yale University; Thomas S. Gates, Jr., Chairman of the Board, Morgan Guaranty Trust Co.; Oveta Culp Hobby, Editor and Chairman of the Board, *The Houston Post*; Anna Rosenberg Hoffman, President, Anna Rosenberg Associates; Paul J. Jennings, President, International Union of Electrical, Radio, & Machine Workers, AFL-CIO; John H. Johnson, President, Johnson Publishing Co., Inc.; Vernon E. Jordan, Jr., Project Director, Voter Education Project, Southern Regional Council, Inc.; Daniel M. Luevano, Director, Western Region, Office of Economic Opportunity; John A. McCone, Joshua-Hendy Corp.; James H. McCrocklin, President, Southwest Texas State College; John Courtney Murray, S.J., Professor of Theology, Woodstock College; Jeanne L. Noble, Associate Professor, Center for Human Relations Studies, New York University; George E. Reedy, Jr., President, Struthers Research & Development Corp.; David Monroe Shoup, General, U.S. Marine Corps, Retired; Fiorindo A. Simeone, Professor of Surgery, Western Reserve University Medical School, Cleveland, Ohio; James A. Suffridge, International President, Retail Clerks International Association; Frank S. Szymanski, Judge of Probate, Detroit, Mich.; Luther L. Terry, Vice President, University of Pennsylvania; Warren G. Woodward, Vice President, American Airlines.

requirements, the reduction of uncertainty and interference in education and careers, social, economic, and employment conditions and goals, and budgetary and administrative matters.

The Marshall Commission got off to a very shaky start. It took some time to find a staff and to name an executive director. From the time of its appointment in July until the middle of September the Commission met only twice. Dr. John K. Folger, on leave from Florida State University to conduct a two-year examination of human resources sponsored by the National Academy of Sciences, was named Staff Director but forced to resign after a short period of time because he found it impossible to do both jobs. He was replaced in late August by Mr. Bradley Patterson, on leave from the Treasury Department. The original choice for General Counsel, Charles B. Wrangel, also resigned soon after he was named in order to accept an appointment to an unexpired legislative term in New York City. These details would be unimportant except that the President expected the Commission's report by January 1, 1967, and the time element was pressing from the very beginning. The Commission planned no open hearings; it expected to rely instead on staff studies and materials submitted by various institutions, educational bodies, and private individuals.

Once before, in 1964, President Johnson had solicited Congressional action on the draft. In the spring of 1964 members of both houses had introduced legislation to form a bipartisan Congressional committee for the purpose, but very shortly after President Johnson announced that the Department of Defense would conduct the now-famous study of Selective Service and the idea for a bipartisan committee was dropped. Now, however, the President was dealing with the Chairman of the House Armed Services Committee, L. Mendel Rivers, a man who takes very seriously the Congressional prerogative not just to legislate but, more important, to initiate exclusively any and all legislation concerning the military establishment. Chairman Rivers spoke forcefully about this issue on a recent *Meet The Press* program:

Mr. Childs.   Chairman Rivers, you have interpreted Article VIII of the Constitution of the United States as saying that Congress has the exclusive right to deal with the military. Is that your view of the powers of your Committee?

Mr. Rivers.   Article 1, Section 8, says the Congress shall provide an army and a navy and make rules for the government thereof. I take that as what it means. If the Congress did not provide a military, Mr. Childs, there would be none. This is one area where the Constitution does not delegate to the Congress; it directs the Congress to provide for a military. And we take it that the Congress alone shall provide the military and make the laws for it, and nobody else, and that the Commander-in-Chief shall be the President.[2]

Early in the fall of 1966 Chairman Rivers initiated correspondence with an old friend, General Mark Clark, President Emeritus of The Citadel, in which he asked that the General chair a civilian advisory panel on the Selective Service System to report to the House Armed Services Committee. General Clark accepted and the panel was formally constituted on November 1, 1966.[3] If the time strictures were pressing for the Marshall Commission, they were virtually strangulating for the Clark Panel, which was asked to report "no later than March 1, 1967,"[4] although it did not formally convene in Washington until January 4, 1967. Between November 1 and January the Panel "functioned informally through correspondence and independent research."[5] The group was provided with "a variety of background information on the procurement of military manpower and tentatively assigned subject areas in which Panel members were to become especially knowledgeable."[6] We can only speculate about what amount of time eight busy men would be able to spend on such a broad matter in a six-week period (assuming at least two weeks to publish the report in time to meet the March 1 deadline.) The Panel did not hold public hearings or solicit information from any groups. Its one staff member was Lieutenant Colonel Dennis Nicholson, Jr., U.S.M.C. (Ret.), Executive Assistant to the President of the Citadel. A cynic might have predicted, without great strain, that the Panel would receive much of its guidance from the professional staff of the Rivers Committee — but more about that later.

NATIONAL CONFERENCES ON THE DRAFT

As these two study commissions were hard at work, other spectacles were being staged in the public arena. President Johnson, aware of the serious unrest over the draft, particularly among students, was trying to communicate his

[2] *Meet the Press, April 30, 1967,* Vol. II, No. 18, Merkle Press Division of Publishers Co., Washington, D.C.

[3] The other Panel members were Dr. Frederick L. Hovde, President, Purdue University; Dr. Jerome Holland, President, Hampton Institute; Vice Admiral Maurice S. Sheehy, U.S. Naval Reserve, Retired; Robert D. Murphy, Chairman of the Board, Corning Glass International; W. Sterling Cole, Director General, International Atomic Energy Commission; Earl H. Blaik, Chairman, Executive Committee, Avco Corporation; Charles E. Saltzman, partner in Goldman, Sachs & Co.

[4] *Civilian Advisory Panel on Military Manpower Procurement Report to the Committee on Armed Services, House of Representatives,* U.S. Government Printing Office, Washington, D.C., February 28, 1967, p. 2.   [5] *Ibid.* p. 1.   [6] *Ibid.* p. 1.

feelings on the subject. In an address on August 18,1966, to nearly 14,000 students who were in Washington for the summer to work as interns in various government agencies, the President called the draft, "a crazy quilt" system in need of change. He took great pains to point out that "we have inherited that system but are not wedded to it," adding rhetorically, "Can we, without harming national security, establish a practical system of nonmilitary alternatives to the draft?" Some thought the statement ill-timed, since it was made while the Presidential Commission was hard at work on the very problems the President was prejudging.

By the fall of 1966 a number of colleges and universities — through faculty senates, local chapters of the American Association of University Professors, and the like — were issuing strong statements against deferments in general and against deferments based on rank in class and test scores in particular. Among the institutions taking positions were Cornell, Iowa, Michigan, Wayne State, San Francisco State, the University of Buffalo, State University of New York at Stony Brook, and New York University.

Interest and involvement in the question continued to grow, and on November 11-12 a National Conference on the Draft was held in Washington, D.C., under the sponsorship of the American Veterans Committee (AVC). More than 200 representatives from government, the professions, education, labor, church groups, and business were present for the two days of sessions. The Conference was educational in orientation, intended to stimulate thinking and debate about the draft, not to pass resolutions or take votes. As pointed out by its Chairman, Gus Tyler, everyone had an opinion about the draft, but so far there had been much wrangling but little actual dialogue. The object of the Conference was to provide a "blueprint for debate so that Americans will be intelligently informed in advance of Congressional hearings to be held in the spring of 1967."

The delegates who came to the Conference hoping to hear divergent views expressed were not disappointed. The division between the Department of Defense and Selective Service was a dramatic and dissonant one. Dr. Harold Wool, Director of Procurement Policy of the Office of the Assistant Secretary of Defense, came out strongly in favor of inducting the youngest men first by some system of random selection or lottery. This was a new position for the Department of Defense and had been enunciated for the first time several days before in an interview with Secretary McNamara reported in the *Harvard Crimson*.

The spokesman for Selective Service was not slow to challenge this view. Daniel O. Omer, its Deputy Director, and a staunch defender of the status quo, replied: "I need not tell you. . .that we in Selective Service are opposed to the idea of a lottery." He defended drafting the oldest men first and predicted (quite rightly, as it turned out) that "in the foreseeable future we will have no drastic changes in the law."

The Selective Service System came in for some severe licks at the Conference. Harris Wofford, then Associate Director of the Peace Corps, delivered a scathing denunciation of the present draft system:

"We are here to appraise the Draft, but in due course I hope that the President's Advisory Commission and the Congress will not only appraise the present Selective Service System but bury it. A system which corrupts American higher education, encourages a cynical avoidance of service, discourages real volunteer services, relies primarily on compulsion, discriminates in favor of students enrolled in formal education, uses class standing or grades as the criterion for who will go to kill or be killed, turns college or graduate school into a refuge, turns upside down the sensible order of calling younger men first, throws a shadow of uncertainty over most men until they are 26 or older, differently treats men in the same category according to the vagaries of local boards, permits the calling home for induction of Peace Corps Volunteers still serving overseas, drafts former Peace Corps Volunteers while others who have not served at all are deferred or passed over, provides no alternatives for men with a conscientious preference for non-military service, requires conscientious objectors to prove some kind of direct line to God, leaves women out, and leaves unmet, so many national needs for service — requires fundamental reform." [7]

Woffard went on to advocate one of the two major alternatives to the draft presented at the Conference: a system of national voluntary service in which young men and women can choose to serve in either the armed forces or such nonmilitary services as the Peace Corps and VISTA.   .

The other alternative was championed by Joseph McMurray, President of Queens College who vigorously opposed the present coercive system of Selective Service and came out in favor of a voluntary army.

The conference was presented with a careful analysis of local draft boards by Dr. Roger Little, one of a small group of sociologists who are doing significant work on many aspects of the military as a social organization in our society. Little maintained that the local board, which served a real function for emergency manpower procurement in a relatively rural society, has become obsolete in an urban society at a time when the Federal government has a pervasive array of agencies in every local community, it is simply no longer a valid instrument. The county, the political subdivision on which the concept is based, plays a remote and insignificant role in the lives of most Americans today.

[7] *Dialogue on the Draft: Report of the National Conference on the Draft,* edited by June A. Willenz, American Veterans Committee, Washington, D.C., 1967, p. 81.

More important, according to Little, the Selective Service System was not designed to be the permanent monitor of the early adulthood of American men, but it has usurped that function; for example, Little goes on, the classification schedule was originally introduced as a simple administrative device for sorting the manpower pool into categories of relative availability for the duration of an emergency that was never longer than four years. Classification actions had little aggregate impact because the decision was based on the registrant's status at the moment of his registration. The basis for a deferment could not be foreseen before registration and was unlikely to change after classification because the emergency was of limited duration; but when the classification schedule is used over a longer time period, its effects become much more pervasive in the social structure of American society. Moreover, the System's channeling activities imply that one status has a higher value than another. The schedule itself becomes a series of approved behavior patterns with profound implications for affecting occupational choices. This should not be the function of a military manpower procurement agency.[8]

The delegates were given the facts. Indeed, they were overwhelmed with them from all sides throughout the two-day Conference. One newsman covering the Conference for the *Washington Star* took an informal poll of the conferees and came to the conclusion that

". . .no one is satisfied with the present set up – but that no single alternative was universally acceptable. Majority opinion favored national service, with the voluntary army a poor second. There was almost no support for Universal Military Training and little for a lottery, unless tied to national service."[9]

We should remember that the purpose behind the Conference – that of fact-finding – had been admirably achieved, even if no consensus was reached. The growing isolation of the Selective Service System from other groups both in and out of government was clearly manifested at this Conference. Warren Hoge remarked: "Capital observers noted with interest that the Selective Service System now seems isolated in its opposition to alternative conscription procedures."[10]

Later that month, from November 17 to 20, the National Collegiate Conference on Selective Service was held at Antioch College. Though but one of many college conferences, it was typical of its kind. The Conference was attended by about 100 student delegates from 35 colleges and universities. A majority of the conferees were able to decide on a series of proposals, although some of

[8] *Ibid.* p. 28.
[9] Article by Ernest Ostro, *The Sunday Star*, Washington, D.C., November 13, 1966, p. 1.
[10] *The New York Post*, Saturday, November 12, 1966, p. 6.

the delegates from Yale and Lawrence College walked out of the debates because they felt the Conference proposals went beyond draft reform and far beyond the purpose and scope of the Conference. Among the proposals were the following:

A limitation on voluntary military service "except in times of grave national peril."

A reduction in the size of the projected military force, with adequate financial incentives and an annual turnover in the ranks to "protect society against the dangers of a professional army distinct from the general society."

Exemptions from the draft for those with conscientious objections, based on moral, religious, or philosophical grounds, to war or to service in a particular war.

A system of universal national service with options such as the Peace Corps for those rejecting military service.

Abolition of the present deferment of students and of class ranking to establish eligibility for deferment.

Now the road show made its last stop on the national conference circuit with the Chicago Conference on the Draft, sponsored by the University of Chicago with the help of a Ford Foundation grant. On December 4, 1966, delegates gathered to begin four days of deliberations on one of the most pressing domestic problems confronting the nation. Impetus for the Chicago Conference came from questions raised in the academic community over the operation of the present draft system. The first speaker, Bradley Patterson, Executive Director of the President's National Advisory Commission on Selective Service, attempted to assure his audience that although the report was due in less than a month the Conference might still influence the Commission's decisions. When he informed the delegates that the report had not yet been written, the reaction was one of dismay that the Commission was not further along with its business. Patterson was confused; he had only been trying to reassure the delegates that their deliberations were important.

Early on Monday, the first full day of the Conference, Bruce Chapman, a young author and one of the founders of the liberal Young Republican Ripon Society, interjected a note of partisan politics by ripping into the "Administration" for its "secret studies" of the draft, enumerating as his examples the "secret Pentagon study," the full text of which was never released, the "secret Presidential Commission" now in session, and the "secret Clark Panel" also presently functioning. Several days passed before the reasons for Mr. Chapman's tactics became clear. On the morning of the last session, Wednesday, December 7, two statements were on the delegate's desks when they arrived. The first document was a letter from Governor George Romney of Michigan to Burke Marshall in which he discussed the secrecy of all the draft studies and their time limitations and called for the establishment of an Ad Hoc Joint House-Senate Committee to conduct a thoroughly open and complete study of the draft. The second statement came from the Office of Representative Curtis (a long-time draft critic and voluntary army enthusiast) in which he applauded and echoed the Romney statement. The Chapman statement on Monday clearly set the stage for this "happening."

The Conference itself reached some consensus on certain issues, although under rules adopted before the final session no official votes or recommendations were accepted. It was clear that delegates agreed that the present system was arbitrary and should be drastically revised or eliminated. Speaker after speaker recited the litany of its shortcomings. The spokesman for the System, Colonel Dee Ingold, Special Assistant to the Director of Selective Service, tried to defend Hershey and the System by hitting the group at its weakest point: its inability to provide an adequate substitute.

The bewildering array of questions fired at Ingold from all sides clearly showed that the draft, once a symbol of national unity, was now in the minds of many a symbol of uncertainty, the same uncertainty that exists concerning the war for which young men are being drafted. The conferees felt that better records could be kept, information provided, and research stimulated if the System were to utilize automatic data-processing equipment. Ingold replied that this had been tried in 1942, but inaccurate information had been fed into the machines, and, besides, the machines made errors! The paper submitted to the Conference by General Hershey comes closer to the heart of the System's objections to automation. It read, in part: "If a successful method [for using computers] were adopted, it would destroy local [board] autonomy."

This autonomy, however, came in for much criticism. Morris Janowitz, Roger Little, and others concluded that sociological, economic, and other demographic differences among areas of the nation had produced substantial inequities. They stressed also lack of Negro representation on local boards. Asked if it was true that there was not a single Negro draft-board member in Mississippi, Ingold replied, "I think this is so." The differing interpretations and applications of the rules by local boards were also cataloged.

To all these criticisms of weaknesses in the local board system the answer was the same: local autonomy is the heart of the system, the basis of the supervised decentralization of which Hershey is so proud. It enables draft boards to grant occupational deferments according to local and regional fluctuations in the demand for skilled labor. It permits close consideration of individual cases in which questions arise. It preserves the warmth and neighborliness of the human being against the encroachments of the cold, impersonal machine. Another interesting, if somewhat macabre, argument in Hershey's paper was that in the event that atomic attack destroyed part of the country, or that the enemy occupied part of the country, the local board system would permit the national government to continue to call up men. Little had the last word when he pleaded for complete reorganization of the local boards to make them "more compatible with reality."

Deferments also came in for serious criticism, and almost unanimous consensus was reached concerning educational deferments. President Keast of Wayne State University in Detroit, as well as others, attacked the test score and rank in class criteria for deferment as meaningless and irrelevant. Wayne Booth, Dean of the University College at Chicago, and Eugene Groves, President of the National Student Association, submitted evidence that tests of academic ability are meaningless and prove only that some students will always do well on tests.[11] The sole dissent regarding deferments was expressed by myself. I urged continuation of deferments coupled with a tightening of regulations and a limitation of local board autonomy on the grounds that student deferments are not equitable, but inequity is always present in any draft system, at least until such time as all, rather than just some, men are called.

One of the most surprising results of the Conference was the strong endorsement of an all-volunteer force as an alternative to the present system. As mentioned in Chapter 5, at least 64 of the approximately 100 delegates signed an information resolution that favored a volunteer force, and more might have signed had they not been representatives of organizations or Federal employees. Friedman, Oi, Chapman, Rumsfeld, and others presented their case excellently. Oi demonstrated clearly the economic feasibility of such a system under peacetime conditions, and the other proponents sketched in the remainder of the picture, particularly with regard to a "transitional system" designed to bring more volunteers into the military until the changeover was completed. This, in part, silenced those critics who felt that a change in the system of military manpower procurement during a war was folly.

National Service was the second alternative that received significant support – indeed, more than any other alternative – at the four-day session. Unfortunately its proponents were unable to agree on the form the program should take. The highly respected Margaret Mead felt that all young people should register at age 18 and, among other things, have "their teeth checked." She was not at all concerned about the impact that such regimentation might have on young people, saying that in 38 years of teaching, "I saw no sign of. . .brainwashing, no signs of subservience to authority." On the contrary, she remarked, it was her experience that most men came out of the service "on the whole disliking authority."

[11] Philip Price, Calvin Taylor, James Richards, and Tony Jacobsen, "Measurement of Physician Performance," *The Journal of Medical Education,* Vol. 39, No. 2, February 1964, p. 203.

Others advocated a totally voluntary program of National Service. A third group, led by Harris Wofford, proposed a combination voluntary program and a draft lottery at age 18. This lack of agreement on the essential elements of the National Service program was to continue to plague its adherents throughout the next six months of the debate.

It was agreed, virtually unanimously, that the youngest men should be taken first. This point was stressed most eloquently by Dr. Harold Wool of the Defense Department and by Senator Edward Kennedy. Both expressed the conviction that military service is in large part a young man's job and that to take men at 19 would put an end to the uncertainty and career interruption that exists under the current "oldest first" system. Kennedy went further and advocated a lottery as the only fair way to draft young men. The position of the delegates on the merits of a lottery was ambiguous, however, and no clear consensus developed.

Finally the academicians and the spokesman for the military and Defense Department establishment agreed that the present system was antiquated, outmoded, and in need of basic change. Colonel S. Hays, a West Point faculty member, expressed the sentiments of many when he said, "the present system works with some inequity and lack of uniformity." At the end of the Conference Selective Service once again seemed shut off and out of touch with the rest of the conferees.

THE REPORTS OF THE ADVISORY GROUPS

Both study groups, presumably, were busy preparing their reports. The contrast between the operation of the two groups was striking. No information at all was available from the Clark Panel, although it is known that individual members of the Panel communicated informally with various groups; for example, Dr. Frederick Hovde, President of Purdue University was in touch with members of the scientific community. Most of these groups stressed the necessity of continued student deferments.

The Marshall group, on the other hand, was in communication with all segments of American society concerned with the draft. Numerous consultants, among whom were Don Eberly, an expert on National Service, and Morris Janowitz, an authority on the military in general and local draft boards in particular, were called in to prepare papers on their special subjects. To illustrate the way the Marshall group worked, David F. Bradford, an economist from Princeton University, prepared a paper on the deferment of college students. This paper was read by unofficial consultants involved with the problem, myself included, and at a formal meeting Bradford, members of the staff, and the unofficial group of consultants met and discussed the paper. If revisions were called for, they were made before the position paper was presented to the Commission. As thorough an investigation of the System as possible was accomplished within the time limits imposed by the President.

The Executive Order that established the Presidential Commission asked the group to report "on or about January 1, 1967," but because of the complexity of the problem considered the report was late. The time strictures on the Clark Panel were even more severe. Though the group did not convene formally until early January 1967, Chairman Rivers wanted the report "not later than March 1"! On February 28, then, the Clark Panel Report was published. It is not an impressive document by any standards. (The complete report appears in Appendix I.) It is 30 pages long, but, if we eliminate the Introduction, Approach to the Problem, Panel Philosophy, and Appendices, as well as some tedious restatement of the conclusions, it amounts to no more than 20 pages. We should not, of course, be interested primarily in quantity in a report on so serious a problem. Obviously the value of such a document depends on what is said, how it is said, and how conclusions are reached, but on this basis, too, the report fails.

To understand this failure we must first consider the administrative procedures surrounding the Clark Panel. The time element has already been mentioned but it bears repeating: eight busy men, in less than eight weeks (minus whatever time it took to write the report and have it published by the U.S. Government Printing Office), tackled this assignment. Had they met continuously, they might have accomplished a great deal, but to the best of my knowledge they met formally only about six times to discuss substantive issues. An adequate staff might have offset this weakness, but the Panel staff apparently concisted of one man, retired Marine Lieutenant Colonel Dennis D. Nicholson, Jr. Since 1958 Colonel Nicholson has been Public Relations Director at The Citadel and since 1965 Executive Assistant to the President. In other words, one staff man, who probably held another fulltime job, worked with the panel. (I attempted to obtain information from various members of the Panel but all referred me to General Clark. I wrote to General Clark explaining that I was writing a book and asking specific questions concerning the Panel but never received an answer. After a second letter I received a perfunctory reply from Colonel Nicholson but no answers to the questions I had raised.)

Even so, these time and staff limitations might have been overcome if the Panel had heard from qualified experts in the problem areas, but here, too, strong evidence exists that such was not the case. The complete list of 13 expert witnesses (given on page 27 of the Report) indicates that only three groups were represented. Four of the witnesses were intimately involved with the House Armed Services Committee. Three witnesses, including General Hershey, were from Selective Service. Four, including Secretary Morris, were from the

Department of Defense. The other two witnesses were staff members of the Committee. No one can deny that these men are well informed and deeply involved with this issue, but when Chairman Rivers appoints a Civilian Advisory Panel "charged with analyzing and evaluating the equity and effectiveness of existing laws and policies relating to military personnel procurement,"[12] we expect a rather more extensive and heterogeneous list. Not one public witness was heard. No one from the academic community or from an educational organization or a civil libertarian organization was asked to testify. Not a single member of the United States Congress was heard except, of course, Messrs. Rivers and Hall (R. Missouri), Chairman and Committee member. The Panel philosophy, as enunciated in the Report, was that "the interest of the nation would best be served by conducting Panel deliberations in executive sessions and that selected experts be requested to present their views to the Panel, either in person or in writing." The term "executive session" here seems something of a euphemism for the "secret hearing" label used by Chapman, Romney, and Curtis.

Despite these grave shortcomings, the Report might still have had some value had methodology, scientific data collection, and research of the Panel been above reproach. Unfortunately, the opposite seems to have been the case. The entire report contains not one single reference. The Preface of the Report has a section entitled "Advance Studies of the Panel." No such studies are documented. The Report says merely: "From its studies of available information on the subject. . .and from the extensive aggregate experience of Panel members with various phases of military manpower employment, the Panel early in its initial formal meeting arrived at a consensus concerning its approach to accomplishing its mission." The Report speaks of interviews with various people such as local board chairmen, but nowhere are these interviews listed or summarized nor are the names of those interviewed provided.

Congressman Curtis, a critic of Selective Service policies and procedures, wrote to Rivers on May 16, 1967, asking for the Panel's "working papers."[13] Rivers replied on June 21 that the materials being considered by the Panel were primarily the 1966 House Hearings on the Selective Service System (discussed in Chapter 3) and that the testimony received by the Panel was oral rather than a matter of written record. Curtis was primarily interested in those deliberations concerning the voluntary army, and the Panel's handling of this subject is an apt example of the way in which apparently all its conclusions were reached. The Report dismisses the voluntary army concept in three short paragraphs, citing as

---

[12] *Civilian Advisory Panel on Military Manpower Procurement Report to the Committee on Armed Services, House of Representatives, op. cit.* p. 1.
[13] *Congressional Record,* July 24, 1967, pp. H.9199-9202.

reasons for its rejection the lack of flexibility, the high cost, and the danger that a voluntary army would become a professional military corps divorced from the rest of American society. The Panel reached these conclusions on the basis of the highly controversial Department of Defense Draft Study, itself a scant 24 pages in length, only a small portion of which was devoted to the voluntary army concept. The only additional information utilized by the Clark Panel appears to have been oral testimony of witnesses from the Defense Department, the same agency responsible for the study in question. All in all, it is not unfair to say that the research was flimsy, the data nonexistent, and the findings undocumented. Most people would feel that the conclusions reached by such a methodology were not worth much, but, as we shall see, they formed the basis for most later Congressional decisions.

The conclusions of the Panel are divided into recommendations to the President and recommendations to the Congress. Far from being the broad pronouncements that one would expect, given the weaknesses just enumerated, they are precise and detailed. To take, for example, their handling of the local board problem: critics of the System say that the autonomy of the more than 4000 local boards creates serious inequities and disparities, whereas those operating Selective Service regard this autonomy as the essence of democracy. What does the Clark Report have to say on the subject? It makes three recommendations to the President: first, that Selective Service schedule periodic regional meetings of local board members to exchange ideas and discuss common problems, with a representative of the Director of Selective Service present to ensure the effectiveness of such meetings; second, that the title of the Chief Clerk of each board be changed to "Executive Secretary"; third, that the tenure of local draft board members be limited to 10 years. With such trivial recommendations do they "take care of" one of the most critical issues in the entire draft debate.

Other significant recommendations to the President were as follows:

1. The order of call should be changed to draft the youngest men first. Men eligible for induction (19-20, plus men whose student or other deferments expired) are exposed for one year, then revert to a lower order of call. Also known as conveyor belt or modified young age class system.

2. Draft card burners and draft evaders should be dealt with harshly.

3. The Department of Defense "Project 100,000," which would provide service opportunities to those who would not ordinarily meet the physical and mental requirements, should be supported.

To the Congress the Panel recommended that the present Act should be extended intact but that its name be changed to the Selective Service Act. They also suggested that the Congress maintain surveillance of the administration of the System through the Committees on Armed Services, that student deferments be continued until age 24, [14] and that the National Security Council determine which occupations should be allowed deferments, an assignment that would place a heavy burden on this Council.

One of the Panel's most extreme recommendations — though not, perhaps, a surprising one in light of the public statements of Chairmen Rivers and Russell concerning the decisions of the Supreme Court — was that the wording of the legislation regarding conscientious objectors be changed because the Supreme Court decision in the *U.S.* v. *Seeger* (380 U.S.163, 1965) "unduly expanded the basis upon which individual registrants could claim objections to military service." Moreover, the Department of Justice should complete action on these cases within 60 days. In short, a Congressional Advisory Panel of less than eight weeks' duration took it upon itself to recommend legislative changes that would not only narrow a Supreme Court decision, but also upset the Court calendars of the entire Federal judicial system.

Finally, the Panel made a series of recommendations on other issues. Universal Military Training, National Service, and a voluntary army were all dismissed as being impractical. Local board autonomy should remain intact, no lottery should be instituted, and the utilization of an electronic data-processing system was unnecessary.

It seems clear enough that Chairman Rivers, jealous of Congressional prerogative, saw the Advisory Commission appointed by the President as another attempt by the liberal establishment to centralize and modify one of the most venerable of American institutions, the Selective Service System, a last proud vestige of local and state autonomy in an era of galloping Federal encroachment. As a countermeasure, he appointed his own Advisory Panel, asking it for an independent study but taking no chances on the results. It was his staff and the Selective Service System that testified and provided information, that cooperated closely with the Panel, and that ultimately, virtually dictated the recommendations of the Report. In light of evidence, particularly the Report itself, this judgment, however disagreeable, is not unfair.

THE MARSHALL REPORT

The final report of the President's Advisory Commission on Selective Service was released in a most unusual manner. Ordinarily, the Administration and the President in particular prepare for the release of any important statement with

---

[14] This decision was justified by the use of statistics I had never seen before. They are undocumented figures that apparently are incorrect and so general as to be meaningless, "In recent years sixty percent of the college student group has served in the armed forces either as volunteers or inductees, whereas fifty-seven percent of the non-college students were called to or entered military service." See p. 11 of the report.

utmost care, paving the way for its acceptance. But the Commission Report was released over the weekend of March 4, 1967, two days before the President sent his message to Congress. It was suggested in the press that the reasons for this departure from the norm were that the President was willing to give the Report precedence even over his own proposals and that he was inviting a comparison between his proposals and those of the Marshall Commission (as well as those of the Clark Panel).

The contrast between the procedures of the President's Commission and those of the Clark Panel could not be more vivid. The Commission Report was based on an extensive six-to-seven-month study. Its members met formally for more than 100 hours. Although the group was large and unwieldy, they were able to read hundreds of papers and reports on various aspects of the problem. They invited more than 120 organizations to give their opinions. College student leaders, editors of 250 student newspapers, cabinet officials, the 50 state governors, heads of various government agencies, and mayors of major cities – all were involved with the Commission. Questionnaires were sent to the State Directors of Selective Service and to the more than 4000 local draft boards and the 97 appeal boards. Individual members of the Commission solicited information and advice from their contacts in many sectors of national life. Staff members complained that the size of the group, wide differences in interests, and varying degrees of preparation stymied the Commission on occasion from going into depth on some issues. The staff attempted to make up for this weakness, however, by assuming the informational burden. Members of the Commission staff attended and reported on the major draft conferences held throughout the country.

The Commission, apparently not sharing General Hershey's horror of the machine, effectively utilized computers to facilitate the analysis of information received. The data made up almost three-fourths of the 219-page Report, which certainly constitutes the most detailed analysis of Selective Service ever published. Moreover, it is literate, well-reasoned, and persuasive. (A summary of the Report is contained in Appendix II.)

Taken together the recommendations propose a radical reorganization of the draft and the agency primarily responsible – the Selective Service System.

Finding no immediately viable alternative to the system presently in operation, the Commission recommended extension of the existing draft authority for four years. In calling for a form of random selection among eligible 19-year-olds, its reasoning was simple and clear-cut:

"A dramatic population growth has increased the supply of eligible men available for military service. . . . Of the nearly 2 million men now reaching draft age each year, our Armed Forces are likely to need only from one-half to one-third of them, varying with the circumstances. . . . And of those, only a portion must be selected for nonvoluntary induction." [15]

The number needed will vary with circumstances affecting voluntary enlistments but will be between 100,000 and 300,000 men who will come from a pool of about one and one-half million men qualified for service. [16] This situation will continue at least into the middle 1970's when the post-World War II birth rate will level off. Thus the apt title of the Report, *Who Serves When Not All Serve?*; more precisely, the Report is concerned with how those men will be selected. Induction at age 19 is recommended to reduce uncertainty about career planning. More important, the military feels younger men respond better to training. The fairest way to select those reasonably few men necessary is by some system of random selection that would work impartially on a nationwide basis and that would enable a young man to determine his status at the earliest possible date. The young man would face a one-year period of "maximum vulnerability." If he were not called during that year, his name would move to the bottom of the list, and the current annual crop of 19-year-olds would precede him. With each passing year the young man would become progressively safer from induction *but* still available in case of a national emergency.

The Commission also recommended that Selective Service be consolidated under a more centralized administration. Under this plan the national headquarters should "issue clear and binding policies concerning classifications, exemptions, and deferments to be applied uniformly throughout the country." [17] Eight regional offices would be aligned with the eight regions of the Office of Emergency Planning in order to facilitate national security planning. The 4000 local boards would be replaced by 300 to 500 area offices, established on the basis of population, with at least one in each state. These offices would register and classify men according to policy directives from national headquarters (and would be administered by the eight regional offices.)

Processing, registration, and classification would be facilitated by the use of modern data-processing equipment; for example, a young man could change his registration from one office to another if a change in permanent registration were made. This change is, of course, impossible under the present system.

The area offices would operate as the registrant's court of first appeal. Their composition would represent all elements of the public; members would serve for five years only; women could serve; and the President's power to appoint

[15] *In Pursuit of Equity: Who Serves When Not All Serve? Report of the National Advisory Commission on Selective Service,* U.S. Government Printing Office, Washington, D.C., February, 1967, p. 3.
[16] *Ibid.* p. 37.
[17] *Ibid.* p. 5.

would not be limited to those citizens nominated by the governors of the states.

The appeals procedure would be strengthened in a number of ways if the time of appeal were extended from 10 to 30 days. (This recommendation was quickly implemented by a Presidential Executive Order issued in March 1967.)

The Commission also called for improved public information procedures on the part of the Selective Service System. The reasoning behind the suggested changes is that the characterization of local boards as little groups of neighbors, who through long association with a registrant evaluate his ability to perform, is no longer valid, except perhaps in rural areas. A team of researchers reported to the Commission that "Very little evidence exists to suggest that the fact of drafting by local boards has more than symbolic significance, if that, in urban settings." Since roughly seven out of ten Americans today live in urban areas, the system as presently constituted is an anachronism. In fact, the personal touch that is made so much of by Selective Service does not exist: the Report found that in most urban areas the identity of local board members is a well-kept secret.

The Commission also found wide variation not only in the way that local boards operate but also in the degree and kind of guidance they receive. Furthermore, directives from the state director sometimes directly conflict with directives from the national office; for example:

"In 1966, 39 state headquarters issued 173 directives, bulletins or memoranda to their local boards dealing with deferment policies. This means, of course, that some states sent no such guidance; of those that did, several sent only 1 or 2, several 7 or 8, and 1 headquarters dispatched 13."

The same variation exists with respect to appeal boards. The Report shows that within the same state appeal boards may make completely opposite decisions on similar cases.[18]

It is obvious that the issue of student deferments gave the Commission the most trouble. According to Commission-watchers in Washington, first one side and then the other got the upper hand. The decision to urge abolition of student deferments was carried by a small majority, led by Chairman Burke Marshall and President Brewster of Yale. Their argument was that all otherwise eligible 19-year-olds should be subjected to one simultaneous risk of induction for at least one year's time, that the educational process would not be harmed by an interruption, and that only a portion of college men would be selected if a random selection system were used. There is no question but that the majority was swayed by the thought that postponing service now might mean the difference between serving during a wartime period and serving later when, it is

[18] *Ibid.* p. 107.

to be hoped, the war would be over and that it was grossly unfair to require the noncollege youth to bear the greatest risks. Overshadowing all other arguments was the realization that some of the worst inequities in the entire draft system are connected with student deferments.

The minority, led by George E. Reedy, Jr., President Johnson's former press secretary and now president of the Struthers Research and Development Corporation, remained adamant in favor of continued student deferments. Essentially, their position was that criticism of student deferments is directed more at the manner in which deferments are administered than at the principle itself. Moreover, they argued, those who were deferred to finish college would, at the end of the period of study, be placed in the pool with the draft-eligibles of that year.

The Commission was unanimous in favor of ending graduate deferments. Deferments beyond the undergraduate degree for potential doctors, dentists, or others pursuing courses in the national interest should be granted only if there is "an irrevocable commitment for military service at the time of the completion of the advanced degree . . . made by each student so deferred."[19]

The Commission spent a significant amount of time on the question of conscientious objection. The majority felt it was not necessary to change the law in light of the Supreme Court's 1965 *Seeger* decision, which widened the concept of religious training and belief to include "a given belief that is sincere and meaningful [and] ocupies a place in the life of its possessor parallel to that filled by the orthodox belief in God of one who clearly qualifies for the exemption." A minority wanted even further liberalization of existing laws; they felt that a conscientious objector should be able to refuse military service on the basis of his opposition to a particular war.

The Commission went beyond the obvious issues connected with Selective Service and into areas of far greater controversy by recommending (a) that more opportunities in the armed forces be made available for women in order to reduce the numbers of men who must be called to serve involuntarily, (b) that insofar as possible, volunteers who do not meet induction standards be given an opportunity to serve, and (c) that a study be initiated to determine the feasibility of allowing 18-year-olds selected for induction to decide themselves when, between the ages of 18 and 23, they would serve.

Finally, in considering the draft's effect on and fairness to the Negro, the Commission came to several interesting conclusions. Although Negroes do not serve out of proportion to their percentage of the population, their participation is in other ways disproportionate; for instance, Negroes are drastically under-represented on local draft boards (1.3 percent, although they make up 11

---

[19] *Ibid.* p. 46.

percent of the population.) Moreover, although the proportion of Negroes rejected is about twice as great as the proportion of whites (50 percent compared with 25 percent), eligible Negroes are drafted at a proportionately higher rate (30 percent) than eligible whites (18 percent.)

Comparisons between the two groups and their respective reports are inevitable. Both groups were composed of busy people with limited time available. The Marshall Commission was a little larger, but this was compensated for by a dedicated, hardworking staff. On the other hand, the Clark Panel, although much less unwieldy, was hampered by an almost nonexistent staff. Almost no formal meetings were held by this group.

One report was literate, well-written, documented, and broad in its scope. The other exactly the opposite, yet it had by far the greater impact. No matter how one judges the two, the ultimate test must be the impact. Using this measure, the Clark Panel Report was more successful, as we shall see later.

THE PRESIDENT'S MESSAGE

On Monday, March 6, the President's message on Selective Service to the Congress was released. The President praised the Commission for providing "the most penetrating analysis of Selective Service in our history." He then made nine specific proposals to the Congress:

"1. The Selective Service law under which men can be inducted into the Armed Forces be extended for a four-year period, upon its expiration on June 30, 1967.

"2. Men be inducted beginning at 19 years of age, reversing the present order of calling the oldest first, so that uncertainties now generated in the lives of young men will be reduced.

"3. Policies be tightened governing undergraduates college deferments so that those deferments can never become exemptions from military service, and providing for no further post-graduate deferments except for those in medical and dental schools.

"4. Firm rules be formulated, to be applied uniformly throughout the country, in determining eligibility for all other types of deferment.

"5. A fair and impartial random (FAIR) system of selection be established to determine the order of call for all men eligible and available for the draft.

"6. Improvements in the Selective Service System be immediately effected to assure better service to the registrant both in counselling and appeals, better information to the public regarding the System's operation and broader representation on local boards of the communities they serve.

"7. A study be conducted by the best management experts in the government of the effectiveness, cost and feasibility of a proposal made by the National Advisory Commission to restructure the organization of the Selective Service System.

"8. The National Commission on Selective Service be continued for another year to provide a continuing review of the system that touches the lives of so many young Americans and their families.

"9. Enlistment procedures for our National Guard and Reserve units be strengthened to remove inequities and to ensure a high state of readiness for those units."

On balance, the President's proposals do not go so far as the Marshall Commission had recommended in the matters of college deferments and the abolition of local boards. In a remarkably ambiguous statement on undergraduate deferments the President called for a national discussion of the issue. He said:

"An issue so deeply important, with so many compelling factors on both sides, cannot be decided until its every aspect has been thoroughly explored.

"I hope and expect that the Congress will debate the questions this issue poses for the Nation's youth and the Nation's future.

"I will welcome the public discussion which the Commission report will surely stimulate.

"I shall await the benefits of these discussions which will themselves be a great educational process for the Nation.

"I will then take that Presidential action which, I believe, will best serve the national interest."

On the matter of Selective Service reorganization the President was less than emphatic. His failure to accept totally the Marshall Commission's recommendation that the local board system be overhauled is understandable. Not only has Selective Service, by and large, been an effective part of the American democratic process – and as the President said, "We cannot lightly discard an institution with so valuable a record of effectiveness and integrity" – but also (and this point the President did not mention) an all-out attack on such a venerable institution whose Congressional friends are equally venerable – or at least powerful – might have shattering political repercussions. The President's message, however, did say: "Neither can we afford to preserve [such an institution], if we find that in practice it cannot adapt to the new controlling concept of equal and uniform treatment." The President solved the dilemma confronting him by saying that the restructuring proposal of the Marshall Commission should be studied further and then naming a Task

Force – made up of the Secretary of Defense, the Director of Selective Service, and the Director of the Bureau of the Budget – to undertake this review. The White House message did not come to grips with the Commission's revelation that a far higher proportion of eligible Negroes than of eligible whites is drafted.

THE PRESS REACTION

Both the Marshall Report and the President's message received considerable favorable comment from the national press. A *New York Times* editorial on March 6, said: "President Johnson's National Advisory Commission on Selective Service has made generally admirable proposals for eliminating the inequities of the present military draft." Two days after the President's message, however, the same newspaper editorialized: "President Johnson has set forth with great clarity all the reasons why the military draft must be made more equitable, but his message to Congress shows a puzzling absence of insistence on swift action to get rid of the unfairness." The *Washington Evening Star* likewise felt that the Marshall Report and the President's message were "on balance...tailored to improve a system never well designed for brush-fire wars." But the *Star* also twitted the President for a "remarkably muted message," particularly with reference to student deferments.

The working press, particularly those familiar with the Washington political scene, were at the same time raising storm signals that heralded adverse Congressional reaction. On March 7 J. Y. Smith of the *Washington Post* indicated clearly that key legislators were cool to the President's plan. Congressman Hébert (D. Louisiana), long-time critic of the lottery, said flatly, "There is not going to be any lottery," and Chairman Rivers was quoted as saying in the same article, "We think the present law has too much discretionary authority."

Even more ominous was Richard Wilson's syndicated column of March 8, entitled "Congress Leaning Towards Its Own Panel on Draft":

"The Congressional advisory panel is dead set against the lottery system and abolishing college deferments. So are a good many influential members of Congress and they may change the law before letting the President bring about any drastic change in the Selective Service System under his discretionary authority."

The interested segment of the American public, the executive branch of government, and one committee of Congress had engaged in a public debate on the draft. Now the arena moved back to the legislative branch. The conflicts between the various positions had been clearly established. Only the compromises had yet to be reached.

SUMMARY

The period of dialogue from the summer of 1966 to the spring of 1967 represents a transition from the general discussion stage to the legislative showdown. During that period public debate on the Selective Service System widened; educators, government officials, and others held conferences to find the facts and establish the issues, and two study groups addressed themselves directly to the problem. The reports that these two groups produced are polarized not only in their methodologies but also in the tone of their recommendations: The Clark Report was highly laudatory in its praise of the present Selective Service System, the Marshall Report highly critical. Although he praised the Marshall Report as the "most penetrating analysis of Selective Service in our history," President Johnson, in his March 6 message to Congress, was cautious in his seconding of its recommendations, particularly with respect to student deferment and the reorganization of the Selective Service System. In fact, the President's message represents the perfect transition point: he passed the responsibility to the Congress.

7 | THE KENNEDY HEARINGS

In February 1967 Senator Edward Kennedy discussed with Senator Richard Russell, the Senate Armed Services Committee Chairman, the possibility of the Senate Labor and Public Welfare Committee's holding hearings on problems of the draft directly related to employment, labor, and education. Certainly these facets of the issue are more directly a concern of the Labor and Public Welfare Committee – and more specifically, the Subcommittee on Employment, Manpower, and Poverty of which Senator Kennedy is a member – than of the Senate Armed Services Committee. Senator Russell agreed about the propriety of the hearings, but both men publicly reiterated that the primary legislative jurisdiction for all matters pertaining to the draft law rested with Russell's Armed Services Committee. Regardless of what the Subcommittee hearings disclosed, they would not become a part of the legislative history of the draft law revision. Joseph S. Clark, Chairman of the Subcommittee on Employment, Manpower, and Poverty, agreed to turn the chairmanship of the hearings over to Senator Kennedy, a relatively junior member. So Kennedy was given the opportunity to conduct hearings several weeks before the Armed Services Committees' hearing for, among other things, whatever publicity value would be attached.

As we shall see, however, the senior Senator from Massachusetts accomplished much more. The hearings, which ran for seven days during the period from March 20 to April 6, are an interesting contrast to those hearings previously held by the Rivers' Committee in 1966 and to those subsequently held by the Armed Services Committees of both houses later in the session. To be sure, because no resultant legislative action was contemplated, they were able to cover a far broader range of problem areas and to delve more deeply into peripheral issues ordinarily overlooked. The fact remains that they did a more than creditable job in providing information and in eliciting the opinions of knowledgeable public figures who were never asked to testify before the Committees that had direct responsibility for pending legislation. Among these public figures were Secretary of Labor Willard Wirtz, Commissioner of

Education Harold Howe, and Director of the Office of Economic Opportunity
Sargent Shriver. An excellent example of the Kennedy Committee's
exploration-in-depth of various peripheral topics ordinarily passed over was its
discussion of the conscientious objector problem; here, the witness was Arlo
Tatum, Executive Secretary of the Committee for Conscientious Objectors and
probably the most authoritative person in the country on this subject. A true
pacifist who served two prison sentences in 1941 and 1947 for refusal to register
for the draft, Tatum was able to present a side of the question seldom accorded
a listening in Congressional hearing rooms. When the hearings took up the
question of National Service, the witness was Donald J. Eberly, Executive
Director of the National Service Secretariat, and Milton Friedman, one of the
foremost proponents of the voluntary army concept, was heard on that subject.
Although they did not result in legislation, the hearings provided Senator
Kennedy with the information he needed to make his subsequent statements
before the House and Senate Committees much more authoritative. What is
more important, Kennedy's later testimony did become a part of the legislative
history.

On March 20, 1967, before turning the gavel over to Senator Kennedy,
Senator Clark made a statement which set the tone for the hearings:

"In summary we face two urgent problems: First to accomplish a drastic
revision of the law to eliminate for once and for all the inequities and injustices
that now flaw its operation; and second, to transform the Selective Service
System into an agency with a responsibility to make its own specific
contribution to the economic health and internal strength of our nation and
with policies shaped toward the goal of full employment and the assurance of
jobs for those who have fulfilled their military obligations and are resuming
civilian careers.

"Our young men have an obligation to serve their country. Their country, in
turn, has an obligation to help them return to a productive life and a future of
economic security and opportunity." [1]

At least one of the witnesses before the Subcommittee was no
stranger – General Lewis Hershey. The directness, forcefulness, and specificity
of the questioning – particularly by Senator Kennedy – unnerved the General
somewhat and prevented his falling back on the usual filibustering tactics.
Clearly uncomfortable, as he never was in appearing before the friendly Armed
Services Committees, the General nonetheless was careful to discuss only those

[1] *Hearings before the Subcommittee on Employment, Manpower, and Poverty of the
Committee on Labor and Public Welfare, United States Senate,* U.S. Government Printing
Office, Washington, D.C., 1967, p. 3.

issues that the President in his Selective Service message had indicated were still open to discussion. It was obvious that the Marshall Commission Report, with its recommendation that his Selective Service System be completely reorganized, was not Hershey's favorite reading material. In his opposition to this recommendation the General was quite clear. With great feeling he expressed the thought that all change is not necessarily for the good. He lauded Selective Service as a truly "federal" system, with the states and the Federal government cooperating in carrying out the law. Finally he said:

"I have not yet arrived at the place where I think the machine which operates on cards with punch holes in them will necessarily have any more wisdom, and certainly not as much compassion, than a human being." [2]

The questioning turned to deferments, and Senator Kennedy elicited Hershey's agreement that deferment policies should vary with the particular situation. In conditions of extreme emergency every able-bodied man should be called, and, conversely, during peacetime student deferments at least up to completion of the undergraduate degree should be permitted. The real problem is what to do during a limited-war situation. Hershey cited World War II experience as the basis for the current policy. During that period almost everyone went into service. Postwar reaction, however, was that "we lost the race to the moon or stars or some other places because we had inducted the individuals we should have been making scientists out of." Hershey is correct that, as a result of this experience, the Trytten plan was developed and the current policies emerged, but the analogy between World War II and the current conflict is not a good one, for now there are far more eligible men than are needed. Since circumstances have changed so drastically, we can conclude that a new basis for deferment policy needs to be worked out.

Very predictably, General Hershey made clear his distaste for any type of random selection system. He did admit one could be instituted; all that was needed was, in his words, a signal from his quarterback.

A series of rapid-fire questions from Senator Kennedy finally elicited the General's agreement that the number of young men reaching age 19 every year was increasing dramatically and that the problem was to select some when not all were needed. Using, for purposes of discussion, a figure of 1.9 million men who would reach age 19 in a hypothetical year, [3] they went on to estimate that in this group a million would be qualified and 900,000 unqualified — reasonable

[2] *Ibid.* p. 12.

[3] This is not really such a hypothetical figure. According to the figures used in the Department of Defense Draft Study, released in June 1966, the number of men reaching age 18 will be more than 1.9 million in 1970. Other studies indicate that the 1.9 figure has already been reached.

proportions if history is any guide. Hershey tried desperately to avoid admitting that only a relatively small number would actually need to be drafted, even with the Vietnam buildup and current strength levels. He talked about enlistments, the National Guard, the Reserves, and the like. Finally he said, very tentatively, that inductions "probably are somewhat less than half." Kennedy cut in: "I believe the figure is that 27 percent are inductions." Hershey answered, "I wouldn't quarrel with that." Even granting that the present Selective Service System encourages many to enlist in the armed forces before the draft catches them, there would still be large numbers of men who would not be needed. Reluctantly General Hershey said:

"I am willing to admit that after you take out everybody you want you are going to have somewhere between 250,000 and 350,000 every year that you can't take. There is no place for them."

After further discussion, the following exchange took place:

Senator Kennedy.   You don't think, therefore, it would be very difficult and time-consuming or complicated to establish [a system of random selection]?
General Hershey.   Maybe I am underestimating but I will not admit it will take very long to do it when we decide to do it.[4]

The second witness was Assistant Secretary of Defense Thomas D. Morris. Although the face was familiar, the testimony was very different from that given before the Rivers' Committee less than a year earlier. What were the differences? Chiefly, the Department of Defense had come out in favor of a lottery in the interim between the hearings, as indicated first in the McNamara interview in the *Harvard Crimson* and then by the position taken at the American Veterans Committee Conference by Harold Wool, McNamara's able deputy (see Chapter 6 for a fuller discussion). Why had such a change of attitude occurred? As has been indicated, General Hershey's resistance to any suggestion that the Selective Service System needed changing or was unable to deal with the current situation had led to a gradual drawing away by agencies and persons previously supporting his policies and practices and the increasing isolation of the System. More than any other issue, the lottery — or any system of random selection — pushed the Defense Department and the Selective Service System apart.

Morris, after a careful analysis of a post-Vietnam manpower situation, said that "about one out of seven of the men...available for induction each year would need to be drafted." Even in a Vietnam situation there are many more

---

[4] *Hearings before the Subcommittee on Employment, Manpower, and Poverty of the Committee on Labor and Public Welfare, United States Senate, op. cit.* p. 25.

men than are needed. Senator Kennedy asked about the potential decline in enlistments that might result if a system of random selection were initiated, his point being that a young man might be inclined to wait (some might say to gamble) to see if his number came up rather than to enlist to secure certain advantages, as young men were doing under the draft system. Morris's answer is important because it indicates that the Department of Defense does not feel a system of random selection will cause a dramatic decrease in volunteers. Morris said:

"We have considered it, Mr. Chairman. It is our judgment, I must admit this is a matter of judgment, that we will continue to receive this volume of volunteers. Many men volunteer between ages 17 and 18½. In fact, today the average age of the volunteer is just over 19, 19.2. So, we believe this is a realistic forecast."

Senator Kennedy then asked about possible obstacles to a system of random selection. "We see no obstacles, sir," answered Mr. Morris. Finally Kennedy made his last point:

"The most fundamental – and I think this is an extremely important point – the most fundamental point, which is generally agreed on by the Marshall commission, the Clark panel's report, the Defense Department's own study, and by the military commanders in the field, is to draft the youngest first. In order to implement that recommendation, other than in the Vietnam buildup situation, we must devise an equitable system which is going to take some, while not take all, young men."

Mr. Morris.	Yes, sir.
Senator Kennedy.	The recommendation made by the Marshall commission – random selection – is the one deemed by it the most equitable.
Mr. Morris.	Yes, sir. [5]

On Tuesday, March 21, a new voice was heard. Secretary of Labor Willard Wirtz, who until this time had not expressed his opinion on the draft issue publicly, spoke with obvious conviction, unencumbered by any necessity to hew closely to the administration line. In very quick time Senator Kennedy obtained from Secretary Wirtz his position on two important matters: inequities and random selection. Wirtz went on to pinpoint his views on matters of special interest to him as Secretary of Labor, namely the plight of the noncollege man and the characteristics of the job market. According to Secretary Wirtz, the youth of the nation feel a discontent approaching contempt over the way the

[5] *Ibid.* p. 45.

burden of the draft is being distributed. His stand was clear and unequivolcal:

"I support. . .a method of selection for military service that is FAIR — as fair to the sons of economically and politically weaker parents as to the sons of parents with more immediate influence." [6]

When asked why he thought that random selection was the most equitable system that could be devised, his answer, delivered with great feeling, made a strong impression on those in the crowded hearing room:

"This is a hard idea to sell. When I have said what I have said here, it is out of a depth of conviction that we have got to do something to see that this system does not work more to the advantage of those who already have advantage than it does those who have disadvantage. . . .

"I think the poor and the disadvantaged are getting an unfair break as far as the carrying of the present burden is concerned. I think they are being placed in double jeopardy. First, the jeopardy of not having a chance to go on to college, or to go on to good health, or to go on to that kind of thing; and second, the jeopardy of having to assume this military burden." [7]

Secretary Wirtz came out strong on five points:

"The draft call should be made on the youngest men considered qualified for military service — which is now rapidly becoming identified as the 19-year age group. And so far as I know, there is substantial subscription to that. Every element of uncertainty regarding the fact or timing of this call should be removed.

"There is no justification under present circumstances, and especially in view of the prospective shift to a 19-year age group induction priority, for 'occupational deferments.' If deferments are granted, however, for any kind of training — college, for example — they should be granted on comparable terms for all kinds of training.

"Any young man called for military service and found unqualified because of a remediable inadequacy should be given whatever training or treatment is required to make him qualified.

"There should be enlarged emphasis in military service on training which prepares the individual for both military and civilian usefulness.

"There must be procedures which assure the ex-serviceman adequate civilian training or employment opportunity." [8]

On Thursday, March 23, 1967, the Committee heard from yet another high

[6] *Ibid.* p. 59.
[7] *Ibid.* pp. 59-60.
[8] *Ibid.* p. 60.

government appointee, Sargent Shriver, Director of the Office of Economic
Opportunity. Mr. Shriver came out forcefully against deferments of any kind
and in favor of mandatory registration of all youths at age 16. He showed
unusual candor in calling for a rather controversial form of universal
training: registration of everyone, including (shades of Margaret Mead!) women:

"I favor the registration and testing of all young Americans at age
16 – females as well as males. The Peace Corps and VISTA and the Job Corps
have all proven, once again, that women are just as courageous and patriotic and
hardworking as men.

"Thousands, possibly millions, of young women would like a chance to help
their country by performing recognized national service and such service should
not be restricted to combatant military service.

"It is an archaic sentimentalism, I believe, which excludes young women from
selective service, in the generic sense of those words.

"Moreover, if we registered and tested all youngsters at age 16, we would
know who needs what help early enough to do something – time to perform
significant remedial physical fitness, academic education, and motivational
training."[9]

Yet another key figure heretofore unheard from, United States Commissioner
of Education Harold Howe, was the Committee witness on Wednesday, April 5.
The Commissioner directed his attention immediately to the question of
deferments. After indicating that he supported ending graduate deferments, the
Commissioner stated that a substantial case could be made for eliminating
undergraduate deferments as well, although the issue was a complex one and
required additional discussion and study before a final decision could be
reached. He was careful to distinguish between the position of the Department
of Health, Education and Welfare and his own personal views:

"Let me say from the point of view of the Department and the
administration, we want to keep this question open. The President asked for
open debate on this, and I think it is in this spirit that you asked the question.

"I think that with that reservation, and with the feeling that we have a lot to
learn about the results of this hearing and other evidence that will be brought to
the matter, I would personally feel that undergraduate deferment is no longer
justified."[10]

[9] *Ibid.* pp. 153-154.
[10] *Ibid.* p. 215.

SUMMARY

The Kennedy hearings provided a forum for three important witnesses not previously involved in the draft issue. All three were men of stature, well known not only inside the government but also by the public at large. And all three — Secretary Wirtz, Commissioner Howe, and Director Shriver — came out strongly against student deferments. At this point many knowledgeable people in education, particularly in Washington, felt that undergraduate student deferments were in deep trouble. Further, they agreed that if undergraduate deferments were continued young men in vocational apprentice programs should be deferred also. They further agreed that the youngest men should be taken first and that a system of random selection should be instituted.

Otherwise the hearings were remarkable chiefly because, in their course, General Hershey openly admitted that the armed services could not take all eligible young men and that a random selection system would be workable. Though they did not lead directly to legislation then, the Kennedy hearings had considerable impact because of the widespread publicity accorded to the witnesses.

8 | THE CONGRESS WILL DECIDE

The Kennedy hearings ended on April 6. About a week later the Senate Committee opened its hearings – the first step in the final stage of the process that was to end with the signing into law of the Military Service Act of 1967. All that had gone before, the 1966 House hearings, with the questions raised there about the adequacy of the Selective Service System, the public dialogue, the conferences on the draft, the work of the two study groups and their reports, the President's message to Congress, and the Kennedy hearings, may be regarded as a prelude to the hearings of the two Armed Services Committees. During the some two and a half months following the conclusion of the Kennedy hearings, during the two Committee hearings, the subsequent debate in both houses of Congress, the appointing and meeting of a joint conference committee, and the final consideration of the Conference report by both House and Senate we watch the spectacle of the legislative process at work.

THE SENATE HEARINGS

Until the Senate Committee on Armed Services began its hearings on April 12, 1967, its members had not been publicly recorded on this issue to the same extent as the members of the House Committee. A generally conservative and hawkish group, it is chaired by the venerable and highly respected Senator Richard Russell. The tone of a committee is difficult to describe, but it is sufficient to say that any committee chaired by Russell which has John Stennis (D. Mississippi), Strom Thurmond (R. South Carolina), John Tower (R. Texas), Peter Dominick (R. Colorado), Sam Ervin (D. North Carolina), and Thomas McIntyre (D. New Hampshire) is, to say the least, conservative in its orientation.

The first witness was retired General Mark Clark, Chairman of the Civilian Advisory Panel on Military Manpower Procurement. He was escorted to the hearings by House Committee Chairman Rivers himself. To begin with, Clark summarized the report of his Panel. After the usual accolades for a "well-reasoned statement" Russell got down immediately to one of the major issues of the hearings – student deferments – with a key question about the Clark Panel's recommendations. Under the law then in effect the President had maximum flexibility in dealing with deferments. If he desired to make changes, they could be accomplished administratively by executive order. Should Congress, Russell asked, be more explicit in dealing with student deferments? Clark in his answer was emphatic. Citing his disagreement with the Marshall Commission Report, he said:

"It seems to me that when we are in a limited war, and the training of our youth is so important to the future well-being of our country, and when we need only a small proportion of the available men that we have, that we should go right ahead with the training and educating of our people. The Panel was concerned that this might not be done, and we felt that the law should insure that this educational process be continued."[1]

In connection with his proposed scheme of returning undergraduates to the 19-year-old pool after graduation and limiting graduate deferments, General Clark enunciated his own rather unusual personal philosophy concerning graduate work:

"So many more now are desiring to go on to postgraduate work, to major in such things as musical appreciation and animal husbandry and a lot of things not essential to the military posture of our country; and so we. . .recommended that there be placed in. . .the National Security Council, the identification of truly critical required areas of graduate study so that there would be relatively few who would go on to postgraduate work."[2]

Coming from a college president, the plainly contemptuous reference to courses of study other than those "essential to the military posture of our country" – meaning, by implication, the hard sciences – is unfortunate to say the least.

Ignoring the larger problems facing the Committee, Senator Margaret Chase Smith (R. Maine) turned immediately to the subject of the small number of young people using their aversion to the war in Vietnam as a reason to avoid or defy the call to military service. She asked Clark to elaborate on the soft attitude of public officials toward those seeking to escape military service. Clark replied that the number of incidents of draft-card destruction far exceeded the number that had been brought to trial and that apparently nothing was being done about those who escaped the draft by going to Canada. This exchange was typical of

[1] *Amending and Extending the Draft Law and Related Authorities, Hearings before the Committee on Armed Services, United States Senate,* U.S. Government Printing Office, Washington, D.C., 1967, p. 28.
[2] *Ibid.* p. 29.

those involving Senator Smith; unfortunately she consistently showed a lack of understanding of the essentials of the Selective Service problem. Using tactics reminiscent of those of General Douglas MacArthur who, in his final public speech before the joint session of Congress, related conversations he had had with soldiers who urged more concerted efforts by the United States to bring about total military victory, Clark said that servicemen often questioned him about what was being done about the draft-card burners, protesters, and the like. On the conscientious objector question, he favored a tightening of the language in the legislation because "a breed of cat [is] running around, not the regular religious groups. . .but a lot of people who just don't want to fight, who don't want to go to war. . .I personally don't go along with this business."[3] His personal recommendation was that conscientious objectors be put into service and assigned to noncombatant duty. That many conscientious objectors prefer to go to jail rather than to carry out any duty that helps the war effort is a point that Clark overlooks. Moreover, like many other people, he seems to have rather limited notions about what constitutes "respectable" conscientious objection. Apparently the consciences of persons who do not belong to the "regular religious groups" are somehow not really consciences at all. Clark's attitude is not, of course, unusual, but in light of the Supreme Court's more humanistic and surely realistic conception that attitude is a step backward.

General Clark felt that asking the local board to determine who is and who is not a conscientious objector is placing it in an impossible position. It was the Clark Panel's recommendation that the definition be tightened so that the boards would be able to decide such cases more easily. Yet in other areas the whole thrust of the Clark Panel's recommendations was to give maximum discretion to the local board on the grounds that fixed standards or centralization of function would go against the pattern so successful in the past. Obviously Clark's views on local autonomy are somewhat flexible, as is clearly brought out in his answer to a question from Senator Jackson (D. Washington) pertaining to the lack of national guidelines. Clark's recommendation was that meetings be held, a "watchdog" committee be formed, and a public relations director be appointed. This was the extent of his appreciation of what national guidelines should mean.

Secretary Morris, the second witness, made a short opening statement primarily keyed to supporting the general language of the bill before the Committee. That bill, which would extend the induction authority for four years, did not specifically mention random selection, but the old law left it well within the discretionary authority of the President to establish that alternative. Consequently Morris was questioned repeatedly about the random selection system. He summarized the current position of the Defense Department as follows:

[3] *Ibid.* p. 34.

"When a man reaches 18, he would register with his draft board. He would then be sent for his mental and physical examination at our examining station. They would report their findings back to the draft board. The draft board would. . .classify the man. This would finally leave, then, a group of class 1-A men, just as today, available for induction.

"Since that group of men. . .would in a typical year be about seven times greater than the number we would need to draft each year. . .it seems that the fairest way of selecting would be some kind of random selection system." [4]

It should be noted that Secretary Morris did not go into the details of a system of random selection. His use of the phrase "some kind of random selection" is important in that it provided the basis for Congressional charges that the proposals put forth concerning random selection were vague and difficult to understand. This lack of specificity was a major weakness of the Administration's approach to this phase of the issue. On the other hand, in no way could the critics argue that random selection would take away the discretionary function of the local boards; the random selection process would take place *after* registrants were classified by their local boards.

Mark Clark, titular father of one of the reports concerning the draft, had received a warm welcome and a sympathetic hearing. The reception accorded to Burke Marshall, Chairman of the National Advisory Commission on Selective Service, which had, of course, produced the other report, was somewhat less "friendly." In his opening statement on Thursday, April 13, Marshall summarized the four major recommendations of his Commission: that compulsory service be continued; that the youngest men be taken first; that a system of random selection be instituted; and that college deferments be abolished. Interestingly enough, Marshall did not name the reorganization of Selective Service as one of the Commission's major recommendations.

Chairman Russell immediately indicated the line of attack he meant to take to get at the weaknesses of the Commission's recommendations: his first question was about areas of disagreement within the Commission. Marshall answered that there had been disagreement over the matter of student deferments and, to a smaller extent, over the matter of conscientious objectors. Russell then asked about random selection and particularly about the specifics of such a system. Marshall answered that the details would be left to the operating agencies, the Selective Service System, and the Department of Defense. It is clear from their exchange, which went on for some time, that the Committee Chairman was unable to comprehend how such a system would work, or rather, to be completely fair, it is clear that he chose not to be able to comprehend.

[4] *Ibid.* p. 89.

Senator Russell also recognized that Marshall had not mentioned the Commission's recommendation concerning the revamping of the Selective Service System to do away with local draft boards. The dialogue between the two is an excellent exposition of both sides of the local board problem:

Chairman Russell.

It seems to me you give a rather brief treatment to what I regard as one of the most far reaching of your recommendations, that is to abolish the local draft boards and establish this federalized system. Do you care to elaborate on that for the benefit of the committee?

Mr. Marshall.

I will be glad to, Mr. Chairman. The reason that I did not go into it much in the prepared statement was because it is being restudied and is not before the committee.

Chairman Russell.

I beg your pardon, I didn't understand you.

Mr. Marshall.

It is because it is being restudied within the executive branch and was not a part of the President's proposal to Congress.

Chairman Russell.

All these things deferred for debate and study are going to have to be decided by the committee at some time. I don't know when we will get the result of this study. Are you conducting the study?

Mr. Marshall.

No, sir.

Chairman Russell.

I didn't even know who was conducting it. There were two or three of your recommendations not included in the recommendations for legislation from the executive branch.

Mr. Marshall.

Yes. I would be glad to go into that, Mr. Chairman. We made an extensive study of the way that the system now works, and the conclusions are stated at length with a great many statistics in the report, but they come down to this. The local boards, in the judgment of the Commission, do not operate now the way that they were set up to operate. For example, in the city of Baltimore, which is one example that I just remember, there are 17 local boards. Those 17 local boards share an office. The office is populated basically by the chief clerks for those local boards. The boards themselves meet once a month or something like that.

Mr. Marshall.
(continued)

Under the way the system is now designed, therefore, you have one office in the city of Baltimore with 17 local boards and 17 clerks operating in response to 17 different organizations, all of which has discretion of their own and can have policies of their own, the way the system is designed. We thought in the first place that giving discretion to local boards in that kind of a situation in an urban society didn't make sense, that there wasn't any reason to have 17 different policies going in Baltimore, which is possible.

Secondly, Senator, from the point of view of management and efficiency and simple administrative principles, it seemed to us to make sense to consolidate them. Now that is the first reason for the consolidation and the reorganization. The second reason is that for some of the same reasons, in particular the increase of population and the shift in population from the rural areas into the cities, we thought that the local boards did not exercise discretion in the sense of knowing young men or anything like that. That what they effectively did was not classify everyone that came before them, and there are a lot of statistics in our report on this. Senator, they did not really classify people, one by one, but they passed on the difficult cases in sort of an appellate fashion, and we thought that that was right and proper, that there should be local citizens, local boards, and not some national centralized office, but local citizens and local boards exercising judgment in hardship cases, and so forth. But we thought there were too many of them and that administratively it didn't make sense the way the system operates in fact now for them to go through sort of the motions which they do now of classifying each individual — so that is the second reason, Senator.

The third reason was that we thought that the policies operated by the boards should be national policies and not local policies. For example, on the question of student deferment, the way it works

Mr. Marshall.
(continued)

now, different States can have different policies on student deferment and how you judge who is entitled to it and who isn't entitled to it. In some States they say, and these are the States, not General Hershey, some States they say you have to take 15 hours a week, in other States it has to be 12 hours a week, in other States it has to be 18 hours a week. In some States there is no policy, and each local board can decide itself how many hours a week there should be, and then they treat class ranking differently. They treat the national test differently.

We thought that the policies on those should be uniform and national, and in order to accomplish that, that the best way to accomplish that administratively as well as for the others, was to put the initial classification under a "civil service" system, with the appellate exercise of judgment to be exercised by the local boards.

Chairman Russell.

In theory, that may be very well, Mr. Marshall, but the original proposal and objective was to keep this matter as close within the range of each of these boards to which you refer, on the premise that they had information about family hardships, good faith, personal problems, and conditions within homes that no computer yet devised could possibly ascertain, and that they would come as near to being fair as any group could be, knowing that they had to live in that community, with the mothers and fathers of the sons with whose lives they were dealing. I don't believe I have ever heard — it may have occurred — of any charge that was sustained of corruption against a draft board member, in all the years this has been in operation.

We have had within the very limited compass of the Reserve organizations within the past several months a number of criminal cases against recruiting officers and others who had, for a consideration, undertaken to get a young man in a Reserve organization where he would be immune, at least temporarily, from active military duty in the field. For some reason I rather shudder to contemplate the

Mr. Russell.
(continued)

recommendation that we establish a rather large Federal bureaucracy to deal with this. The present system has its weaknesses, we are all aware of that, and I think we should find ways to strengthen it if the majority decides to keep it, but it is administered by people who are known to the persons affected by the draft.

A man in his own community is going to have to look a registrant in the eye and tell him he is going to serve. It shouldn't be the responsibility of a person in Georgia to tell a resident of Chicago, "You have been selected and you are going into the service." I don't know the final conclusion of the study by whomever the President has referred this matter to, but speaking as an individual member of this committee, I would have to see a great deal more advantage to this new bureaucratic, computerized system than I have to date, before I could support it.[5]

Senator Stennis also discussed the local board system and the changes in the local board system recommended by the Marshall Commission, although Marshall tried to reassure him that this recommendation was not before the Congress and that the only action the President had taken on it was to appoint a committee to study the matter. Senator Stennis's statement is really a plea for rural America caught in the throes of rapid urbanization which has taken so much of the power and responsibility from what in the past was a dominant part of American society:

"Now I believe I can tell you one reason why this board works so well. They meet on the streets the next day the very men they passed on in the afternoon or the night before. They meet the families, the mothers, the wives, and all the rest in one way or another, some of those members do, and they are conscious of that, in addition to their own patriotic motives. They wouldn't be on there, they wouldn't be serving, willing to serve, unless they had some of those motives.

"In addition to that, there is a day by day and week by week, month by month checkup on what they did, and they know it, and I think it is part of the heart and soul, if I may say so, of the backing of this tremendous military program, even when we are at peace, and the backing of it now when we are at

[5] *Ibid.* pp. 135-137.

war, and the backing of it when, as Secretary Rusk said, we already have 40 worldwide commitments, definite commitments, with reference to military intervention under certain circumstances.

"I believe you would kill the heart and soul of a great part of this whole concept now of worldwide responsibility. We are going into the homes of these communities and taking these men out and it is better to be passed on by people who are there and know something about the circumstances. That is my position at least and I hope that will be the position of this group.

"You can call them various groups or whatever you want to, it is commonsense, and it is the American system too." [6]

Senator Kennedy was the next important witness before the Committee. His statement was a capsule of the hearings recently completed by the Labor Subcommittee under his chairmanship, and all that he said became part of the legislative history. Kennedy followed Burke Marshall's explanation of random selection with his own description:

"The random selection system might work in the following way.

"The 4,088 draft boards would classify the young men. . . . After being classified, the young men would go into a national pool. Their numbers would be selected. Those to be drafted would be those whose numbers come up earliest, and those not drafted would be those further. . .down at the end of the list. At the end of the year of prime eligibility – the 19th year – those not selected would go to the bottom of the list for the next year."[7]

The Senator was not questioned at any great length.

The final witness before the Committee on April 19, 1967, General Hershey, said little in his statement or in reply to questioning that he had not said many times before.

In summary, the members of the Committee seemed very much in accord with the recommendation to draft the youngest men first. They manifested little sympathy, however, for the abolition of student deferments, none for a system of random selection, and marked antipathy to any suggestion that the local board system be changed. They were much concerned about those who sought to avoid the draft by applying for conscientious objector status, by fleeing to Canada, or by burning draft cards and actively opposing the war in Vietnam.

[6] *Ibid.* pp. 142-143.
[7] *Ibid.* p. 179.

A PATTERN DEVELOPS

During the interim between the end of the Senate hearings on April 19 and the beginning of the House hearings on May 2 both sides retired to restructure arguments, review tactics, and generally gird themselves for the next encounter, much as football teams do at halftime. Clearly the forces of the status quo had the advantage. The tide had turned on the question of college deferments; the lack of unanimity within the Marshall Commission, together with the high regard in which the Committee held the Clark Panel and its recommendations, provided proponents with potent arguments for continuation of deferments. Similarly, with respect to random selection, the would-be reformers of the Selective Service System made a major tactical error in failing to advocate a precise program. The idea was clearly articulated by several witnesses, but the description of the mechanics were wildly dissimilar, leaving those who opposed the concept in a position to say that no concrete proposals had been put before them.

THE HOUSE HEARINGS

Difficult though it may be to imagine a Congressional committee that is more conservative and hawkish than the Senate Armed Services Committee, one does exist: it is the House Armed Services Committee. Its Chairman, Mendel Rivers, seconded by Edward Hébert, ably represents the old-line southern point of view. The few liberal members have little effect on the general stance of the Committee, as was abundantly demonstrated during the hearings, which ran from May 2 to 11. Much of the miasma of the witch-hunting fifties pervaded the hearing room. Seated between two small American flags, Chairman Rivers smiled benignly as a member of his Committee asked a witness: "Are you now or have you ever been a member of the Communist party of the United States?" The Chairman himself remarked, "There are only two ideologies in the world, the one the cause of Jesus Christ, and the other Mohammed." (The *New York Times* reported the last part of this sentence as "One is represented by Jesus Christ, and the other by the hammer and sickle. Which do you prefer?") A Committee member, denouncing protesters against the draft and against the war in Vietnam, demanded of one witness who represented a peace-oriented church group that he turn over the names of the directors of the group so that they might be placed in the record. [To his credit Representative Floyd Hicks (D. Washington) objected and the request was dropped.] Perhaps the low point was reached when Congressman Hebert said: "Let's forget the first amendment."

It is not surprising, then, that opponents of the draft were roughly handled.

The first to be subjected to this treatment was Secretary Morris. In his testimony he advocated the renewal of the government's induction authority to introduce incentives that would encourage voluntary enlistments and institute a system of random selection that would operate fairly and uniformly and reduce uncertainty. He was then questioned by Frank M. Slatinshek, counsel for the Committee, in a manner best described as "early Perry Mason." Slatinshek had worked closely with the Clark Panel, and Morris had the temerity to criticize certain aspects of its Report. Morris testified that the Clark Panel proposal that draft boards select each month those registrants closest to age 20 was less fair than the random selection system proposed by the Department of Defense, for two reasons:

"First under conditions of relatively low draft calls, local boards would frequently have more draft-available men approaching age 20 (that is, age 19 and 11 months) than would be needed to fill the monthly call. Thus, those registrants born closest to the first of the month would be the 'oldest' 19-year-olds and have a very high chance of selection. Those born at the end of the month would be the 'youngest' men in this monthly age group and would have a much lower chance of selection.

"Second, draft calls normally fluctuate considerably from month to month for the very reason that they are our residual source of manpower procurement after allowing for enlistments and reenlistments.

"In the past few years the fluctuation has been very wide; the highest monthly draft call has been four to five times as great as the lowest draft call. Even in more normal periods, the risk of being called would vary widely from month to month due to seasonal fluctuations in recruiting, as well as to seasonal fluctuations in births, throughout the year.

"Based on these factors alone, the percent of draft availables called each month in a typical post-Vietnam year could vary from a low of 9 percent to a high of 20 percent for the country as a whole, with much wider variation possible in individual local boards.

"In contrast, the random system applied on an annual basis would involve a 15 percent chance of being selected throughout the year — that is, about one out of seven — and it would, in our judgment, provide a far more understandable and objective procedure for selection of young men under these conditions."[8]

A portion of the Slatinshek interrogation will suffice to indicate the antagonistic attitude not only of counsel but also of the Committee Chairman, since he was presiding.

[8] *Hearings of the Committee on Armed Services, House of Representatives,* U.S. Government Printing Office, Washington, D.C., 1967, p. 1929.

Mr. Slatinshek.	In your statement today, on page 12, you identify two apparent shortcomings in the Clark Panel proposal, which, incidentally, for purposes of the record, is precisely the system that is in effect today. You will agree to that, Mr. Secretary?
Mr. Morris.	Yes, indeed.
Mr. Slatinshek.	The only differentiation is the fact that today we are considering a 7-year span from 19 to 26, and under the Clark proposal we would be applying this system to a group between the ages of 19 and 20.
Mr. Morris.	Yes, sir.
Mr. Slatinshek.	The first shortcoming, as you identified it, was the fact that under conditions of relatively low draft calls those registrants born closest to the first of the month would be the oldest 19-year-olds, and therefore would have a higher probability of selection than those born at the end of the month Could you tell the committee what the basis is for that statement?
Mr. Morris.	Yes. As a matter of fact, we have tried to actually identify and illustrate the problem by going to some local boards. We obtained the records of one board recently which this year had calls in February, March, and April, respectively, of two, five, and one men. This is a typical small board, I would say. They had available in the 19 to 20 age group that would be used under the Clark plan nine, 11, and eight men, respectively, in each of those months. The men who would have been called under the oldest 19-year-old first would in each case have been born before the 15th of the month. The remaining men who would not have been called, and who would have passed out of the system, were born after the 15th of the month.
Mr. Slatinshek.	Are you saying therefore to the committee that induction notices are sent out in the first portion of every month by local boards?
Mr. Morris.	No. And we would think, of course, this would be one of the problems that would have to be faced under the so-called Clark system.
Mr. Slatinshek.	It is not a problem today, Mr. Secretary, and this is the point I want to make. Induction notices are not levied and not sent out in the first part of the month. They are

| | distributed throughout the entire month. Any given board makes no regular levy on its induction notices. It might be the first day of the month in board A, and the next month it will be the 15th or 20th or perhaps the 30th. So there is no basis for your statement that people who are oldest first, are oldest in the group, would be the first to be called. It depends on when the induction notices are sent out by the board, and this varies from board to board. |

Mr. Morris.

We believe this might constitute, in the minds of some, a further inequity. The boards now, as I understand it — and General Hershey should confirm this — are advised several weeks in advance of the month in which the inductions are to occur. Therefore, it is local board procedures in 4,000 locations which determine the actual dates of mailing the induction notices. Since this itself tends to be random it could create a further haphazardness in the system which would ·not be desirable.

Mr. Slatinshek.

You would further change the system by establishing a regular date on which induction notices are sent out?

Mr. Morris.

There are many ways I think this could be overcome. I don't think it is a major problem.

Mr. Slatinshek.

You are making a charge against the Clark system that it is unfair because of this, but you are actually proposing to incorporate into your own system at a future date. . .

Mr. Morris.

That is not our intent, sir. We had assumed probably the rule would be any man who was between 19 years 11 months and 19 years 12 months during the month of the draft call would be exposed to call under the Clark system but that is definitely an assumption on our part. We thought it would be the fairest way to do it.

Mr. Slatinshek.

The point I make here is that there is no basis in fact to your present contention that under the existing system induction notices are sent out throughout the month, consequently there is no higher probability that someone who is older in the first part of the month would be called as opposed to someone later. As a matter of fact, did you, in your appearance before a Senate committee earlier this year, indicate that youngsters born in the later months of the year would have a higher probability of induction than those born in the earlier months of the year?

Mr. Morris.   I believe just the reverse of that, Mr. Slatinshek. Originally, without the explanation we later received, we assumed that the Clark plan would in fact deal with a discrete frozen group of men each year, just as the random plan we had been thinking of it. If that were the case, men born in the earlier part of the year would be the older.

Mr. Slatinshek.   That is what I intended to say; they would be the older. It was your contention and your testimony before the Senate committee that under the Clark plan this would be the probable result that those born in the early part of the year probably would not be called.

Mr. Morris.   Under the assumption that we made.

Mr. Slatinshek.   That was an incorrect assumption, of course, because the Clark system is exactly the system that is in effect today. The second criticism you have made is that due to seasonal fluctuations in manpower requirements the probability of induction may in a post-Vietnam low-call period result in a fluctuating probability range of 9 to 20 percent, whereas under the so-called FAIR system there would be a steady 15 percent probability of call. To begin with the calculation, the probability is based on a probable future set of conditions. What would be the probability under today's manpower requirements?

Mr. Morris.   We have not worked them out precisely. We assume that for the purpose of the illustration we have used that the Vietnam war was over, and we had a stable force of 2.65 million. We obtained the age distribution of young men in the country for the next calendar year. And on this basis, the flow of our draft calls, as predicted, and the flow of men coming to age 20 each month, as projected, ranges from a low of 9 percent inducted in January, to a high of 20 percent inducted in November and December.

Mr. Slatinshek.   But, Mr. Secretary, we are concerned with the situation as it exists today, and it is a question of implementing a system that will apply today, or in the very near future, and consequently it is important to the committee that these figures be provided.

Mr. Morris.   We will be happy to.

[The following information was received for the record:
Under the level of manpower requirements for the current period (FY 1967), it is estimated that the percentage of draft-availables who would be required for induction would average about 70% of the number of draft availables (excluding volunteers), under current deferment rules, and about 55%, under the revised policies affecting graduate student deferments recently announced by the President.]

Mr. Slatinshek.   The second consideration in this area of greater equity is, how do you achieve greater equity as between registrants in different years? Apparently the emphasis here is to even out the probabilities from month to month. How do you even out the probabilities from year to year? And to illustrate my point here, in 1964 we inducted some 116,000; in 1966 we will have inducted some 366,000, or 350,000. So is the equity limited to months and do you disregard the yearly inequities that will result from your so-called FAIR plan?

Mr. Morris.   As we have discussed each time we have outlined the plan, the problem that we are trying to solve is one that will primarily exist under a post-Vietnam stable force structure of 2.65 million, with a group becoming age 19 each year of 1.8 million or greater. Only one-half of those found qualified will be needed for service. After volunteers are deducted, only about 15 percent of the residual will have to be drafted. This is the problem that we fully expect will exist, year after year, under such a stable force structure. The problem of how to be fair and equitable in choosing one out of seven men needs to be solved.

Mr. Slatinshek.   You are projecting a system here that you would, however, visualize as working ideally under a circumstance when there are very very low draft calls, and there isn't any way in the world in which you can predict with any degree of certainty this condition will ever again occur.

Mr. Morris.   That is quite correct, Mr. Slatinshek. We do have recent experience behind us to examine. To go back to the record, from about 1955 on through the buildup period which started in late 1965, you will find that draft calls ranged exactly in the proportions we are talking about.

Mr. Slatinshek.   Mr. Secretary, what would you do in the event we accelerated our draft calls, and assume the FAIR system had been in operation, and you ended up with using up practically all of the men in the pool?

Mr. Morris.   Let's assume we ran 5 years under the FAIR system and had another Vietnam buildup. We would have accumulated five annual classes of men ranked under the FAIR system. They would already be in ranked order and would be called in that order for the buildup period. Thereafter, if we needed to take virtually all men coming into the pool, as we did during World War II, a date-of-birth sequence is by far the simplest system to use, just as it was found to be under the high demands of World War II.

Mr. Slatinshek.   In other words, Mr. Secretary, at a time of maximum strain on the Selective Service System you would have to revert back to a date of birth system; is that correct?

Mr. Morris.   You would not have to, but it certainly would be the simplest administrative machinery, and it would no longer be a question of choosing a few from many.[9]

Mr. Hébert continued in the same vein by characterizing the FAIR (Fair and Impartial Random Selection) system of the Department of Defense as "futile and irresponsible roulette." His questioning makes it obvious that Hébert was confused about the system:

Mr. Hébert.   Mr. Secretary, how long will the individual be exposed to this futile and irresponsible roulette that you propose? Will he come along? He will be exposed for over a year, won't he, to be called up?

Mr. Morris.   He will be liable, sir, until he is age 26. His maximum. . . .

Mr. Hébert.   Don't let's go into that. Let's confine ourselves to 19-year-olds, when he first gets on the wheel.

Mr. Morris.   His maximum period of exposure.

Mr. Hébert.   His maximum would be 26. We are talking about his chances now. We are talking about a year's chances, under the Clark plan. How long would your plan expose that individual?

Mr. Morris.   The Clark plan, as we understand it. . .

Mr. Hébert.   I am talking about your plan. I know what the Clark plan does; that is simple; it is understandable; it is not as confusing as this other system. Under your system how long would he be exposed?

Mr. Morris.   He would be exposed, sir, for 1 full year after his name had been lotteried. The period before his name went into the

[9] *Ibid.* pp. 1938-1941

	lottery could be 9 or 10 months. Let's say 21 months maximum.
Mr. Hébert.	That is correct, he could be exposed almost 2 years. Under the Clark system, he goes on the conveyor belt at age 19, whatever date that occurs, it could occur in the middle of the year, January, or February, March, April, May, right on down the line, but immediately when he is 19 he goes on that belt.
Mr. Morris.	Correct.
Mr. Hébert.	And he continues on there for a year, definite and positive, until he gets 20, and then he drops off the belt.
Mr. Morris.	Correct, sir.
Mr. Hébert.	So then under the Clark system he is only exposed and he knows pretty much as far as he can figure it out, he is exposed for 1 year, between the ages of 19 and 20, because at 20 he falls off the belt and the belt is fed by the others who are 19 coming on. It is as simple as that. This is simple for us country boys to understand.[10]

Senator Kennedy, testifying on May 4, 1967, was given a respectful but not friendly hearing. The most revealing exchange of the hearings took place on May 5, when Fred M. Vinson, Assistant Attorney General in the Criminal Division of the Justice Department, was the witness. His appearance was the result of a letter of April 24 from L. Mendel Rivers to the Attorney General, in which he indicated deep concern over the apparent reluctance on the part of public officials to prosecute citizens who evade the draft, presumably by illegal means. Representative Hébert's questioning concerned the line between dissent and treason. He said:

"I will stand in the forefront to defend any man a right to dissent but. . .I am afraid we are going into an area of what is certainly treason and sedition as being exhibited on public platforms throughout this country today and on the university campuses of our nation."

In attempting to answer the question, Vinson raised the point that much of the Constitution was written to protect minorities and dissenters. Hébert sarcastically commented that he was aware of the Supreme Court interpretation in the last few years on this point and continued to bore in on the issue of dissent:

Mr. Hébert.	Now, these utterances – and I am sure you are familiar with them since the general public is well acquainted with

[10] *Ibid.* pp. 1972-1973.

them — of individuals standing before crowds arousing those crowds to treasonable heights, to mutiny against the Government, to defiance of the laws, and supposing we were at war on a formal declaration, would these utterances and these actions be indictable?

Mr. Vinson. I don't think the existence or nonexistence of a war has any legal relevancy. It obviously might have some psychological relevancy.

Mr. Hébert. Wait, never mind, let's don't wander into the field of psychology and all this sort of thing. Let's get down to the facts. I am a country boy like my chairman.

Chairman. Let me read this, then I will give it back to you. Under title 18, section 2388 of the code, among other things, these are the words of that section, quote:

> Whoever, when the United States is at war, willfully causes or attempts to cause insubordination, disloyalty, mutiny, or refusal of duty in the miltary or naval forces of the United States, or willfully obstructs the recruiting or enlistment in service of the United States to the injury of the service or to the United States, or attempts to do so, shall be fined $10,000 [and so forth] 20 years.

Then I am finished. Could we make this applicable to the Selective Service and Training Act? This says "enlistment." The Selective Service and Training Act says "procurement." Why isn't this applicable now?

Mr. Vinson. I would not like to answer that off the top of my head, Mr. Chairman. You definitely and distinctly have first amendment problems.

Mr. Hébert. This is existing law, Mr. Vinson. This thing Mr. Rivers has pointed out and read was the section I had in mind when I asked these questions, what does it say, the exact language?

Chairman. ". . .when the United States is at war."

Mr. Hébert. "At war."

Chairman. I think that is the only thing that might proscribe your capacity to enforce the intendment of this statute.

Mr. Bates. There is an amendment to include the present emergency in a later section, title 18, section 2391 of the Code.

Mr. Hébert. That is what I am trying to get at. Of course, now the refuge there is when the United States is at war. Technically, and when there is no desire to prosecute these individuals, technically the lawyer and the law can stand behind that technicality, and I am sick and tired of technicalities when we

	have treason in this country and sedition. What I am trying to find out is this: If that is the prohibition, because it says "at war," and the technicality is we are not at war, wouldn't it suffice to say "are engaged in armed conflict"? Three little words. Or "in armed conflict"? Wouldn't that bring these individuals to the bar of justice?
Mr. Vinson.	Well, my previous statement was keyed to the first amendment.
Mr. Hébert.	The first amendment, as Justice Holmes said.
Mr. Vinson.	The first amendment I stated really wasn't relevant, as to the first amendment, whether you are in war or not in war. I was not referring to this statute.
Mr. Hébert.	Let's forget the first amendment, I know that will be the refuge of the Supreme Court, I recognize that. But at least the effort can be made and the demonstration given to the American people certainly that the Department of Justice, and most assuredly the Congress, is determined to eliminate this rat-infested area in this country. But if we are going to stand idly by and merely say we can't do it and all of a sudden go back to the first amendment, as Justice Holmes so well said you can't cry fire in a theater. Free speech ends there. This begging the question of the first amendment continuously rather upsets me a little bit, and upsets not only me but millions of American people. They want to know a very simple answer to the question, why can the Carmichaels and why can the Kings, and other individuals of that ilk stand before the American people and institute riot, incite defiance of the law, while the Justice Department stands idly by and the Congress takes no action to strengthen that law? Now, all we can do is strengthen the law. We can't enforce it. That is not our jurisdiction or our problem. But we can give you the weapons to use.[11]

Comment here is really not necessary. Mr Hébert speaks eloquently for his position, however narrow that position might be.

The Committee's cordiality toward General Clark, who appeared on Tuesday May 9, to give essentially the same testimony as he had given before the Senate Committee, comes as no great surprise. The Committee had appointed General Clark to study Selective Service, and he had come up with just the answers they

[11] *Ibid.* pp. 2505-2507.

wanted. He favored the continuation of student deferments. So did they. He was against random selection. So were they. He felt that dissent should be stifled and draft protesters severely prosecuted. So did they. Congressman Hébert agreed with every word the General said, "down to the dotting of the i's and the crossing of the t's." Chairman Rivers did not even question the witness; he merely congratulated him. General Clark, a former college president, again revealed his educational philosophy this time in more detail, when discussing the necessity for deferments in the national interest:

". . . We do provide for exceptions for graduate work but very few. After their 27th birthday or after they have secured. . .their degree, then only those that are studying in the medical, dental, veterinary, or related fields would be exempted, plus limited additional students that were going into scientific and other essential and critically needed occupations and professions, needed for the security of the country, as designated by this National Security Council, and that board we recommended be set up.

"We feel that is so important that some go on for a space program and for some of these scientific programs, we didn't want to cut if off. But we did want to stop this business of having professional students, and that is what has been going on, where he goes there and he stays and he gets to be 26 and then he goes on or if he is 24, he goes into graduate work in music appreciation or animal husbandry or some of these things that contribute nothing, and he escapes the draft."[12]

In response to a question by Congressman Fisher (D. Texas) on deferments, Clark said: "Yes, sir. Well, the deferments would be the same. I mean, a man would be permitted to make his choice, and go to college."

Mr. Fisher.   He does that now.

General Clark.   He does that now, so that would be the same, but we find in college, colleges vary. Some of them let them stay there for 5 years or 6 years, as long as they are paying. The standards differ between colleges. And then there is permission to go on to postgraduate in unimportant subjects that have no relationship whatsoever to the security of our country.[13]

One member of the committee who was opposed to student deferments, Otis Pike of New York, challenged the meaningfulness of the statistics used by General Clark to show that college men serve in larger proportion than other groups:

[12] *Ibid.* p. 2560.
[13] *Ibid.* p. 2571.

Mr. Pike.	General Clark, we have had a lot of discussion this morning about the number of college graduates who serve as compared with the high school, or lower categories of education. I wonder whether the statistics we have gotten are really meaningful, because don't we disqualify about one-third of all of the people in the age bracket from serving, because of either mental or physical limitations?
General Clark.	It is about one-third.
Mr. Pike.	Now, are not the greatest percentage of these disqualified for mental limitations?
General Clark.	I wouldn't know. How is that broken down, Frank?
Mr. Slatinshek.	I don't know how the figures are broken down.
General Clark.	I don't have any figures as to the mental against the physical, how that is broken down.
Mr. Pike.	It seems to me if we disqualify a third of all people before we start, for either mental limitations, or physical limitations, certainly you are not disqualifying graduates for inability to pass the mental exam on a selective service test, at least I would hope not. The question then becomes not whether 74 percent of the high school graduates and 71 percent of the college graduates have served, but what percent of the qualified high school graduates and qualified college graduates have served. Do you have any figures on that?
General Clark.	Well, I would say that your percentage of 71 given for your men with undergraduate degrees, would be the qualified people. I mean it would be 71 percent of those.
Mr. Pike.	Well, what about the 74 percent?
General Clark.	Well, that applied to the high school?
Mr. Slatinshek.	High school graduates.
Mr. Pike.	These are the percentage who actually have served, but my point is this: Wouldn't you naturally expect the college graduates to have a higher percentage serving, simply because they are not going to be disqualified for lack of mental capacity?
General Clark.	The mental would be the only thing. He might be physically or morally – but mentally, you are correct.
Mr. Pike.	You could expect the physical limitations to be the same pretty much throughout the whole gamut of our population, wouldn't you?

General Clark.	Yes. I say the mental and moral.
Mr. Pike.	I don't think the figures are particularly meaningful when you simply talk about who has served. I expect if you threw out the mentally not qualified from your figures, you would find that in actuality a lower percentage of the college graduates had served than of the population generally, wouldn't you agree with that?
General Clark.	Well, I am not sure I would. I don't − it seems to me we ought to take our percentages from those who are eligible to serve. The people that are not eligible to serve our country, I think we ought to forget about those fellows. They are not going to serve, so they should not be included in our computation.
Mr. Pike.	Well, General, it seems to me that if you pay no attention to the mental level of the people that you are looking at, of course you are going to have a better figure for your college graduates in serving, but you do have to pay some attention to it, it seems to me, as a national problem. And we are dealing with it as a national problem here.
General Clark.	But wouldn't that be another problem to be solved, rather than through the military?
Mr. Pike.	Certainly, it is, but my point is I think the figures are a little misleading. Now, General, we are going to be confronted with a bill which will probably last for about 4 years. I have a son who is going to enter college next year. And I just wonder about the basic fairness in a time of war saying to the boys who enter college next year, or who are of an age to enter college next year, "You have your choice of going to college or going to war." You have made a very eloquent plea for the necessity of education, but in response to a question from Mr. Philbin, you said that a person can resume his graduate studies after he returns from the service. Wouldn't the same apply to his undergraduate studies?
General Clark.	Sure; many of them do.
Mr. Pike.	So it isn't a question of whether he gets the education or not; it is a question of whether he gets it before his military service; is it not?
General Clark.	Yes. But I feel this is an obligation to serve your country, and you ought to be eager and anxious to do it.

	You are going to be a much better citizen if you go to college after you have had your military service than before.
Mr. Pike.	If you are going to be a better citizen, if you go on to college after you have your military service, why not make them better citizens; why not have them after the military service?
General Clark.	We don't need them all. We don't need a fraction of them.
Mr. Pike.	The question is whether you take any of them out of college or not. What is the justice today in a time of war, of saying to a 19-year-old boy, you have your choice, you serve your country, or you go to college?'
General Clark.	I think there is a lot of justice in it in the present situation when a small percentage of the people are needed to fight this war. And the processes of education are so important to the future well-being of our country, that we ought to continue them, and why not give the boy the opportunity of either going to college, getting his baccalaureate degree, then going into service, or doing it first, the other way around? I think it is perfectly equitable.[14]

When General Clark was asked whether the same considerations apply to apprentice machinists, he answered, "We didn't go into that, only one in three will go anyway."[15]

General Hershey testified on May 10. In his prepared statement the General asked the Committee "to recommend to the Congress enactment of the legislative proposals submitted by the President."[16] During questioning the General made it clear that he did not favor the lottery, even though he said facetiously, "There is no question about the fact that I am here to defend the lottery."[17] On the other hand, since the President had not specifically backed the Marshall Commission recommendation on complete reorganization of the Selective Service System, Hershey had no compunctions about saying of it, "I completely disapprove."[18]

[14] *Ibid.* pp. 2582-2584.
[15] Mary McGrory column, "Point of View," *Washington Evening Star,* May 9, 1967, Washington, D.C.
[16] *Hearings of the Committee on Armed Services, House of Representatives, op. cit.* p. 2613.
[17] *Ibid.* p. 2616.
[18] *Ibid.* p. 2641.

Burke Marshall, was the final witness. He was accompanied by George Reedy, Jr., who represented the minority of the Marshall Commission favoring undergraduate deferments. The main thrust of the questioning was an attempt to determine which was the better system of selection: General Clark's "conveyor belt" method or the random selection system favored by the Commission. Neither side would budge, and the hearings ended on that inconclusive note.

The hearings indicated that the Senate and House were in general agreement about the vital issues. Both favored deferments on the undergraduate level as well as limited graduate deferments in fields of study vital to the national interest. Both were against any type of random selection, both opposed any significant changes in the operation of the Selective Service System.

Each Committee met in executive session to "markup" its bill. The Senate version, which was completed first because the Senate hearings had been held about a month earlier, was simply an extension of the military draft in the broadest possible language. It also extended other statutes pertaining to military manpower needs; for example, the doctor draft. The House bill, drawn up in mid-May, was another matter. It specified Congressional intent in a number of areas; in many instances it delineated what the President could and could not accomplish by executive order: for instance, in the matter of the lottery, which President Johnson had suggested be set up, the law stated that Congress had to be given notice of intent; if it did not act within 60 days, such a program could be initiated. The Committee also accepted an amendment by Congressman Schweiker of Pennsylvania that "national criteria" be established "for all local boards to follow." On May 10, when the bill was finally reported out of committee, four recalcitrant members – Representatives Otis Pike, Robert Leggett (D. California), Frank Evans (D. Colorado), and Floyd Hicks – filed a minority report, in which they dissented with the majority chiefly on the question of student deferments.

Following a unanimously favorable Committee Report on May 4, Senate debate on S. 1432 began on May 10. The bill was introduced by Senator Russell, who spoke in favor of drafting the youngest men first, although he personally felt that there should be a two-year transition to that system. He delineated the arguments on both sides of the student deferment question fairly but said that the Committee had been more persuaded by the Clark Panel recommendation that such deferments be continued; they would, moreover, be extended to various apprenticeship programs. On the touchy question of random selection Russell made clear the Senate Committee's antipathy to such a system; he added, however, that Congress did not intend to tie the President's hands. Finally Russell expressed complete disagreement with the Marshall Commission recommendation to do away with the local draft board system as presently constituted:

"What I am attempting to say is that there is almost irreconcilable conflict between the power to exercise a local judgment and the attainment of a uniform application of deferment policies."[19]

Senator Kennedy, who commended the Committee for its work, and particularly for the flexibility maintained for the executive, was the first to question Russell, and his questions were obviously designed to go on the record as part of the legislative history of the bill; for example, the Senator said:

"I understand there was some feeling on the Committee that if we were going to continue student deferments we should also favorably consider deferments for those who are in apprenticeship training or on-the-job training." [20]

Russell answered in the affirmative. Thus the point had been made and clarified for the record. Senator Javits (R. New York) questioned Russell in a friendly way about Negro participation in the armed forces. In response Russell quoted the figures from the Marshall Report which indicated that Negroes serve in about the same proportion as their percentage of population.

As the debate continued the next day, Senator Hatfield (R. Oregon) introduced an amendment to move to a voluntary system of military manpower procurement after a transitional period.[21] The amendment was defeated, 69 to 9. He then proposed a second amendment to provide only a two-year, rather than a four-year, extension of the law. This amendment was defeated, 67 to 13.

Senator Gruening (D. Alaska) introduced an amendment that would require a draftee to volunteer for assignment in Southeast Asia before he could be assigned there. This amendment was defeated, 75 to 2. Senator Young (D. Ohio) introduced an amendment to reduce the period of service for a draftee from 24 to 18 months and supported his argument with evidence that a number of nations which use conscription have found this shorter period a workable arrangement.[22] This amendment was defeated, 74 to 4. Then although the hour

[19] *Congressional Record,* May 10, 1967, p. S.6663.
[20] *Ibid.* p. S. 6665.
[21] Senator Hatfield's prepared remarks and the material he submitted for the Record provides the reader with a good statement of the advantages of such a system, *Congressional Record,* May 11, 1967, pp. S.6734-6747.
[22] Conscription in Allied and European nations (country and length of service): France, 16 months: West Germany, 18 months: East Germany, 18 months: Netherlands, 18 months for Army; New Zealand, 12 months; Belgium, 12-15 months; Italy, 15 months for Army; Australia, 24 months; Canada, no draft; England, no draft; Sweden, 10-12 months (universal conscription); Norway, 12 months for Army; 12-15 months for other services; Spain, 24 months; Austria, 9 months; Luxembourg, 6 months; Hungary, 36 months; Czechoslovakia, 24 months; Russia, 36 months for Army; 36-48 months for other services; Denmark, 14 months for Army; 12-14 months for other services; Portugal, 18 months for Army; 18-30 months for other services; Turkey, 24 months; Greece, 21-24 months for Army; 21-30 months for other services; Rumania, 24 months for Navy; 16 months for other services.

was late and the Senate did not plan to meet the next day, Senator Morse introduced three more amendments. The first, which provided for the setting up of "national criteria for classification" to eliminate state draft quotas, was defeated, 68 to 6. The second, an attempt to protect Peace Corps and VISTA volunteers from being drafted while serving in these programs, was defeated, 65 to 7. The final Morse amendment, which would provide legal counsel to registrants protesting their classification, was defeated 55 to 17. (The legal fraternity in the Senate swelled the minority vote in this instance.)

Finally the Senate passed the Administration bill, 70 to 2, with Senators Morse and Gruening casting the only negative votes.

THE HOUSE DEBATE

The House began its consideration of the Selective Service bill at 5:30 p.m. on May 25. It had just finished three days of furious debate, which included a marathon night session, on the Elementary and Secondary Aid bill; the next day marked the beginning of the Memorial Day weekend and a Congressional break was planned; all in all, the time did not appear to be auspicious for the introduction of such important legislation. Rivers, however, turned all these factors to his advantage with a rhetorical flourish: "I come here to work. Those boys in Vietnam do not work by the clock." Under the rules established for the legislation a three-hour time limit was placed on debate, with additional time for consideration of amendments.

Eleven of the proposals in the new bill represented major changes from existing legislation:

1. The bill recommended a uniform system of blanket deferments for undergraduate students until they finish college, reach age 24, or no longer pursue their studies.

2. It recommended that the youngest be taken first – a reversal of the existing order of induction.

3. It required the President to inform Congress if a program of random selection was deemed necessary. The new system would go into effect in 60 days unless Congress adopted a resolution rejecting it.

4. It established a National Manpower Resources Board to recommend future deferment of individuals in occupations or professions deemed necessary to the national interest.

5. It required more stringent enforcement of the draft act by giving automatic top priority to cases concerned with the act.

6. It provided that, whenever practical, the President should establish national criteria for the classification of persons under the act.

7. It recommended that tenure of draft-board members be limited to 25 years or age 75, whichever occurs first, and that women be permitted to serve as members.

8. It recommended the establishment of a Deputy Director of Selective Service for Public Affairs.

9. It recommended that Selective Service submit quarterly reports on the administration and operation of the System.

10. It recommended that alien physicians and dentists be liable for service until age 35, if admitted to permanent residence.

11. It recommended that all conscientious objectors selected for induction be required to serve in some capacity.

After he had recited the highlights of the bill, Chairman Rivers was questioned about its provisions. To Representative Holifield's (D. California) assertion that the uneven classification system resulted in inequities he responded that the quarterly reports from Selective Service and the President's authority to establish national standards, whenever practical, would ensure greater uniformity. Representative Gross — the conscience of the House on all matters of expenditure — asked where the money would come from to pay for the proposed National Manpower Resources Board and how many high-paid employees the agency would utilize. Rivers answered that the manpower function would be removed from the Departments of Labor and Commerce and the Department of Health, Education and Welfare and placed under the aegis of the supreme bulwark of the country's interests, the National Security Council; no high-paid executives would be employed.

Otis Pike, one of the dissenters on the House Committee, continued to speak out strongly against college deferments:

"I suggest that in time of war there is no justification whatsoever for saying to a group of our citizens which is wealthier than the rest of our citizens, 'Others will take their chances on dying now, but you will take your chances on dying four years from now.' "

Next the advocates of a voluntary army spoke at length, interrupted by cries of "Vote! Vote!" from impatient House members who knew how futile it was to oppose the bill.

Debate ended and the proposing of amendments began. Congressman Hall of Missouri, a member of the Armed Services Committee, offered the first amendment. It was intended to do away with the practice of giving military service credit to Public Health doctors on duty with the Peace Corps, the World Health Organization, the Food and Drug Administration, the Office of Economic Opportunity, and other agencies outside the traditionally accepted public health areas, such as the National Institute of Health, the Coast Guard, and the Merchant Marine. The rationale was that the Congress did not intend service with these agencies to constitute military service or to discharge a physician's military obligation. The amendment was accepted. Mr. Rivers then offered an amendment on behalf of his own Committee to delete from the bill the language on which the Supreme Court had based its decision in the *Seeger* case, the reasoning here was, in the words of Mr. Rivers, that this language unduly expands the basis for conscientious objection. The amendment would speed up the investigative process surrounding the status of a conscientious objector and would also require all conscientious objectors technically to enter military service before being assigned noncombatant duty. The amendment was accepted.

Representative Pike attempted to strike from the bill the language that allowed for some graduate deferments in the national interest. Chairman Rivers said of his proposal, "This is a dangerous amendment arrived at after a great deal of confusion. I ask that it be rejected." It was. As a sop to the voluntary army advocates, Representative Rumsfeld offered an innocuous amendment — which was accepted — in which he declared it to be the policy of Congress that the obligation to serve in the armed forces be enforced through the legislation only when necessary to ensure the security of the nation. Other amendments, all of which were rejected, proposed that inductees serve in a foreign country only after authorized to do so by Congress, that the legislation be limited to two years, that reserves be called up after 300,000 men were inducted, that discharged servicemen receive a bonus in the amount of earnings lost while serving, that the ceiling of military manpower be reduced, and that Negroes and other minority groups be provided adequate representation on local draft boards.

Several attempts were made to recommit the bill. At one point the House majority leader, in a most infrequent appearance, spoke against a preferential motion (a move to report the bill back to the House committee with the recommendation that the enacting clause be struck out) made by Representative Ryan of New York and a motion by Representative Rumsfeld to extend the law for only two years. Finally, after all maneuvers had failed, and as House members continued to register their impatience with cries of "Vote! Vote!," the yeas and nays were ordered and the bill passed 382 to 9, with 61 members not voting.

The members departed on their holiday junkets; one large group flew to

Paris — at government expense — for the Paris Air Show. The conferees for the House were named immediately; they were Messrs. Rivers, Philbin (D. Massachusetts), Hébert, Price (D. Illinois), Bates (R. Massachusetts), Arends (R. Illinois), and O'Konski (R. Wisconsin). The Senate conferees, who had already been named, were Messrs. Russell, Stennis, Symington (D. Missouri), Jackson, Smith, and Thurmond.

THE CONFERENCE COMMITTEE

In general, Congressional Conference Committees, which take place in executive session, are mysteries to all but the participants and sometimes, one imagines, even they are mystified by them. If records of Conference Committee proceedings are kept, they are never released publicly. Consequently any account of the Conference Committee's actions must be based on speculation and on whatever inferences can be drawn from a comparison of the final Conference Committee Reports with the two bills that went into the Committee.

It could be predicted from the beginning that the House bill would "win out" over the Senate bill. First, the Senate conferees were in a poor bargaining position: their bill was no more than a general extension of the draft, whereas the House bill contained specific provisions and restrictions, particularly of the President's authority in a number of particulars. Moreover, the Senate conferees were undoubtedly sympathetic with many provisions spelled out in the House bill; for instance, the Senate Committee's report on the bill strongly endorsed the deferment concept:

"The Committee believes that under normal circumstances undergraduate student deferments should continue to be authorized until the recipient receives a bachelor's degree, reaches age 24, or ceases to pursue a course of study satisfactorily, whichever occurs first. . . .

"The Committee refrained from prescribing student deferment policy in order to adapt to changing military conditions. . . . In the Committee's opinion student deferments should be viewed in light of their importance to the nation, instead of on the basis of whether they constitute an inequity in draft procedures."

Similarly, the Senate Conference Report echoed the House's doubts about the effectiveness of a random selection system: "The Committee is not convinced that a random selection will really result in a fairer sharing of military service, but" — and the language here is crucial in light of subsequent events — "it is not so opposed to a trial for a random selection system that it has recommended a prohibition against such a system." The House bill, it will be recalled, would have allowed the President to initiate a random selection system if he so informed Congress first and if Congress did not react adversely within 60 days. The Administration, however, through one of the conferees, let it be known that it would not accept what amounted to a Congressional veto. The Conference Committee solved the problem by making it mandatory for the Administration to come to the Congress with a system of random selection.

The House and Senate versions of S. 1432 differed in 14 particulars. The Conference Report shows that of the 14 differences the Senate adopted nine of the House provisions completely and accepted three in modified form, whereas two of the Senate's provisions were accepted by the House. In short, the Conference Report substantially supports the more detailed and restrictive House bill.

Many of the compromises were on minor and relatively unimportant points. The Senate, for example, accepted the House language that changed the title of the legislation to the "Military Selective Service Act of 1967" and the title of the local draft board clerk to "executive secretary." The Rumsfeld amendment of the House bill, which gave lip service to the principle that obligated service in the Armed Services (meaning the draft) should be used only when necessary to ensure the security of the nation, was dropped when the Senate Conferees objected to it on the grounds that it added nothing to the legislation and could in fact create ambiguities, particularly in the interpretation of "the security of the nation." The House also accepted the language in the Senate bill that gave the President the authority to order reservists to active duty if they failed to discharge their reserve training obligation properly; the House bill contained no such language.

SENATE DEBATE ON THE CONFERENCE REPORT

Although the Conference Report is dated Thursday, June 8, it apparently did not reach Congressional desks until the next day. Under the rules of the Senate, a Conference Report has the status of a privileged matter, and Chairman Russell asked the Senate leadership that it be considered on Monday, June 12. Chairman Russell realized, as did every member of the Senate, that debate on Senate Resolution 112 – the censure motion against Senator Thomas Dodd   (D. Connecticut) – was scheduled to begin on June 13.

Under such pressure the opponents of the bill had to move swiftly. By Monday, June 12, Senator Edward Kennedy had sent a letter and an attached statement of particulars to each Senator in which he indicated his strong reservations about the Conference Report. His letter said in part that "instead of a balance being struck the bill was further changed to further discourage all hope of reform. . .I do not believe the Senate should act in haste on this vital legislation."

After some preliminary debate during which it became apparent that some members of the Senate were unwilling to have the Conference Report shoved through with such unseemly haste, the majority leader, Senator Mansfield (D. Montana), came up with a compromise reluctantly accepted by both sides. It was agreed that a two-hour period from 4:00 to 6:00 p.m. be set aside on Wednesday, in the midst of the Dodd debate, to discuss and vote on the Conference Report. Senator Kennedy had won a key delay which gave him an additional two days to marshall support, to prepare his arguments, and possibly (though the prospects were not bright) to force an adverse vote on the Conference Report. In the ensuing two-day period his strategy became clear. Should the Conference Report be rejected, the senior Senator from Massachusetts intended to move that the conferees be instructed to report back a bill extending the induction authority just one year. He also made it clear that a vote against the Conference bill was not so much a vote against the draft as against specific items which the Senate conferees had agreed to and pointed out that there was ample time – 16 days – to complete another Conference Report.

In his letter of June 12 Senator Kennedy listed eight objections to the Conference Report. First, he felt that it was a mistake to give the National Security Council responsibility for setting policy on occupational deferments and critical occupations, since that body was established to advise the President on broad policy questions affecting national defense. Also, the Interagency Advisory Committee, the agency currently handling questions of occupational deferments, had apparently been working well.

Second, the language of the Conference Report precluded the initiation of a system of random selection without the President's getting Congressional approval first. Because the House had been emphatic in its disapproval of such a plan, any system of random selection was highly unlikely under the provisions of the bill as accepted by the Conference Committee.

Third, the provision written into the Conference Report would cut down the supply of Public Health Service doctors to agencies outside the military who utilized these skilled professionals.

Fourth, the precise language of the Conference Report froze undergraduate deferments into the law and provided a loophole that would allow graduate deferments to continue by Presidential executive order or by the decision of the National Security Council.

Fifth, by striking from the law the language on which the Supreme Court based its 1965 decision in the *Seeger* Case the Conference Committee over-ruled that decision. In essence, such a provision would make it impossible for anyone who was not a member of an established religious group to qualify for conscientious objector status. Senator Kennedy wisely pointed out that such a provision would seem to violate the equal protection clause of the United States Constitution.

Sixth, the Conference bill prohibited judicial review of local-board classification procedures, except as a defense in a criminal prosecution. Thus, no matter how a person was classified, the only way he could obtain a court ruling would be to refuse induction and to appeal to the courts as a criminal.

Seventh, the Conference bill had two aspects that would adversely affect Federal court procedures: first, the Selective Service cases be given absolute precedence on the court dockets at both trial and the appellate level, and, second, that at the request of the Director of Selective Service the Department of Justice prosecute a particular case or let Congress know in writing the reasons for nonprosecution. This last provision would rob U.S. attorneys of this discretion in deciding which cases to prosecute and which to dismiss.

Finally, a minor point, but certainly a valid one, given the backgrounds and attitudes of the chairmen of the respective Armed Services Committees, the law would allow women to serve on local draft boards for the first time but did not state in the usual boilerplate language that there would be no discrimination based on race.

In the short period of debate that took place on June 12 Senator Russell, "hitting the highlights of the Conference Report," took the offensive by commenting on many of these same points. Senator Edward Kennedy directed his arguments against the language in the bill concerning conscientious objectors, desperately fighting for a delay and attempting to gain the interest of the Senators on the Judiciary Committee:

"I think that there are many Senators, including members of the Committee on the Judiciary and members of other committees, who are deeply interested and concerned about the whole problem of conscientious objectors. They ought to have an opportunity to express themselves in view of the history of this provision, as well as the Supreme Court decision. There is serious doubt as to whether the Judiciary Committee would or would not feel there has been an overruling of the *Seeger* case, which was based on the provisions of the Selective Service Act and the belief in a Supreme Being.

"This is certainly one of the areas which I hope we would have a chance to examine further, both this afternoon and in the future."

In his prepared statement Kennedy cited the opinion of Attorney General Ramsey Clark that this change "may tend to proliferate litigation by opening new issues concerning the interpretation and constitutional impact of the statutory standard." [23]

[23] *Congressional Record,* June 12, 1967, p. S. 8055.

During the two-day postponement that followed Kennedy secured additional statements on particular provisions of the Conference bill, met with several other people who advocated real reform of the draft legislation, and worked with his staff to decide which issues to concentrate on. Two hours of debate, to be equally divided between Russell and Kennedy, were all that were alloted.

On June 14 the debate over Senator Dodd ended earlier than expected, and final debate on the Conference Report began at 3:15. A large number of Senators were present because of interest in the Dodd debate and because the draft bill required a yea-nay vote. Kennedy, realizing the time limitation, indicated that he would keep his arguments short.

There was some confusion over Kennedy's strategy of requesting that the Conference Report be rejected and the conferees then instructed to limit extension of the Act to one year. His reasoning was that this action would honor the agreement that the Senate conferees had made but at the same time would represent the whole Senate in the Conference. Because the current draft law was to terminate on June 30, 1967, and the war in Vietnam made some sort of draft legislation essential, Kennedy suggested that the new law be accepted for a one-year period. He also placed in the *Record* numerous letters in support of the objections he had raised. Ramsey Clark, the Attorney General, expressed the reservations mentioned earlier. Jack Vaughn, Director of the Peace Corps, said the provision in the law that would deprive the Peace Corps of Public Health Department doctors would "deal the whole Peace Corps program a fundamental blow," a point echoed by Sargent Shriver. All of these men were, of course, connected with the Kennedy wing of the Democratic party.

Next, Kennedy bore in on the very complicated question of drafting youngest men first. Under the present law a local board calls its oldest available men under age 26 first, and so on down the line. Under the plan approved in Conference the President could tell local boards that they must make draft calls first from a "prime age category" such as the 19-year-olds. The Conference Report, however, also provided that within any prime age group the oldest available youth must be called first. If the President did not designate a "prime age category," which he probably would be reluctant to do, for it would single out one age group (say 19-year-olds) to assume the full burden of a particular draft call, the Selective Service System would continue to call the oldest first. Under the new law college students, after they had graduated, would probably be among the oldest eligible registrants in most draft boards. It is conceivable, that particular groups of draftees for some months would be made up entirely of college graduates. Kennedy stressed this point and quoted part of a letter from Cyrus Vance, Deputy Secretary of Defense:

"We estimate that as many as 100,000 college graduates who would normally be going directly into graduate schools each year will lose their deferred status next year under the new policies. If the present system is continued, most if not all of these men would be drafted immediately, and for several months nearly all draftees would be college graduates under the present "oldest first" system."

Several senators began to get testy: they did not clearly understand Kennedy's points and time was growing short. When Senator Symington asked that the time limits be extended to allow for discussion of the matter, Majority Leader Mansfield said no, only 30 minutes remained for each side. Symington, a member of the Armed Services Committee and also a conferee on the bill, exploded: "I say with all respect to the. . .majority leader. . .a good many millions of Americans are interested in this." He indicated his participation in the hearings and Conference, but admitted "the point the Senator. . .is bringing up at this time is not clear to me. I would like to ask him some questions."[24]

Both Kennedy and Russell tried to prevent well-intentioned but obviously poorly informed Senators from interrupting with questions that would take precious time to answer.

Although admitting that he preferred the original Senate bill, Russell attacked Kennedy's objections as "vastly overstated" and, with specific reference to the supporting letters, remarked:

"It is significant to me. . .that we have not had anything from General Hershey objecting to this bill. He has not expressed displeasure with it. He has not said it would cripple the. . .system. I suspect General Hershey knows as much about the subject as anyone here. I think I know a little bit about it, but he knows a great deal more than I."[25]

This rebuttal was effective in its implicit charge that the letters came only from people who were "reformers," who knew little about Selective Service, and who, more plainly, were Kennedy's friends.

On the point that the law prohibited discrimination based on sex in determining the composition of local boards, but still permitted discrimination based on color and creed, Kennedy won the admission that the bill's failure to prohibit race discrimination was an oversight and did not represent the intent of the Conference Committee.

The debate ended when the Presiding Officer, Senator Mondale (D. Minnesota), announced "All the time has expired." Senator Javits attempted to secure unanimous consent to continue, Senator Eastland (D. Mississippi)

[24] *Congressional Record,* June 14, 1967, p. S. 8165.
[25] *Ibid.* p. S. 8171.

objected, the Presiding Officer called for the question, and the Conference Report was approved 72 to 23 with five members necessarily absent and not voting.

Senator Kennedy lost. He had not had sufficient time to present his case, and the pressures of other business prevented the Senate from granting such time. He did pick up 21 negative votes on the Conference bill (the initial vote on the bill was 70 to 2) primarily from Senate doves who were looking for a legitimate reason to vote against the draft-law extension but also from some who sincerely felt that his arguments were well taken.

HOUSE CONSIDERATION OF THE CONFERENCE REPORT

On June 20 the House considered the Conference Report. Debate was limited and centered primarily around the decision of the Conference to delete the provision for mandatory national standards (an amendment proposed by Representative Schweiker and accepted by the House Armed Services Committee). After Representative Rumsfeld had discussed briefly his amendment (dropped in Conference), which advocated the use of the draft law only "when necessary to insure the security of the nation," the vote was taken. It was 397 yeas, 29 nays, 27 not voting.

SUMMARY

The debate was over – at least temporarily. Congress in its wisdom, speaking for the people, had acted. There had been conflict between contending positions and there had been compromise. The compromises, however, were not between conflicting alternatives because the senior members of both Committees were in complete control. They were matters of degree after the decision on an issue had been reached; for example, in the case of random selection the decision was that no such system be instituted. The compromise concerned the way in which this decision could best be implemented. The answer was that separate legislation would have to be introduced to achieve the goal of selecting draftees by lot. The same situation prevailed with respect to other issues.

9 | THE NEW LAW

On June 30, 1967, President Johnson signed into law the Military Selective Service Act of 1967. The Executive Order implementing the new law was released at the same time. (Both documents appear in Appendix III.) Thus the 1967 draft debate became a part of history. During the preceding year ideas had been generated, evaluated, and for the most part discarded, especially if they were controversial or radical. The tough question of equity, discrimination, and centralization versus decentralization remained moot until the very end; they were, in fact, still being discussed during Edward Kennedy's last stand in the United States Senate on June 14. The end came abruptly with the conclusion of the two-hour debate allotted to the Conference Report. House consideration of the bill a week later was perfunctory, the resistance against it only token, its passage a foregone conclusion.

Criticism of the old law had been nationwide and had involved many segments of society. In response to growing dissatisfaction President Johnson had taken the initiative and appointed the Marshall Commission to conduct a comprehensive study of the system. This group went about its task with energy and thoroughness, calling on experts on various aspects of military manpower procurement and listening to and evaluating new ideas. Meanwhile the national and college conferences on Selective Service involved a wider range of people. They, too, were active in considering and weighing new ideas. Sometimes these ideas were quickly discarded, as was the case with the voluntary army concept at the AVC Conference and the universal military training concept at the Chicago Conference. The Clark Panel, a study group appointed by Congress, was also functioning at this time, but it had little concern with new ideas except to reject them as quickly as possible so that it could turn its energies to defending and preserving the status quo.

The Marshall Commission centered its attention on the area of equity, and the title of its report, *Who Serves When Not All Serve?* manifests its intent. In general, the President favored its recommendations and specifically, in his message to Congress, endorsed the ideas that the order of call should be reversed

139

so that younger men would be called first and that some form of random selection system should be used. Acutely aware of the political realities facing him in the Congress, however, he did not explicitly accept the Commission's recommendation that the Selective Service System be completely reorganized to end local-board autonomy and centralize the system. Indeed, here he went no further than to name a task force to study this recommendation.

On the issue of deferments, too, the President drew back somewhat. Essentially, the Marshall Commission recommended that college-student deferments be terminated. This recommendation was weakened by the presence of a strong minority on the Commission who felt that undergraduate deferments, at least, should be continued. In his message to Congress the President stated emphatically that graduate deferments would end but he added that the question of undergraduate deferments could not be so easily decided and must be given further consideration. In his *New York Times* column of May 5 James Reston said that the termination of undergraduate deferments was opposed "high in the Administration." The reason he gave was that because of the general opposition to the Vietnam war in colleges and universities it was feared that the abolition of undergraduate deferments would result in massive defiance on the part of college students inducted into the armed services. Reston reports that one estimate indicated that as many as 25 percent of college men might refuse to serve. It is only fair to comment at this point that this estimate has never been substantiated and that it appears highly unlikely that anything like one-quarter of the male college students in this country would go so far as to defy the government publicly. Some young men will refuse to serve. Others may serve and hope that they will not be sent to Vietnam. If they are ordered there, undoubtedly some will refuse to go. The figures are, to say the least, problematical.

To understand more fully the climate surrounding passage of the Military Selective Service Act of 1967 it is necessary to be aware of the Congress's anxieties and uncertainties about the Vietnam war and about the increased internal divisiveness over that war. Some felt that the struggle was morally repugnant to the conscience of the nation. Young people – from the hippies with their "flower power" to the peaceniks with their "Hell no! I won't go!" attitude – were increasingly defiant. National magazines featured articles about the growing number of young people moving to Canada to avoid the draft. The publicity given the case of Cassius Clay (Mohammed Ali), the snide remarks about George Hamilton's draft status, the alleged deferment of professional athletes, the refuge of many in National Guard units, and above all the inflammatory speeches of Stokely Carmichael, H. Rap Brown, and others like them created a reaction that often expressed itself as patriotic hysteria and permeated discussion of the issue in Congress. The New York City Peace March, which culminated in the burning of an American flag as well as of many draft cards, took place at the time that the draft hearings were being held. Indeed, the House hearings opened with Federal marshals and Capitol police guarding the Committee against a threatened sit-in and demonstration by antiwar elements.

The Congress, and in particular the senior members of both Armed Services Committees, sought reassurance for the position that they were determined to take. They received this reassurance from the Clark Panel, whose Chairman — a retired general — could say the things that they wanted to hear about the moral degeneracy of the younger generation and the virtues of military discipline. They were reassured also by the continued tacit support of the other general in the affair, Lewis B. Hershey, whose response to suggested change was always, at best, reluctant. He shared with most members of the two Committees the conviction that what has worked well in the past will work well in the future, that any protest from young people is a type of aberrant behavior symptomatic of the weak moral fiber of the nation, and that those who waiver or carry dissent too far should be punished. Rapid urbanization, speeded-up communications, the student revolution, the civil rights movement, hippie alienation — these are trends far beyond their comprehension, and they reacted to them, as elders often do, in a crotchety, narrow, and even vindictive fashion. In such an atmosphere the hearings took place and the bill became law. Thus were the advocates of change defeated and thus do the inequities of the American draft continue unabated.

THE NEW LAW

As mentioned before, the 1967 law does not represent any great departure from the law that existed, but those of its provisions that do incorporate changes or were particular targets of controversy deserve comment. When pertinent, those portions of the Presidential Executive Order that are necessary to implement the changes are mentioned.

Name of the Act

The name of the Act was changed from the "Universal Military Training and Service Act" to the "Military Service Act of 1967." The reason for this change is obvious: military service was not universally required of all qualified men and therefore the new name more correctly identifies and describes the legislation.

Induction Authority

The induction authority [Section 17(c)] of the draft law was extended for four years when the President signed into law the Military Selective Service Act of 1967 (Public Law 90-40. 62 Stat. 604. 50 App. U.S.C. 481 et seq.) On the same day the President signed Executive Order 11360, which amended existing Selective Service Regulations (32 Federal Register 9787).

Administration

The new law requires that Selective Service submit to Congress periodic written reports covering the operation of the System. During the House hearings and floor debate Chairman Rivers would refer to this provision whenever anyone suggested that portions of the law might result in inequities. The Committee was aware of this weakness, he would say, but it would be taken care of by this requirement for periodic reports. On August 1, 1967, Chairman Rivers established a special subcommittee to monitor and review the operation and administration of the new law. He promised Congress that this "watchdog" committee would, among other things, act as a legislative overseer by reviewing the semiannual reports, initiating pertinent inquiries into alleged irregularities and inequities, publicizing its own existence so that everyone would be aware of its purpose, and submitting an annual report to the chairman. The members of the subcommittee are Messrs. Hébert, Chairman, Pirnie (R. New York), and Walker (D. New Mexico). The term watchdog, when applied to this group of Congressmen, undoubtedly means protection of the System by adherence to the status quo.

Personnel

The maximum term of service for all board members shall be 25 years. They may not serve after they have reached age 75. If a local-board employee (clerk) has supervision over other employees at one or more local boards, the title of this employee shall be executive secretary. The term of employment in such positions shall not exceed 10 years, although there may be a reappointment. Women may be named to serve on local draft or appeal boards. The exact language of the law [Section 8(b)] is: "No citizen shall be denied membership on any local board or appeal board on account of sex." There is no explicit statement that prevents discrimination based on race or creed, however, and this omission gave rise to much discussion in the Senate Conference Report debate. There is sufficient legislative history to prevent such discrimination but the law is plainly silent.

Students

Under the law the President may provide for the deferment of undergraduate students who are satisfactorily pursuing a full-time course of instruction at a college, university, or similar institution of learning and who request such a deferment. The deferment continues until the student (registrant) completes the requirements for his baccalaureate degree, fails to pursue satisfactorily a full-time course of instruction, or attains the age of 24, whichever comes first. The President carried out this provision by executive order.

Satisfactorily pursuing a full-time course of instruction means that the student taking a four-year course should earn 25 percent of his credits each year and the student taking a five-year course should earn 20 percent of his credits each year. These figures are intended as guidelines, set up to ensure greater uniformity in certification by educational institutions and in classification by local draft boards. The word "should" rather than "must" was deliberately used in order to give boards discretion in continuing the deferment of students who have failed to earn the required credits because of illness or some other circumstance beyond their control. It also provides some leeway for the institution to exercise discretion when, for example, a first-year student has earned somewhat less than 25 percent of his required credits, but the institution is convinced that this deficiency will not delay the expected date of completion of his course of study. The intent of the executive order is to indicate that a student should receive his degree in the normal and specified length of time. The student's academic year is now the 12-month period following his matriculation. The law makes no provision for part-time college students.

When a student accepts a Class 2-S (student) deferment, he is no longer eligible for a fatherhood deferment, and he remains liable for service until age 35. Moreover, the student himself must request the deferment in writing; it is not automatically granted to him.

Graduate Students

The language in the legislative history and in the law itself allows the President to permit deferments for graduate study if such study is in the national interest. Only the study of medicine, dentistry, veterinary medicine, osteopathy, and optometry are specifically written into the law as deferred categories of study in the national interest. The law gives responsibility to the National Security Council to advise Selective Service concerning other critical areas in which graduate deferments may be granted. The executive order provides for what amounts to a one-year moratorium on graduate deferments. Although the Congressional intent was to end graduate deferments in general, the language of the Act permits deferments in specific subject-matter areas in the future. The executive order stated that those students who by October 1, 1967, were entering their second year of graduate study may continue to receive a 2-S deferment if the institution certifies that they are satisfactorily pursuing a fulltime course of instruction leading to a degree.[1] The total deferment, however,

---

[1] Note. These students entered graduate school under the old law and therefore are not affected by the new regulations, except as to the total length of their deferment.

shall not exceed five years, inclusive of the years already spent in such course of study. A student pursuing a master's degree only may not be deferred for more than a total of two years. The reasoning behind this specification is that a master's degree should be completed in two years and the Ph. D. in an additional three years.

The executive order further stated that the student who has graduated from college and who will attend graduate school for the first time by October 1, 1967, may also be given a 2-S deferment. This deferment, however, is for one year only, or until he ceases to pursue satisfactorily the course of instruction, whichever comes first.

Section 4(g) of the new law is clear (as is the legislative history) that the responsibility of the National Security Council shall be to advise the Director of Selective Service periodically and to help him coordinate the work of state and local volunteer advisory committees which he may establish to aid in identifying those individuals who should be deferred and those categories of occupations that are crucial to the national interest. It seems clear that graduate deferments *may* continue but on a *selective* basis. The only way to avoid selective deferments is to have Congress pass a system of random selection before the one-year moratorium ends. If such a system were initiated, uncertainty would end: some graduate students would be drafted and some (in all fields) would be able to continue their studies.

Enlistment in the Reserve

Registrants may enlist in the National Guard or Ready Reserve at any time before the date scheduled for their induction, provided (with respect to the National Guard) that the state governor has issued a proclamation to the effect that the authorized strength of any organized unit of the Guard of that state cannot be maintained by the enlistment or appointment of persons who have not been issued orders to report for induction and (with respect to the Ready Reserve) that the President has made a similar determination.

The new law also gives the President permanent authority to order reservists to active duty if they fail to discharge their reserve training obligation properly.

Conscientious Objectors

In many ways the changes in provisions for conscientious objectors represent a classic example of dramatic irony. In the new law the definition of religious training and belief has been amended to strike the words "religious training in this section means an individual's belief in a relation to a Supreme Being involving duties superior to those arising from any human relation." The Conference Report states that it is the conferees' intent to "more narrowly construe the basis for classifying registrants as conscientious objectors." Therefore it was their feeling that the term *religious training* should not include "essentially political, sociological, or philosophical views, or merely personal moral codes."

It is clear enough why General Clark and the members of the Committees wanted to make this change. In 1965, in the famous *Seeger* case, the Supreme Court interpreted the religious requirement broadly enough to include nontheistic beliefs. Seeger himself said he believed "the cosmic order does, perhaps, suggest a creature intelligence." He also said, however, that he felt that an ethical belief in intellectual and moral integrity even "without belief in God except in the remotest sense" should be respected as true conscientious objection.

The Clark Panel found that the number of persons claiming the status of conscientious objector had more than doubled between 1954 and 1967. Further, there was a backlog of cases being processed by the Justice Department. To Clark's way of thinking something had to be done. He set the record straight when during the Senate hearings on April 12 he said: "But now you have got a breed of cat running around, not the regular religious groups that we have recognized for so many years as being sincere, but a lot of people who just don't want to fight, who don't want to go to war. They are the kind who are anti-Vietnam all the time, who are using this and being taught to use the escape route as conscientious objectors...I personally don't go along with this business." He also complained that the *Seeger* decision places the determination that a man is a conscientious objector on the man himself. (We could wonder who else has a better right to decide about his own conscience.)

So the offending language was removed and the language remaining stressed "religious training and belief." The legislative history going back to 1917, however, shows that under that draft act only those who belonged to religious groups (Quakers, Mennonites, etc.), whose existing creed or principles forbade its members to participate in war in any form, achieved conscientious-objector status. In the 1940 act this stipulation was changed to grant conscientious-objector status to those outside the recognized peace churches, *provided* that their objection was a result of "religious training and belief." In 1948 the Supreme Being requirement was added to *tighten up* the clause and restrict the number of men who could qualify as conscientious objectors. So, ironically enough, by removing the Supreme Being clause in an attempt to offset the *Seeger* decision the Congress probably liberalized the section.

The new law also eliminates the requirement for a hearing by the Department of Justice when there is an appeal from a local-board decision that denied conscientious-objector status.

Sequence of Call

The new law enables the President to establish the order of induction for registrants within various cohorts. The President has the right to reverse the order of call from oldest men first to youngest men first. He may not, however, effect any change in the method of determining the order of induction for individual registrants within the age groups ordered for induction; for example, he may say that 50 percent of those drafted will be 19-year-olds. Within the 19-year-old age group, however, he must take the oldest 19-year-olds first. He may not introduce a system of random selection unless Congress, at his request, passes a law that would allow such a method to be used.

Under the old law the President had the authority to put a system of random selection into operation. The Senate bill would have allowed him to keep this prerogative. The House, which initiated the limitation, argued that Congress has Constitutional responsibility for "raising armies" and thus should play the affirmative role in deciding the method of selection. (That the President had been granted flexibility in this matter under the previous legislation without Congress's feeling left out did not apparently enter into their consideration.) Further, the Conference Committee did not seem to be aware of the tremendous demographic changes that have occurred since World War II, to recognize that even under Vietnam conditions the military requires only a small proportion of the young men reaching draft age each year, and that, given this circumstance, almost any system except random selection will produce inequities.

Even more startling, in the eyes of many people, is that the language decided on during the Conference was entirely new and had never been considered or discussed before. The Senate version of the bill had contained no limitation on the President's prerogative to introduce a system of random selection. The House version had specified that if the President wanted to institute a system of random selection he must advise Congress and that the new system would go into effect within 60 days after such notice unless Congress had, in the interim, adopted a resolution rejecting the proposed change. There is evidence that the Administration, through certain members of the Conference Committee, let it be known they did not like the idea of a Congressional veto.

Enforcement Procedures

There were several changes in the matter of enforcing the Act. First, a registrant who reaches age 26 and is still engaged in attempting to fight induction by legal or administrative action will continue to be liable for induction and when or if he becomes available will be inducted.

Second, a registrant can obtain judicial review of classification only as a defense to a criminal prosecution. In other words, a man must refuse to be inducted and be charged as a criminal before the courts will consent to review classification procedures.

Third, all cases arising under the Selective Service law, including appeals, receive precedence on the dockets of Federal courts. Moreover, the Justice Department must prosecute violations of the act on request of the Director of Selective Service or furnish a report to Congress explaining failure to do so.

Public Health Service Medical Officers

The new law prevents Public Health Service medical officers from receiving exemption from military service for duty with the Peace Corps, VISTA, the Office of Economic Opportunity, and similar organizations. The intent is clear: if a doctor serves with one of these organizations, he is liable for a term of military service.

THE WIDER IMPLICATIONS OF THE NEW LAW

Laws are not made in a vacuum; they are very much the product of their time, shaped by the impact of often conflicting forces and bearing the imprint of the personalities of those who formulate them. So it is with the Military Selective Service Act of 1967. A number of generalizations can be made about the wider implications and indirect effects of the new law — how it reflects this period in history as well as more permanent features in our system of government. First, the law represented a significant setback for the Administration. Second, it was a victory for L. Mendel Rivers, Chairman of the House Armed Services Committee. Third, General Hershey emerged once again not only as an immovable object in his resistance to any suggested change in the administration and operation of Selective Service but also as one of our nation's sacred cows, accorded absolute and unquestioning respect by most members of Congress. Fourth, the intellectual community and American higher education received an interesting lesson in the differences between informed criticism, public debate, Congressional hearings, and Congressional action. Fifth, the pervasive effects of the seniority system — which often brings to positions of great power people whose chief virtue is their having been elected to Congress for long periods of time, very probably from "safe" districts — were strikingly demonstrated.

To examine each of these generalizations in turn: there is no question but that the draft act finally passed was a severe blow to the Administration. During the preceding year it had issued all sorts of statements to indicate that equity should be the ultimate objective of a new draft law. President Johnson called the draft a "crazy quilt," Secretary McNamara talked about National Service as a worthwhile goal, and Secretary Morris spoke out in favor of random selection at the AVC Conference. Following the lead given by President Johnson in his message to Congress, the Senate produced a broad and generalized bill that gave the Administration considerable discretion. The House, on the other hand, went its own way. Unwilling, perhaps, to accept legislative recommendations from a Presidential commission, task force, or any other nonlegislative group, and jealous of the Constitutional provision that allowed Congress the authority to legislate in all matters concerning the military, the House Committee produced a bill that contained many inhibiting features; and, when the going got rough, the Administration was silent. It stood by while Burke Marshall and Secretary Morris, the Administration's own witnesses, faced Chairman Rivers alone.

The proponents of random selection (and that includes, of course, the Administration) made a serious tactical and political error in failing to prepare a single well-thought-out scheme of implementation to present to Congress. The concept of random selection was lucidly explicated by Marshall, Morris, and Kennedy, but the details of the process were left unspecified. So the Committees, neither of which favored the system, could honestly say that the system was "vague" and could raise spurious objections that went unrefuted because of the lack of a specific scheme. In consequence, the law as it was passed leaves the President with much less flexibility than he had had in the past in dealing with the procurement of military manpower.

When the bill was sent to the President late in May, a few diehards, including myself, were still hopeful that there might be a slim chance he would veto the law. Such a veto would not have hampered the flow of men into the armed forces. If the law had been allowed to lapse, the only result would have been to terminate the Selective Service System's authority to classify new registrants. Those men already classified could still be called. Such a termination would have permitted a smooth transition to the introduction of a random selection system or to the practice of taking the youngest men first. Aware that such a veto might be looked on as a lack of resolve over Vietnam, a "letting down" of the nation's fighting men, the President did not exercise his veto power. Thus recognition of political "realities" resulted in the Administration's failure to salvage a worthwhile bill and its acceptance of a much more restrictive and reactionary bill.

The heavy in the controversy was self-styled country boy L. Mendel Rivers of South Carolina, the conservative southerner whose target is anything that might be regarded as liberal, enlightened, or reformist—from the Supreme Court to the Eastern Establishment, from Secretary McNamara to whatever egghead happens to be around. At times his charm and courtesy can disarm his most ardent opponents; at other times his hortatory harangues and red-baiting tactics can cause unfortunate witnesses to squirm. At all times, however, he is an astute politician. His appointment of the Clark Panel was a masterful stroke; it gave him the weapon he needed to ward off the critical recommendations of the Marshall Commission.

During the entire period of the controversy General Hershey proved a most elusive target. Unquestionably this man deserves commendation for having served his country so long and so well, but the fact remains that he, as well as many of the conservatives on both the House and Senate Armed Services Committees, lives in an era that has long since passed. He believes quite sincerely that local draft boards still base their decisions on personal knowledge of registrants, although the Marshall Commission clearly showed that the urbanization of America has made the local board an anachronism. Whether rightly or wrongly, he has remained consistent in speaking out — sometimes almost alone — for the continuation of college deferments. At one point in the spring of 1966 some members of the House Armed Services Committee had had just about enough of General Hershey's practice of answering questions concerning the draft with long, anecdotal speeches that deftly avoided coming to grips with the issue. As a result of this attitude and because of a refusal to accept valid criticism, the Selective Service System alienated itself from much of its previous support. It was not Until L. Mendel Rivers appointed the Clark Panel that the tide began to run in favor of the General and the status quo. It is reasonable to say that no significant reform in Selective Service operations and procedures will ever be attained until General Hershey retires.

The intellectual community participated in widely publicized fun and games during the year preceding the passage of the new draft law. They spent a great deal of time making a lot of unproductive noise, arguing and exploring all aspects of the draft controversy — from the war in Vietnam to pacifism, from conscientious objection to mandatory national service. Everyone had an opinion, everyone had a position, but when the arena of debate switched from protest magazines and national conferences to the Congress the intellectual community had had its day. None of its recommendations and proposals found their way into the law. Almost none of the leading exponents of change in the Selective Service System were asked to testify except before the Kennedy Committee, which had no status as far as the legislation was concerned. Neither Mendel Rivers nor Richard Russell was interested in hearing Arlo Tatum, Margaret Mead, Roger Little, Milton Friedman, Samuel Huntington, Morris Janowitz, or any of a hundred assorted members of academia. American higher education did not cover itself with honor either. There was no unanimity regarding the portions of the new draft law that affected colleges and universities. Mostly there was complete silence from those in responsible positions. Certainly Kingman Brewster and a few others spoke out against deferments, but what were they and others in favor of as alternatives? No one ever knew their position.

Finally the Congressional seniority system assured southern conservatives of positions of authority on the committees with ultimate responsibility for the legislation. They wanted no change in the Selective Service law. Even if there had been no Vietnam war to rally their old-school patriotism, it is not likely that either committee would have acted to pass a law containing any of the recommended reforms. The senior members of both committees feel that Selective Service, as presently constituted, is the last vestige of local participation in government.

SUMMARY

The 1967 Selective Service law is certainly more old than new. When it does differ from the preceding law, the difference is often minor and unimportant; for example, the change in the name of the Act itself and the change in the title bestowed on local-draft-board clerks. On most significant points the situation is the same as it was before. Local boards still function in the same manner, undergraduate deferments are granted more freely than ever, oldest men are still being taken first, and General Hershey is still the Director.

The most important difference between the old and the new laws is that the new law is more specific in its language and contains several narrow, restrictive provisions. The language relating to conscientious objectors was changed to make the provision tougher, or at least such was the intention. The Presidential power to initiate a random selection system was taken away, for no such system can be effected unless Congress passes a resolution on the proposal. Changes in the enforcement procedures and in the status of Public Health medical officers who serve certain nonmilitary governmental agencies furnish other examples of the specificity of the new law. In short, the inequities of the draft remain and the flexibility of the previous legislation has been lost.

10 | OVERVIEW

This chapter is divided into two parts: conclusions about various issues connected with our military manpower procurement policies and recommendations based on the evidence contained in earlier chapters and on my own opinions.

THE SYSTEM ITSELF

The Selective Service System, as presently constituted, is outmoded and archaic. It represents something less than the best efforts of a democratic society to secure the military manpower needed in times of national stress. The system was inaugurated to fulfill the requirements of a nation involved in a total war, but it failed to keep pace with the profound changes in American life that have taken place since that time. National needs have changed, and, given the nuclear capabilities of the probable adversaries, it is questionable whether the need for total mobilization will ever again exist. The System must be able to expand to meet potential crises. For the present, however, emphasis must rest on the limited mobilization necessary for Vietnam and other potential trouble spots like Korea.

The concepts of "supervised decentralization" and of local-board autonomy are outmoded. Local boards do not reflect the constituencies they were set up to serve because the population has shifted to the cities, in which approximately 70 percent of the nation now live. The Marshall Commission Report showed, for instance, that New York City has 68 local boards — more than 27 states and territories have at the present time — which average more than 21,000 registrants per board. These figures are paralleled in many other large cities in this country. Moreover, there is a great variability in local board standards; 90 percent of the boards in Alabama and Washington were inducting married men in 1965; during the same period no married men were drafted by boards in Connecticut. The argument for the local-board system is that it is the essence of "democracy in action." Vital decisions affecting the lives of citizens are left in the hands of their neighbors serving on the draft board, who are at least acquainted with the young men with whom they deal and who therefore have a fuller sense of personal responsibility. Such is the idealized picture in the minds of Hershey and his supporters. Yet the Marshall Report found that urban board members often work in anonymity. A team of researchers reported to the Commission that drafting by local boards has little more than "symbolic significance" in urban areas. Academic researchers, among them Roger Little and Morris Janowitz, working independently of the Marshall Commission, have substantiated this point.

The most important single unit in Selective Service is the local board. If it fails to meet the needs of the nation, the whole system fails. I submit that this has happened. The Marshall Commission Report conclusively demonstrated the need to centralize the local-board system. Hershey, Rivers, and Russell disagree with this assessment. But the rural America for which they claim to speak is now largely a fiction.

PROFESSIONAL PERSONNEL WITHIN THE SYSTEM

The Selective Service staff at the state and national levels is recruited from a very narrow base. Only "selected" reserve officers from the various armed forces are given the opportunity to serve in key positions within the System. The *1966 Annual Report of the Director of Selective Service* indicates that 89 percent of the state directors hold military rank, and every key office at national headquarters is held by a reserve or retired officer on extended active duty.

It is not my intent to demean the services rendered by these men, but it should be borne in mind that the Selective Service System makes manpower decisions that vitally affect the future of the nation. Not only are these decisions made without reference to national standards but they are also made by a staff whose expertise is limited. If persons with backgrounds in economics, sociology, and other pertinent subject areas were employed, we should have more assurance that manpower decisions were based on hard data evaluated by experts. Interestingly enough, the Marshall Commission was able to produce the first in-depth study of the Selective Service System in only six months, because the staff, though small, was made up of competent, highly specialized persons capable of accurately evaluating the data that came out of the computer and to present the results in a cogent manner.

STUDENT DEFERMENTS

Student deferment is the most difficult and emotionally charged problem connected with the draft issue. The essential question, stripped of emotionalism and irrelevancy, comes down to this: does the nation during a time of limited war wish to give to those young men able to attend college the option of serving now or serving in the future? To answer this question affirmatively we must be sure that the deferment of undergraduate students is in the national interest. In my opinion some student deferments can be justified on these grounds. The leaders of American higher education did not, however, present an effective case for the continuation of these deferments. Indeed, in many cases, college and university presidents spoke out firmly against student deferments. Undoubtedly, student and faculty reaction against both the war and the draft inhibited some administrators who might otherwise have taken a broader view of the issue. For almost a year General Hershey stood virtually alone as a proponent of student deferments, though later in the debate he was backed by the Armed Services Committees.

On the other hand, Commissioner Howe, Secretary Wirtz, Sargent Shriver, a small majority of members of the Marshall Commission, and many others made a strong case for ending such deferments, the most compelling argument being that the system operates unfairly and in fact fosters a class society based on ability to pay for a college education.

The main argument of those who urged continuation of student deferments was that college graduates served in the armed forces in proportions equaling or exceeding that of other groups and that therefore the deferment process does not operate unfairly by allowing students to avoid service. This is a difficult assertion to prove or disprove. One can only say, "it depends" – it depends on which statistics you use for which period of time. There are several safe conclusions that can be reached however. First, not many college graduates have been drafted up to the present time. One Department of Defense table, supplied to the House Armed Services Committee during the hearings in June 1966, showed that in a study of the educational level of a 5 percent sample of army inductees on active duty as of February 28, 1966, it was found that less than 2 percent were college graduates. Second, both the Department of Defense and the Marshall Commission statistics show that in relation to persons who have never done graduate work significantly fewer (only about 27 percent) students who have attended graduate school ultimately serve in the armed forces. Third, it is from the college-graduate group that junior officers are drawn: each year the armed services need approximately 40,000 new officers, and about 90 percent (36,000) are recent college graduates, but service by 36,000 men a year would not seem to justify deferment of a total of 1.7 million.

Other conclusions are more tentative. Each year more than 300,000 men graduate from college. Given the fact that a large number (about 100,000) go on to graduate school, others receive occupational deferments, and still others fail the physical examination, it does not appear that college graduates serve in overwhelming proportions in relation to other groups. Therefore continued deferment of college students on the grounds that they will serve at some later date is probably justified only in time of war, when draft calls are high.

RANDOM SELECTION

On the basis of the evidence presented in the Department of Defense study released in 1966, we can estimate that there will be at least an 84 percent increase in the number of young men reaching age 18 by 1975. Because the requirements of the armed forces, even in a Vietnam situation, are such that only about one out of every seven qualified men must be drafted, there is no fair and reasonable alternative for procuring military manpower other than a random selection of the men needed. This is not to say that random selection is the *best* way to select men to serve. It does mean to say that under existing conditions it is by far the most equitable method. Further, it follows that a system of random selection is necessary simply because local boards cannot apportion the burden of military service uniformly and consistently. The opponents of random selection have a misguided notion of how it operates and are motivated by conservatism, a desire to cling to the past, in their opposition.

VOLUNTARY ARMY

Congress is not likely to give serious consideration to a voluntary army as an alternative to the draft in the immediate future. Its reasons are both pragmatic and philosophical. From a practical point of view it would be folly to change the whole complexion of the army during a war, however limited. Moreover, there are many who have grave doubts that such a force would be flexible enough to meet unknown expanded military commitments in the future. On the philosophical level many persons feel that the whole concept is antithetical to democratic principles. No one can object to increasing salaries, substituting civilian personnel for military in certain jobs, and instituting any other innovations that would improve the lot of those serving their country in the military. What is objectionable is the notion of a democratic society's placing a price on serving in the military and thereby hiring those most susceptible to such emoluments, knowing full well that many who would take up such a career would come from those groups unable to obtain social mobility any other way. Finally, the white-officer caste system, which would develop along with the noncivilian aspects of a voluntary army, would also appear repugnant.

DEPARTMENT OF DEFENSE STUDY

The Department of Defense study, released after several years of temporizing, was inadequate. Its omissions were appalling; it failed to address itself to the basic questions of equity in the application of the draft law. What was included did not significantly add to the information available on the subjects covered. The main intent of the document was to prove that a voluntary army was not economically feasible, but the research methodology used to do so was highly questionable. The argument presented in the study was refuted by several competent economists, among whom was Walter Oi of the University of Washington. In short, the Department of Defense produced a meaningless document that did nothing to help solve the various draft problems.

THE CLARK PANEL REPORT

The Clark Panel Report is surely one of the most blatant travesties ever foisted on the Congress of the United States and thus, indirectly, on the American people. Its over-riding weaknesses are its lack of hard empirical data or testimonial evidence and its failure to come to grips with the essential problems of the draft. Its conclusions apparently were made beforehand and its Report written in an attempt to substantiate them. That the Congress should accept such a document at face value and use it as the basis for formulating the new law is sad comment indeed on the good sense of this nation's chief legislative body.

THE MARSHALL COMMISSION REPORT

Given the time limitations imposed on the Marshall Commission by the President, this document is the finest in-depth study of the Selective Service System ever produced. Its major shortcoming is that because of the division of opinion among its members on the difficult question of deferments its arguments in this area are weak. The Report, which was based on the research and testimony of experts, concludes that the Selective Service System as presently constituted is in need of drastic reform and, indeed, complete reorganization; for example, on the basis of competent evidence, the

Commission concluded that the draft law operates to discriminate against the Negro. Although it is true that Negroes serve roughly in proportion to their numbers in the population (11 percent), it is also true that roughly 50 percent of the Negro registrants fail the physical or mental examination before classification. Therefore the proportion of eligible Negroes who serve (30 percent) is far higher than the comparable figure for whites (18 percent). The Negro is also seriously under-represented on local draft boards (1.3 percent), although there is some evidence that Selective Service has taken tentative steps to remedy this situation. (Other conclusions of the Marshall Commission are discussed under other subheads in this chapter.)

THE ADMINISTRATION'S ATTITUDE

The Administration went through all the motions of favoring changes in the Selective Service System. A blue-ribbon commission was appointed, and a Presidential message endorsing most of its findings was sent to Congress, but when matters came to a head the Administration began to backslide. President Johnson studiously avoided committing himself on certain key issues and exerted no apparent pressure on Congress to adopt the Commission's recommendations. During and after the hearings the Administration became a spectator by staying well clear of the arena. The Administration so consciously excluded itself from meaningful participation that it has only itself to blame for the new law.

RECOMMENDATIONS

The Selective Service System in its present form should be abolished. Selective Service performs two roles: it makes vital decisions affecting the allocation of the military manpower resources of the nation and, because its decisions determine draft status, has a profound influence on the lives of individuals and thus on the whole of society. This second role, though often overlooked, is every bit as important as the first. The military excludes roughly 50 percent of all applicants for physical and mental reasons. Thus Selective Service determines who will receive the advantages of military service: the G.I. bill, educational opportunities within the service, occupational training, upward mobility, and so forth. Conversely, it has at least indirect responsibility for consigning many in the rejected group to socioeconomic exile outside the mainstream of American society. As presently constituted, the System is poorly equipped to fulfill these responsibilities.

A Federal manpower agency should be established and held responsible for the utilization of military and civilian manpower. It should inherit all the duties of Selective Service as well as the manpower functions of the Department of Labor, the Department of Commerce, the Office of Economic Opportunity, and the Department of Health, Education and Welfare.

If this solution proved too drastic, the Selective Service System could be made a bureau of the Department of Labor.

The internal composition of the agency should also be changed. On the retirement of General Hershey a civilian should be named director. The narrow selection policy that permits only reserve officers to serve in key positions should be ended. The staff should be recruited without regard to military background, and appointments should be determined on the basis of a person's education and experience, thereby ensuring that important decisions will be based on the competent and thoughtful evaluation of experts.

In 1940 President Roosevelt selected Dr. Clarence A. Dykstra, a civilian, as the first Director of the Selective Service System. This appointment was made to bolster public confidence in the draft. Public confidence is once again at stake. Because Selective Service deals with the American public and performs a civilian service, it should be a civilian agency. Only after a man is inducted does he become a part of the military establishment. In keeping with the civilian image of the System, no member of the armed forces is permitted to serve on local draft boards; this civilian image should be extended to all higher echelons within the agency. There is nothing wrong with the military, but in this sensitive capacity the relationship with the public should be built on trust, not on the suspicion with which many members of the general public view the military.

The evidence indicates that the local board system should definitely be revised, whatever other changes are made in the over-all System. The degree of autonomy exercised by each board has caused serious inequities and an uneven administration of the law which have gone a long way toward destroying the effectiveness of the System. Because of the urbanization of the nation, local boards no longer function effectively as little groups of neighbors sending local boys off to war; they are an anachronism. The Marshall Commission's recommendations that all parts of the System be consolidated and centralized and that uniform rules and regulations be established should be implemented. Such reorganization would help to provide equal treatment for all registrants. Under this system there would be eight regional offices and 300 to 400 area offices established on a population basis in each state. The area offices would replace the local boards. Centralization of the System would facilitate the use of modern data-processing equipment and would enable the processing, registration, and classification of registrants to be carried out more effectively.

FINIS

The offhand manner in which both Houses of Congress dismissed the reforms proposed by the Marshall Commission is bound to increase cynicism and disrespect among segments of the public. The burdens of military service continue to be borne disproportionately by low-income families. The new law, like the old, favors white middle-class society. How long this undemocratic and discriminatory system can prevail is at present unknown. Perhaps the summer of 1967 — or, as it is sometimes referred to, the summer of our discontent — holds a clue to the answer. It may well be that the results of the 1968 national election will give hope for early reconsideration of this vital issue.

11 | EPILOGUE

When President Johnson signed the 1967 draft bill into law on June 30, 1967, many people breathed a sigh of relief. To be sure, the reform-minded were chagrined that the law contained more that was old than new, but Congress and those within Selective Service responsible for the day-to-day operation of the law felt that at least the pressure was off – for a little while, in any event.

In response to Congress's urging that more effective communication with the public be established, Selective Service initiated a weekly newsletter, with a question-and-answer format, in July 1967. Almost immediately, the newsletter produced some highly provocative public information:

Question. In regard to college student deferments, is a junior college considered an institution of higher learning?

Answer. Yes, if the credits given by the junior college are acceptable toward the granting of a baccalaureate degree by a college, university, or similar institution of learning.

This answer implies, of course, that any junior college student who is not pursuing a program that will eventually lead to his transfer to a four-year degree-granting institution is not eligible for a 2S deferment; students engaged primarily in vocational or technical fields of study (which are usually two-year or shorter nontransferable programs) are in a different category and will be treated in a different manner.

The newsletter, which reached various Washington-based educational organizations on July 15, 1967, immediately set off a chain reaction of indignation. Particularly incensed was the American Association of Junior Colleges (AAJC) which is highly sensitive to the seemingly second-class position of the junior college in American higher education. The American Council on Education and other organizations joined with the AAJC in an attempt to have this stand changed privately by consultation with appropriate people in Selective Service. Their first request was for a clarification of the answer given in the newsletter. Had a final decision been made, they asked, concerning this

159

situation? The answer was quickly forthcoming: on August 9, 1967, General Hershey, on the advice of Colonel Daniel O. Omer, Deputy Director and General Counsel of Selective Service, issued an advisory bulletin to all local draft boards that henceforth, junior college students in nonbaccalaureate (occupational) programs would be considered eligible for 2A occupational deferments, not 2S student deferments. His explanation for this change was that Congress had failed to specify the status of junior college students in the 1967 draft law, which read:

"The President shall, under such rules and regulations as he may prescribe, provide for the deferment from training and service in the Armed Forces of persons satisfactorily pursuing a full-time course of instruction at a college, university, or similar institution of learning and who request such deferment. A deferment granted to any person under authority of the preceding sentence shall continue until such person completes the requirements for his baccalaureate degree, fails to pursue satisfactorily a full-time course of instruction, or attains the twenty-fourth anniversary of the date of his birth, whichever first occurs."[1]

The language that Selective Service depended on was "requirements for his baccalaureate degree." Since junior college students in nontransferable programs do not receive the baccalaureate degree, they are not to be considered eligible for the 2S student deferment. The AAJC argued that Hershey's interpretation of the law was too literal and that under previous legislation all junior college students had received 2S deferments. Moreover, the policy discriminates against more than 50,000 students throughout the nation:

"The policy is especially discriminatory against students from lower-income and middle-income families, those from disadvantaged urban and rural areas, and members of minority groups. For many such students, a two-year occupational, technical, or business-related program may be their only chance for an education beyond the high school. Many of these students are hard-working young men, already disadvantaged for economic or other reasons."[2]

When the Washington-based educational organizations attempted to dissuade Hershey from making this change, they were not listened to with much sympathy. The General had in the past received a buffeting quite regularly from various college presidents over a number of issues, particularly deferments, even when he had followed the advice of national education organizations; for example, the American Council on Education (ACE) had strongly urged that the draft test and class rank be reinstituted as a basis for student deferments. As a

---

[1] Public Law 90-40, June 30, 1967, 81 STAT. 102 (h) (1).

[2] A statement on *Selective Service and the Junior College,* William G. Shannon, Associate Executive Director, American Association of Junior Colleges, Washington, D.C., December 7, 1967, p. 1.

military man, the General assumed that the ACE had control over its membership and that therefore this decision would not be opposed. Various representatives of higher education told him, however, that the policy concerning junior college students was a bad one. Hershey reacted by saying he was not sure whom they represented or did not represent. When Jack Morse of the ACE explained that the Council was an umbrella organization representing all of higher education, Hershey replied: "Your umbrella leaks and I got wet before, but not again."

In my judgment such a Selective Service policy has several important ramifications. First, it tends to pressure students into programs that may be inappropriate to their capabilities and interests. Take, for example, a high school senior with a marginal academic record who seeks the advice of a guidance counselor about his educational opportunities. If he were basing his advice entirely on the student's capacities and scholastic achievement, the counselor would probably recommend that the student take some kind of occupational training. But he would also have to point out that the student would then be in a nontransferable program and would receive not a 2S deferment but an occupational deferment, which could be honored or not, depending on local-draft-board judgment based on the advice of the National Security Council in regard to occupations in short supply and essential to the national interest. In such circumstances the student might decide to enter an academic program that would in the long run be of no benefit to him.

Second, this kind of a ruling opens up a new classification for "students" – one that would probably make it difficult for a young man to transfer from one program to another. A student might not be able to obtain a 2S deferment once he had a 2A, and vice versa, because of the unfamiliarity of local boards with the great variety of occupational and educational programs.

Third, it is highly undesirable that a government agency should decide who is and who is not a college student. Both as a matter of principle and as a matter of practice, government agencies – especially Selective Service – lack the know-how to make such distinctions.

For several months the junior colleges fought the Hershey directive, even carrying their case to the White House staff, whose chief refrain was, "Have you talked to the General?" Meanwhile Selective Service did not stand idly by as the educators lobbied for change. After consultation they asked for and received a letter from Mendel Rivers which bolstered their ruling on 2A deferments by stating that Congress had intended to defer only four-year college students.

Finally the Justice Department, in a legal memorandum of opinion requested by the Office of Education, indicated that although there were tenable legal arguments on both sides it agreed with the position of the junior colleges. It offered two alternatives: Hershey could rescind his advisory memorandum (the easier and more preferable of the two) or the President could deal with the matter by executive order. General Hershey publicly and privately indicated that if he were to be over-ruled it would have to come from the top. So far the President has not issued such an order.

Again, Selective Service has by administrative fiat made a decision without considering its possible consequences for the manpower situation. True, it may have been intended to protect junior college students, but such protection probably was not needed to begin with. More important, this change in deferment policy seriously complicates the problems of training necessary skilled manpower on less than a college-degree basis.

While the junior college issue continued to occupy the time and energy of many people, a second happening occurred. It was discovered that on October 26 General Hershey had suggested in a letter to local boards that persons who engaged in illegal interference with the draft or military recruiting might lose their deferments on the grounds that any action which violated Selective Service laws could certainly not be in the national interest. If evidence of violation of the draft law were established, a local board could declare the registrant to be delinquent, thus moving him to the head of the list of draft-eligibles. Although it is true that, under the law, local boards are not bound to follow the recommendations set forth in the Hershey letter, it is equally true that this type of pronouncement is generally interpreted by local boards as orders from the boss.

Once again, the reaction was violent; once again, various groups called for the retirement of the 74-year-old general. Those who protested against the contents of the letter argued that, reprehensible as the harassment of military and other recruiters might be, the proposed "solution" was even more reprehensible. The Selective Service Act is not a penal statute, those who operate the System are not judges, and local boards are not courts or juries. As the American Association of University Professors put it in a telgram to General Hershey, the provisions of the letter "would allow penalty without regard for...due process.... More importantly your letter sets down such a vague standard that local boards may induct persons for the exercise of constitutional rights."

In response to the outcry from members of Congress, the press, and many national organizations, General Hershey held a news conference at which he said, among other things, that he had "talked with somebody at the White House" before issuing the letter. One can imagine the shudder that greeted this statement in Administration circles. Throughout the entire controversy the executive branch had been only too happy to see General Hershey take all the heat and abuse that arose from the problems surrounding the draft. When reporters pressed the White House staff to reveal the person with whom Hershey had checked, they received no answer. At the news conference the General not only stood by his statement but amplified it by stating that a draft registrant caught interfering with military recruiting would be offered the choice of military service or jail. His argument was that once a man has been registered and found qualified, he knows he has an obligation to serve. He has a right to fulfill that obligation by volunteering rather than waiting to be inducted. When a recruiter tries to enlist such a registrant and his efforts are interfered with, at that point there is a violation of the law.

During the period of stunned silence that followed the administration attempted to determine the legality of this latest "Hersheyism." Various sources within the Justice Department indicated that it would be difficult to support in a legal case brought on Constitutional grounds. Finally, on December 9, after weeks of negotiation, the Selective Service and the Justice Department issued a joint statement intended to clarify their respective roles in handling draft protesters. Registrants would not be subject to special action by either agency if their protests were lawful. The Justice Department would establish a new unit to deal quickly with criminal violations such as draft-card burnings. The Selective Service would retain its authority to handle those personal actions that affected the draft status of the registrant, such as failure to carry a draft card or refusal to report for a physical examination.

One would have thought that this statement solved the problems occasioned by the Hershey letter, but unfortunately the General stepped in again and said, in an interview with the *Washington Post,* that the statement "strengthened" the position taken in his letter. Not surprisingly, the Attorney General was reported to be surprised and disappointed by Hershey's "amplification." Certainly any fair reading of the joint statement leaves the impression that it was intended to allow the Justice Department discretion in deciding whether a particular protest incident warranted legal action.

In February 1968 an Oberlin College student (aptly named Dove) was declared delinquent by a local board for interfering with military recruitment on campus. The board cited the October 26th letter from General Hershey as its authority. The faculty and student body at Oberlin were naturally aroused. After several days of negotiations by telephone between the college, the Justice Department, and Selective Service, in which the American Council on Education acted as intermediary, the delinquency notice was rescinded verbally by the National Headquarters.

In addition to stirring up moral indignation over the punitive tactics employed by Selective Service, this issue makes clear the tragic shortsightedness of the policies enunciated by a governmental agency charged with the function of supplying necessary military manpower. That the Director of this system can state publicly that the law has penal provisions never envisioned by the Congress which passed it is almost incredible.

The third and final happening under the new law — at least so far — pertains to the status of graduate students. To reiterate: the President in his Executive Order No. 11360, issued July 3, 1967, stated that after a one-year moratorium to end at the close of the 1967-1968 academic year, no more 2-S deferments would be granted to graduate students except those specifically written into the law. Under the existing "oldest-eligibles first" system such a policy would mean that most of those drafted would be 1968 college graduates, students finishing their first year of graduate school, and students with master's or doctoral degrees – in short, the most highly trained men in our society. To look at it another way, after June 1968, and until further change was instituted, the enrollment in the first two years of graduate school would consist of women, veterans, foreign students, men over the age of 26, and physically unqualified and otherwise deferable men.

Recognizing the potential dangers in such a situation, those involved in higher education tried in vain to make contact with someone in the administration similarly involved. But no one knew who had the ball, where the ball was, or even if the ball existed. At one point Douglass Cater, Special Assistant to the President on educational matters, was rumored to be considering various alternatives; later, Joseph Califano, another of the President's confidants, was named; still later, Harold Wool of the Defense Department was said to be working on a detailed alternative plan.

Early in October the prime movers in the educational establishment met with representatives of the Office of Education, the Bureau of the Budget, the Federal Council of Science and Technology, and, of course, the Department of Defense. Meanwhile, panic mounted as Washington-based educational organizations sent memoranda to their member institutions in which they emphasized the dire aspects of the situation they were about to face. On December 1 the American Council on Education, with the complete agreement of other educational organizations, urged a four-point program to help avert the chaos that would surely occur if the policy were not modified.

1. That for the immediate future a prime age group (age 19) be designated as first to be inducted and that those past age 19 without military service and not entitled to deferment be treated as if they were 19. The order of call within this pool would then begin with the oldest first, by month and day of birth.

2. That legislation be introduced to provide a random selection system as a long-range solution.

3. That deferments in additional fields of graduate and professional study be provided only in narrow and critically needed specialities such as metallurgy, for example, if there were a severe shortage in that field, rather than in the broad field of the physical sciences.

4. That local boards be urged to postpone the induction of students and

teachers classified 1-A until the end of the term in which they are studying or teaching. By term is meant a quarter, a semester, or a trimester, not an academic year.

The first break came when the press leaked a report that the Federal Interagency Committee on Education had recommended to the National Security Council that graduate deferments be continued for students in certain fields, namely, the sciences, engineering, and mathematics. Although such a compromise solution is certainly consistent with the biases of Generals Hershey and Mark Clark, it would have disastrous consequences for higher education. Not only would students be pressured into fields they might otherwise not have selected, but also graduate schools would become bitterly divided, with top-heavy emphasis given to the "hard" sciences and technology at the expense of the social sciences, the humanities, and other areas less "essential" from a military standpoint.

The press accounts, however, proved somewhat inaccurate. True, the Committee made the recommendations mentioned, but it sent them not to the National Security Council but to the Departments of Labor, Commerce, and Health, Education and Welfare. At this point the influence of Willard Wirtz, Secretary of Labor, made itself felt. Instead of forwarding the recommendations to the National Security Council, Wirtz, true to the views he had expressed in his testimony at the Kennedy hearings (see Chapter 7), suggested that all graduate deferments be abolished. According to reports. Secretary of Commerce Alexander Trowbridge agreed to this modification only after he was assured that a "youngest-men-first" system would be instituted. John Gardner, Secretary of Health, Education and Welfare, did not sign the Wirtz recommendations at all. Nevertheless, they were sent to the White House before Christmas.

Meanwhile, a delegation of educational leaders, still relying on the press reports, which were never denied by the administration and which were widely assumed to be trial balloons sent up to gage public reaction, went to the White House to express their opposition to the proposed graduate deferments by category. Ironically enough, the higher education community had finally reached virtual agreement about the draft. Had their position been enunciated a year earlier, during the Congressional hearings, it might have been persuasive. In brief, they argued that categorical deferments would be divisive to higher education and that no one is wise enough to decide which disciplines are vital to the national interest and which are not. Rather they favored some method of achieving equality of liability to the draft, of spreading the risk among all segments of the 19- to 26-year-old group. Under such a method some graduate students would be called but some would be passed over and thus able to continue working on advanced degrees, whatever their fields.

The delegates received a respectful hearing and were assured that their concerns would be reported to the President; but the holidays arrived and no decision had been reached. Graduate deans fumed, admissions officers at both the graduate and undergraduate[3] level quaked, and students grew more and more bewildered. Even those outside the educational community were coming to realize that the new policy might have most unfortunate repercussions for programs in business and industry. Except for the unfortunate death of Australian Prime Minister Harold Holt, which necessitated President Johnson's hasty departure to attend the funeral, a decision might have been reached over the holidays, when colleges were closed and Congress not in session.

The new year opened with mounting dissent and growing pressure on the President. Secretary McNamara, at that point a lame-duck cabinet member, offered a Defense Department compromise plan that would have instituted a modified "youngest first" system, but his recommendations fell on deaf ears, or rather on ears that had already been reached by Secretary Wirtz. A meeting of the National Security Council was held in mid-January, and after he had been assured that the President had considered all sides of the question Secretary Gardner signed the proposal ending graduate deferments (several days later he announced his resignation as Secretary of Health, Education and Welfare, and although the deferment issue was not paramount in his decision some feel it could have been a deciding factor). To make it unanimous Price Daniel, head of the Office of Emergency Planning, also signed, but only after severe pressure to sign or resign. This pressure was verified when staff members of the Office of Emergency Planning made calls to various educators, which indicated that neither the staff nor the director agreed with the decision reached.

On Friday, February 16, Selective Service headquarters announced the final – really final – decision. In a telegram to all State Directors General Hershey said that the National Security Council had informed Selective Service that it was no longer essential to the national interest to defer graduate students except in fields already covered by the law, that no change in the order of calls (to a system of drafting younger men first) was required in the name of fairness, and that the lists of essential activities and critical occupations (which had up to that point provided the basis for local-board decisions) were suspended. Each board, however, retained the right to grant occupational deferments that they felt to be in the community interest. This last provision has since been interpreted to mean that if, for instance, a community has only one automotive mechanic he may be granted an occupational deferment; if the same community has a registrant studying nuclear physics at Harvard, however, he need not be

---

[3] Undergraduate admissions, particularly in universities, may be affected because of the large number of teaching assistants currently used at such institutions. Who will fill these positions if graduate schools are depleted?

granted a deferment, since his activity is not necessarily in the community interest. In any event, the 4000 local boards still had power to make these decisions, independent of any national policy. Along with the telegram local boards received memoranda from the National Security Council and the Departments of Commerce, Labor, and Health, Education and Welfare that explained the reasons for the decision.

In actuality, this final decision was simply a logical conclusion to the decisions made by President Johnson during the preceding spring and summer. His failure to back the Marshall Commission's recommendations more strongly in his message to Congress, his failure to bring pressure to bear on the Congressional Conference Committee when it was formulating the new law, and his failure to exercise the veto were the steps leading to this culmination. The final pronouncement, however, came not from the White House but from Selective Service: thus responsibility again was shifted to General Hershey.

The potential effects of the new policy stagger the imagination. The United States may find itself with the best educated army in the history of the world. Assuming that draft calls remain at the stepped-up Vietnam level, approximately 35 to 40,000 draftees will be called each month, for a total of 400,000 men during fiscal 1969. Most of the oldest draft-eligibles (who are to be called first) will necessarily be recent college graduates and graduate students, since virtually everyone else in this age group will already have served. According to one estimate, the male full-time enrollment in the nation's graduate schools may be reduced by 70 percent in academic year 1969-1970.[4] Those disciplines that are dominated by men – engineering, law, and the natural sciences, for example – will, of course, be particularly hard hit. The real impact on all segments of society, when it finds itself without trained professionals in various crucial occupations, may not be felt until a few years later, but it will be felt. In short, the failure to solve the problem (surely not too difficult or complex) of instituting a system for calling the younger first, but at the same time not allowing the oldest to escape entirely, may have far-reaching and calamitous effects on the national interest.

Many persons were quick to criticize Congress for passing a bad law. Bad it may be, in several respects, but in this particular area it is not. The provisions about deferments and methods of selection were deliberately made general, and almost unlimited discretion was granted to the President. If blame must be assigned, then, it is clear enough where the finger of scorn should point.

Granted that the President was under pressure from many groups who were supposedly advising him – both in and out of government – it is still clear that

---

[4] *The Impact of the Draft on Graduate Schools in 1968-69,* Scientific Manpower Commission, and the Council of Graduate Schools of the United States, Washington, D.C., March 1968, p. 1.

his decision rested on a pragmatic political judgment. A large number of Americans, particularly those who vote, are convinced that the current generation of students is un-American in its opposition to the war and to the draft. Bewildered by the philosophy and folkways of both the hippies and the activists, hurt by youth's rejection of middle-class values, and always suspicious of intellectualism, many older people feel strongly that students deserve to be drafted. General Hershey's "punitive" interpretation of the draft law epitomizes that kind of thinking.

Once again, conflict produced reaction and compromise was arrived at on the basis of what would be most palatable to the voting public. The choice was between the short-range realities of a presidential election year and the long-range needs of the nation and the choice was made. The success or failure of the new policy will without doubt become highly visible in the near future.

CIVILIAN ADVISORY PANEL

ON

MILITARY MANPOWER PROCUREMENT

REPORT TO

THE

COMMITTEE ON ARMED SERVICES
HOUSE OF REPRESENTATIVES
NINETIETH CONGRESS
FIRST SESSION

FEBRUARY 28, 1967

U.S. GOVERNMENT PRINTING OFFICE
WASHINGTON : 1967

HOUSE COMMITTEE ON ARMED SERVICES

FIRST SESSION, NINETIETH CONGRESS

L. MENDEL RIVERS, South Carolina, *Chairman*

PHILIP J. PHILBIN, Massachusetts
F. EDWARD HÉBERT, Louisiana
MELVIN PRICE, Illinois
O. C. FISHER, Texas
PORTER HARDY, JR., Virginia
CHARLES E. BENNETT, Florida
JAMES A. BYRNE, Pennsylvania
SAMUEL S. STRATTON, New York
OTIS G. PIKE, New York
RICHARD H. ICHORD, Missouri
LUCIEN N. NEDZI, Michigan
ALTON LENNON, North Carolina
WILLIAM J. RANDALL, Missouri
G. ELLIOTT HAGAN, Georgia
CHARLES H. WILSON, California
ROBERT L. LEGGETT, California
DONALD J. IRWIN, Connecticut
FRANK E. EVANS, Colorado
FLOYD V. HICKS, Washington
HERVEY G. MACHEN, Maryland
SPEEDY O. LONG, Louisiana
E. S. JOHNNY WALKER, New Mexico

WILLIAM H. BATES, Massachusetts
LESLIE C. ARENDS, Illinois
ALVIN E. O'KONSKI, Wisconsin
WILLIAM G. BRAY, Indiana
BOB WILSON, California
CHARLES S. GUBSER, California
CHARLES E. CHAMBERLAIN, Michigan
ALEXANDER PIRNIE, New York
DURWARD G. HALL, Missouri
DONALD D. CLANCY, Ohio
ROBERT T. STAFFORD, Vermont
RICHARD S. SCHWEIKER, Pennsylvania
CHARLES A. HALLECK, Indiana
CARLETON J. KING, New York
WILLIAM L. DICKINSON, Alabama
CHARLES W. WHALEN, JR., Ohio
JAMES V. SMITH, Oklahoma

SANTIAGO POLANCO-ABREU, Puerto Rico
Resident Commissioner

JOHN R. BLANDFORD, *Chief Counsel*
FRANK M. SLATINSHEK, *Counsel*

LETTER OF SUBMITTAL

CIVILIAN ADVISORY PANEL ON
MILITARY MANPOWER PROCUREMENT,
Washington, D.C., February 28, 1967.
Hon. L. MENDEL RIVERS,
Chairman, Committee on Armed Services,
House of Representatives,
Washington, D.C.

DEAR MR. CHAIRMAN: I have the honor to submit the enclosed report of the Civilian Advisory Panel on Military Manpower Procurement which you established under my chairmanship to commence functioning on November 1, 1966, and which you discussed with me several times prior to that date. The report is countersigned by all members of the Panel to signify the unanimity achieved with regard to the report.

Sincerely,

MARK W. CLARK,
General, U.S. Army (Retired)
Chairman of the Panel.
Hon. W. STERLING COLE,
Vice Chairman of the Panel.
Dr. JEROME H. HOLLAND.
Hon. ROBERT D. MURPHY.
Msgr. MAURICE SHEEHY.
EARL H. BLAIK.
Dr. FREDERICK L. HOVDE.
CHARLES E. SALTZMAN.

CONTENTS

CIVILIAN ADVISORY PANEL ON MILITARY MANPOWER PROCUREMENT

I. INTRODUCTION

A. FORMATION

A Civilian Advisory Panel was formed on November 1, 1966, by the Committee on Armed Services, House of Representatives, and charged with analyzing and evaluating the equity and effectiveness of existing laws and policies relating to military personnel procurement.

B. PRECEPT

The precept of the Panel was enunciated in letters, dated October 10 and 11, 1966, from the Honorable L. Mendel Rivers, Chairman of the Committee on Armed Services, to General Mark W. Clark, U.S. Army, Retired, Chairman of the Panel; and to the following members of the Panel: Mr. Earl H. Blaik, The Honorable W. Sterling Cole, Dr. Frederick L. Hovde, The Honorable Robert D. Murphy, and the Right Reverend Maurice Sheehy. The precept was reiterated to Dr. Jerome H. Holland and Mr. Charles E. Saltzman, also members of the Panel, in letters to these gentlemen from Mr. Rivers on November 10, 1966, and December 13, 1966, respectively.

C. CONVENING

The Panel functioned informally through correspondence and independent research on the part of Panel members until formally convened in Washington, D.C., on January 4, 1967. During the period between November 1, 1966, and January 2, 1967, the Panel Chairman provided members of the Panel with a variety of background information on the procurement of military manpower and tentatively assigned subject areas in which Panel members were to become especially knowledgeable. At the same time, ideas and suggestions relating to the subject were exchanged between the Chairman and the members, and, as a means of acquainting the Panel with local board procedures, the Chairman initiated a series of interviews of local board chairmen by Panel members in their local areas.

D. THE PRESIDENT'S COMMISSION

1. The Panel Chairman conferred with Mr. Burke Marshall, Chairman of the National Advisory Commission on Selective Service established by Executive Order on July 2, 1966, with a view to ascertaining informally for the information of the Panel, the general approach of the Commission. The conference with Mr. Marshall, who was most cooperative, was approved by the Panel and with full appreciation of the separateness of the Executive and Legislative Branches which appointed the Commission and the Panel, respectively, to serve the unique functions of the two Branches. The Panel's position with

1

regard to the Commission was that the Panel should take pains to operate completely independently of the Commission but that a spirit of friendly recognition should prevail between the two entities.

2. Under the precept issued to the Panel by the Chairman of the Committee on Armed Services, House of Representatives, the Panel was requested to review the report of the Commission. Unfortunately, although the Executive Order establishing the Commission stipulated the submission of a final report to the President "on or about January 1, 1967," that report has not yet been available to this Panel. Therefore, confronted with the requirement of submitting its recommendations to the Committee on Armed Services "not later than March 1, 1967," the Panel decided not to delay submission of its report, notwithstanding the lack of opportunity to review the report of the Commission.

II. PREFACE

A. ADVANCE STUDIES OF PANEL

From its study of available information on the subject of the current military manpower situation and the history of mobilizing military manpower in this country, from conferences with State Directors and Selective Service and local draft board personnel, from interviews with individual citizens interested in the subject, and from the extensive aggregate experience of Panel members with various phases of military manpower employment, the Panel early in its initial formal meeting arrived at a concensus concerning its approach to accomplishing its mission.

B. THE PROBLEM

The problem facing the Panel was to determine:

(1) whether the induction authority contained in the Universal Military Training and Service Act should be continued beyond its current expiration date of July 1, 1967;

(2) whether the Universal Military Training and Service Act is sufficiently responsive to national needs and sufficiently harmonious with the national psychology to warrant its continuation in substantially its present form as the legal vehicle for providing military manpower in war and peace;

(3) alternatives to involuntary induction in the event continuation of either the induction authority or the basic law were found undesirable; and

(4) ways and means of minimizing inequities in the law and the administration thereof in the event continuation of the induction authority and the basic law were found desirable.

C. APPROACH TO THE PROBLEM

The Panel's approach to its problem was to isolate for independent study each facet of the University Military Training and Service Act which could be identified as the basis of significant criticism by responsible citizens. Specific problem areas so identified were assigned to one of three sub-Panels into which the Panel divided itself, while general problem areas were reserved for consideration by the Panel as a whole. Recommendations developed by the sub-Panels were submitted to the full Panel for acceptance, modification, or rejection.

2

D. PANEL PHILOSOPHY

The philosophy underlying the Panel's approach to its mission was that:

(1) military manpower is the indispensable ingredient of the defense of the United States in periods of limited war and all-out war, as well as in periods of peace,

(2) the over-all effectiveness of a law is affected by the measure of public acceptance and support it receives.

(3) while giving precedence to maintaining adequate armed strength to ensure the security of the nation, every reasonable effort should be made to achieve equitable sharing of the obligations and privileges of serving in the armed forces and their Reserve components, and

(4) the interest of the nation would best be served by conducting Panel deliberations in executive sessions, and that selected experts be requested to present their views to the Panel, either in person or in writing.

III. SUBJECT AREAS CONSIDERED

A. AGE

1. At the present time youths must register at age eighteen, are classified by age 18½, and at that point become legally liable for induction. However, as a practical matter, the induction of young men between the ages of 18½ and nineteen cannot occur until the available pool of registrants above age nineteen has been exhausted by the local draft board. A provision to this effect is contained in Sec. 5(a) of the Universal Military Training and Service Act. Therefore, the age of liability for draftees can be considered as extending from age nineteen to twenty-six, or in the case of registrants who have been given a deferment, until age thirty-five.

2. From the pool of men classified as available for induction, individual draftees are selected in the chronological order of their birthdays; i.e., the oldest are selected first from the age group of twenty-six years and under. This system has caused unnecessary uncertainty for men in this age group because an individual who is classified as available, or who is reclassified as available after a temporary deferment, is liable from age nineteen to age twenty-six (or to age thirty-five after an expired deferment).

3. The Panel believes that it would be beneficial both to the individual and to the military service if the so-called "Modified Young Age Class System" were adopted in place of the present "oldest first" system. Under the "Modified Young Age Class System" the present deferment system would be unchanged, but instead of selecting the oldest men first for induction, the induction of men from the Class I-A available pool in any one year would be made from a priority category consisting of:

(a) men whose student or other temporary deferments have expired and who are thereafter available for selection to age thirty-five, and

(b) the current nineteen- and twenty-year-olds (young men subject to selection at age nineteen and inducted normally at nineteen or twenty).

4. Men in this category who were not selected for induction by the end of any year would be placed in the next lower order of induction,

below the new class of ex-college students and nineteen-year-olds. While they would continue liable to age twenty-six (or thirty-five if they had formerly been deferred), they would normally not be inducted except in extensive military manpower buildups. Thus, the present uncertainty would be substantially reduced. Furthermore, this system of selecting first from the pool composed of college deferees and the young age group, with equal exposure to the draft being given to all members of the combined pool, would generally draft men at the most favorable time in their educational or career patterns; i.e., between either high school and college or career employment or immediately after college and before they have acquired domestic or career commitments.

5. The Panel has been informed that in the opinion of the Department of Defense the adoption of the "Modified Young Age Class System" would have negligible effect on the procurement of manpower for the active and Reserve military establishments by voluntary enlistments, non-prior-service Reserve Enlistment Programs (REP), or ROTC programs. On the other hand, younger men make good soldiers, and combat commanders generally prefer most of their new recruits from the younger age group.

6. Since the average age of inductees at present is 20.3 years, the adoption of the "Modified Age System" would have little practical effect under today's conditions of larger draft calls due to the Vietnam war. However, if conditions change so that draft calls are considerably smaller, the average induction age under the present system would rise considerably. The Panel recommends that the change to the "Modified Young Age Class System" be effected.

B. SIX-MONTH ENLISTMENT—RESERVE ENLISTMENT PROGRAM (REP)

1. GENERAL

a. Under the Reserve Enlistment Program (REP) men enlist for six months' active full-time training and acquire an obligation to participate in the active Reserve for six years (including the initial active training period). The Panel is of the opinion that in certain respects participants in this voluntary program may escape or mitigate service to which drafted men are subject.

b. When the REP participant enlists voluntarily in that program under present conditions he ensures effectively against his having to serve initially for two years in active training, combat or other full-time military service, since the full-time training period in the REP is basically six months (the recent average has actually been 5.8 months). Under current conditions, he also ensures against his being ordered to additional full-time service because neither Reserve units nor individuals in the Ready Reserve pool are currently being called to active service (see footnote, Par. III. B.1.e.).

c. The foregoing conditions provide the REP a possible means of evading certain service to which draftees are liable. The Panel believed that the man who enlists under the REP should not thereby become entirely exempt from the types of service to which the draftee is subject, and it believed that the present situation in this respect causes legitimate discontent on the part of those who think that REP participants are escaping arduous service.

4

d. When a REP participant finishes his initial, full-time, period of active duty training, he returns to the National Guard or Organized Reserve unit to which he is assigned, and is supposed to engage in its Reserve training program. However, if such an individual moves his residence from the unit's community, if changes in his personal situation occur so that he cannot participate satisfactorily in the unit's training program, or, in case of willful neglect of duty, he is transferred from the National Guard or the Organized Reserve unit to the Ready Reserve pool of such men who, while in the pool, perform no training or other duty. While in this pool he is subject to assignment to a suitable unit and is subject also to being ordered to active duty by the President. However, today only a fraction of such men are assigned to other units and none is being called to active duty (see footnote, Par.III.B.1.e.). A total of 42,000 REP men was recently reported to be in the U.S. Army pool alone, while the number in such pools of the other services was relatively negligible.

e. The Panel believes that it is undesirable for a substantial number of REP men, who have received basic and perhaps additional advanced individual training during their initial full-time period, to remain for an indeterminate period and perhaps until the end of their six-year obligation in an inactive pool in which they are receiving no training and performing no military service. Furthermore, the Panel believes that this pool could provide a haven for REP men who wish to evade military duty responsibilities. Therefore, the Panel believes that some more suitable disposition should be made of REP participants in the pool. To this end, the Panel recommends that the secretary of the military service concerned be required to order to active duty for twenty-four months, including any period of active duty previously performed, any individual REP who, for whatever reason, does not participate satisfactorily in a unit of the National Guard or Organized Reserve during the period of his military obligation if he has at least fifteen months remaining to be served on his active duty commitment. However, the Panel recommends that provision be made for the secretary of the military service concerned to grant an exception in individual cases when circumstances warrant. In these instances, the individual should be discharged from the Reserve component concerned and reported to the Selective Service System as eligible for the draft. In effecting the foregoing policy, provision should be made to ensure that such individual will not, as a consequence of early discharge from the REP, be given reduction in his Reserve obligation. An individual discharged from the service as described above would lose his I–D classification and be subject to reclassification as I–A or otherwise by his local board.[1]

2. Professional Athletes and the Reserve Enlistment Program (REP)

a. The athlete whose draft status is subject to close scrutiny by the public has been discussed at considerable length by members of Congress, the press, and, more importantly, by those who have been inducted. The subject has three facets: the undergraduate athlete, the IV–F professional athlete, and the professional athlete who allegedly avoids the draft. The college athlete is less involved in.

[1] This policy recommended by the Panel has apparently been adopted by the Department of Defense as evidenced by its press release of February 15, 1967, and Executive Order 11327 of the President which authorized ordering reservists in control groups to active duty.

5

the discussion as his draft status parallels that of the normal undergraduate if he is classified as a deferred student.

    b. The subject of physical defects of athletes classified IV–F is often misunderstood by the public. It is the belief of many who understand military requirements and athletic injuries that in a great majority of cases the chronically-injured, deferred athlete is not physically able to meet the full demands of service in a combat zone. Such defects as chronically dislocated shoulders, torn knee ligaments, calcium spurs, perforated ear drums, recurring sacroiliac displacement, and sciatic nerve pressures can be endured by the athlete who, as a player, is under constant medical attention with quick access to whirlpool baths and other modern and elaborate therapeutic devices. The same player, however, would become a distinct liability to a military unit if an equivalent level of military medical resources were required to maintain his limited effectiveness and availability.

    c. The Panel is unaware of any evidence indicating that the medical profession has shown partiality in examining men for the draft, and the Panel does not believe that athletes get preferential consideration by Selective Service medical examiners.

    d. A soldier who breaks down physically in line of duty, whether athlete or not, may become a charge to the government for the rest of his life since a physical discharge carries with it certain compensation for the discharged soldier. This makes it imperative that waivers on physical deficiencies be restricted by examining medical officers.

    e. An athlete may participate in sports but still be a definite liability to the armed forces. Deferment of athletes for physical defects should be more thoroughly understood by the public, and every effort should be made to present fairly the case for the professional athlete who is classified IV–F.

    f. Because of publicity involving the professional athlete vis-a-vis the draft, the Panel found it advisable to comment on this segment of the nation's manpower. The professional game involves millions of dollars and the players, in order to remain with their teams, willingly cooperate with owners who endeavor to enlist their players in the Reserve or the National Guard. Every effort should be made by the Department of Defense to prevent those athletes who are physically qualified from avoiding induction. Unless units of the National Guard or Reserve are called to active duty, enlistment therein may be a means of avoiding the draft. In this respect, regulations were recently issued to eliminate the possibility that athletes could receive preferential` treatment over nonathletes in enlisting in either the National Guard of Reserve. On December 22, 1966, the Department of Defense promulgated the following policies with respect to the Reserve Component Enlistment Standards and Procedures to become effective prior to February 1, 1967:

> It shall be normal practice to accept the earliest applicant for enlistment who meets the minimum qualifications for a vacancy and whose availability to serve the unit is assured. Exceptions may be made when, in the best judgment of those responsible for the procurement of reserve personnel, the individual's prior military service or significant civilian experience in the occupational skill concerned is considered to warrant it.

The Panel believed this departmental policy will diminish public criticism of the Reserve components' recruiting practices, provided that in the case of professional athletes there be added to the departmental regulations a further requirement that in the case of profes-

6

sional athletes no exception be made. The Panel recommended the addition of this provision regarding professional athletes and felt that its adoption would tend to assure equity in the enlistment procedures of Reserve components.

C. UTILIZATION OF RESERVE FORCES BY ORDER-ING THEM TO ACTIVE DUTY DURING PERIODS OF HIGH INDUCTION CALLS

1. The Panel was disturbed by the obvious disproportionate sharing of the Vietnam war between involuntary inductees on the one hand and their Reserve counterparts on the other. The Panel was advised that until the enactment of the temporary authority contained in Public·Law 89–687 (October 15, 1966) the President was unable to order reservists without their consent to active duty without either declaring a new national emergency or securing new legislature authority from the Congress. As a consequence, the President chose to meet the increased military personnel requirements of the Vietnam crises by substantially increasing the number of inductees on active duty. This action was taken despite the recommendation of the President's senior military advisers that he take such steps as would be necessary to call Reserve forces to active duty.

2. The Presidential decision to meet increased active military personnel requirements by utilizing inductees has increased the on-board count of inductees in the military services from an average of approximately 200,000 from 1963 through 1965 to a September 30, 1966, figure of almost 500,000 inductees.

3. Notwithstanding the fact that the Commander-in-Chief has been given temporary statutory authority to order Reserve forces to active duty, there continues to appear to be some reluctance to activate these forces. Therefore, the Panel urges the President to spread the burden of the Vietnam war more equitably between inductees and Organized Reserve Forces by ordering some reservists to active duty.

4. The Panel also believes that situations will recur in which the President will find it not in the national interest to declare a new national emergency even though there exists a genuine need for ordering Reserve forces to active duty. Consequently, the Panel recommends that the President be given permanent statutory authority to order Reserve forces to active duty without the necessity of declaring that a new national emergency exists.

D. LOCAL BOARD PROCEDURES

1. The Panel reviewed in considerable detail the procedures followed by local draft boards, the employment practices of the Selective Service System, and the procedures for appointing local board members. As a result of these studies, the Panel recommended that the tenure of local draft board members be limited to ten years. This would permit greater participation in the operation of local boards by more citizens in the community, thereby tending to create wider understanding of the boards' roles in community life. This change would also reduce the probability of board members handling cases in a perfunctory manner as a result of "getting in a rut."

2. Also, the Panel felt that the title of the position of the Chief Clerk of the local board should be changed to "Executive Secretary" so as to be more nearly reflective of the responsibilities of this position

7

and that the "Executive Secretary" be charged with the additional responsibility of referring to the proper agency for career guidance and counselling registrants who return to their community after completion of their military service.

3. The Panel recommended that the Director of Selective Service schedule periodic regional meetings of local board members, as well as the Chief Clerks of these boards, for the purpose of discussing common problems arising out of classification procedures and related matters, with a representative of the Director of Selective Service present to ensure the effectiveness of such meetings. It is hoped that such meetings will result in an interchange of ideas and discussion of common problems between local draft board members in contiguous geographical areas and thereby promote greater uniformity among local draft boards in the interpretation of Selective Service regulations and procedures.

4. The Panel strongly recommended that in obtaining the uniformity recommended elsewhere in this Report care be exercised to avoid diminishing the discretionary authority of local draft boards since maximum flexibility in this regard is considered essential to protect individuals who have special problems and to provide boards with authority to devote particular attention to such cases.

E. PHYSICAL, MENTAL, AND MORAL STANDARDS FOR INDUCTION

1. General

The Panel reviewed the physical, mental, and moral standards for induction as established by the Department of Defense, and strongly supported recent action by the Department to modify and revise downward these standards in order to permit acceptance by the military services of inductees and enlistees who qualify as satisfactory servicemen, with minimum special instruction and attention by the military services. The Panel did not believe that the military services should be forced to accept inductees and enlistees whose trainability is so limited as to make questionable their value to the military services. On the other hand, the Panel believed that every effort should be made by the military services to ensure that established physical, mental, and moral standards do not needlessly deprive individuals of the opportunity to serve their country, nor provide a means of escaping military service.

2. Physical Standards

As a part of the effort being made by the Department of Defense to revise downward the physical standards, a Medically-Remedial Enlistment Program has been established. Under this program, men are accepted for enlistment when they have physical defects which can be corrected by minor surgery, or when they have a metabolic condition (overweight or underweight) which can be corrected in a short period of time. This program, however, is available only to volunteers who must, as a prerequisite to enlistment, sign a written agreement to submit to appropriate procedures for the correction of their physical defects. The Panel was of the opinion that consideration should be given to extending this program to registrants who may desire to qualify themselves to fulfill their military obligation by availing themselves of these corrective medical services.

8

3. MENTAL STANDARDS

The Department of Defense has made a determined effort to reduce mental standards for admission to military service. This effort, beginning in November 1965, was an important factor in reducing rejection rates at preinduction examinations administered to registrants. The preinduction rejection rate for all causes dropped from about fifty percent in Fiscal Year 1965 to about forty per cent in Fiscal Year 1966, and continued to decrease to a level of about thirty-four per cent in October 1966. The Department now advises that the overall rejection rate on the basis of mental standards applying to all men in the draft-age population has now been reduced to an estimated thirty per cent. The Panel agreed that it would be inadvisable to attempt to train men acquired by reducing this rejection rate below thirty per cent. The Panel commended and supports this recently adopted policy of the Department of Defense of lowering the mental qualifications for inductees to present levels, but recommended that no further lowering of the present standards be considered until experience demonstrates that the lowest group can, in a reasonable time and without excessive costs, be trained to serve effectively.

4. MORAL STANDARDS

The Department of Defense has also recently made a comprehensive study and review of the moral standards which had previously applied for induction and enlistment. This review has resulted in elimination of many technical and administrative procedures which previously had resulted in failure of inductees to be accepted into military service. The Panel strongly supported this action by the Department and recommended continuation of this review for the purpose of precluding unnecessary rejection of inductees and enlistees from military service because of minor civil offenses or because of temporary periods of probation or civil restraint.

5. SUMMARY

The Panel has been advised that changes made in the mental and medical standards by the Department of Defense will, starting in 1967, result in the acceptance of 100,000 men a year more than could meet the standards in effect on September 30, 1966. The Department further estimated that these changes in qualification standards, together with revisions now under consideration, will increase the input of men who previously failed of acceptance by approximately 100,000 (85,000 mental; 15,000 medical) a year starting October 1, 1967.

F. SO-CALLED "DRAFT CARD BURNERS"

The Panel noted with dismay the number of disloyal acts of alleged burning of draft cards or registration certificates, and that there have been reported far more incidents of burning of cards than there have been prosecutions under the law. The Panel, therefore, urged that those who destroy draft cards or certificates be severely and expeditiously punished under authority of existing law.

G. LEGAL ACTION AGAINST DRAFT EVADERS

1. The Panel was deeply concerned by what appeared to be a soft attitude on the part of public officials toward individuals who contrive to escape the privileges and responsibilities of military service to

9

country through evading the draft by illegal means. Manifestations of this attitude were noted in connection with:

(a) individuals who fail to register within the prescribed time after their eighteenth birthday, and

(b) individuals who escape service by leaving the continental limits of the United States, notably by moving to Canada.

2. The Panel inferred that the soft attitude alluded to above existed primarily because officials considered the number of individuals involved to be comparatively insignificant. A correlative attitude seemed to be that ferreting these offenders would be administratively bothersome, time-consuming, and expensive.

3. It was considered by Panel members that, regardless of the difficulties of bringing offenders to justice, no escape from a legal obligation for military service should be countenanced. The Panel reserved for this matter its strongest recommendation that "teeth" be put into procedures for identifying all such offenders and that a vigorous program of punitive action against them be undertaken. This approach should be taken against individuals in the categories enumerated above and all others who employ illegal means to escape military service.

H. THE INDUCTION AUTHORITY OF THE UNIVERSAL MILITARY TRAINING AND SERVICE ACT

The Panel closely questioned experts competent to assay whether the induction authority contained in the Universal Military Training and Service Act should be continued beyond its current expiration date of July 1, 1967. After securing the views of these experts and studying documentary material relating to the question, the Panel concluded that the induction authority should be extended. The Panel was of the opinion that the induction authority should logically be viewed as a permanent feature of the Universal Military Training and Service Act.

I. TITLE OF LAW

Although on the surface it would seem to be of little import, the Panel found that considerable confusion is created by the title of the "Universal Military Training and Service Act," which is a misnomer. Since the law provides for neither bona fide "universal training" nor "universal service" except in times of full mobilization, the Panel was of the opinion that the title of the law should be changed to reflect the selective nature of training and service which is in fact effected under this law. Accordingly, the Panel recommended changing the name of the law to "The Selective Service Act."

J. MONITORING THE SYSTEM

1. The Panel concerned itself with devising some method of achieving and maintaining optimum equity of exposure to induction and optimum uniformity in the implementation of the law throughout the Selective Service System. While endorsing the general principle of autonomy of local boards to handle special cases according to their individual merits, the Panel felt that a mechanism could be created to provide for monitoring the overall operation of the System in a way that would increase the level of uniformity without detracting from

10

the present independnet character of local boards, and thereby enhance public acceptance of the draft.

2. After considering several approaches to this problem, the Panel concluded that the objective could be achieved by Congress, itself, through its Committees on Armed Services serving as the monitoring agency to maintain surveillance over and close scrutiny of the entire administration of the Universal Military Training and Service Act. Such action of the Committees should be developed in a way that effectively supplements the present audit procedures being carried out by the Director of Selective Service, and in a way that permits the Committees to assist in achieving a reasonable degree of uniformity and to take whatever action the Committees deem appropriate to allay to a reasonable extent public suspicion that gross inequity exists.

K. STUDENT DEFERMENT POLICY

1. For many years a large percentage of full-time students registered in institutions of higher learning have been deferred until they terminated or completed their formal collegiate study, at which time they have become available for selection and possible induction.

2. Despite some criticism of deferring full-time college students, it has been a wise and necessary procedure because our national security requires a continuing input of highly educated manpower for both civilian and military needs.

3. The deferment of students has not meant that they have been protected from the draft or received favored treatment compared to non-students. In recent years sixty per cent of the college student group has served in the armed forces either as volunteers or inductees, whereas fifty-seven per cent of the non-college students were called to or entered military service.

4. During the next decade the available military manpower pool (age nineteen to twenty-six) will exceed 12,000,000 men. This is a far larger number of men than will be needed to meet foreseen military requirements. Approximately 2,000,000 eighteen-year-olds register and enter this pool each year, of which more than sixty per cent now qualify under recently-revised physical, mental, and moral standards of acceptability for service.

5. During recent years, a policy of calling the "oldest first," i.e., from the twenty-five-to-twenty-six age group and younger, has been in force. This policy has meant that all deferred, but otherwise qualified, students have been considered for induction by local boards.

6. The Panel recommends and supports in principle the Department of Defense proposal that a "Modified Age System" rather than the present policy be adopted to govern priority of induction (see Par. III.A.). Adoption of this new policy means that the majority of calls will be filled from the youngest age group, mainly those nineteen and twenty. Implementation of this policy, however, must be effected in a way that precludes adverse effects on voluntary enlistment programs and the important requirements of obtaining college-trained men, primarily from the ROTC programs, to serve as young officers. In the Panel's view, it will be necessary to continue granting deferments to all qualified individuals (see Par. III.K.8.c.) who request such deferment to attend post-high school education institutions.

7. We therefore recommend that provision be made for student deferments for all bona fide students of institutions of higher learning

who qualify for such deferment (see Par. III.K.8.c.); this deferment to remain in effect until the student terminates his student status, receives his undergraduate degree, or reaches the age of twenty-four, whichever occurs earlier, at which time the individual reverts to the I-A pool for consideration for induction by his local board with equal exposure to the draft as others then in the pool. By electing to accept a student deferment, students would be required to waive any possible entitlement to a subsequent deferment based on other than student status (for example, paternity) except in extreme hardship cases as determined by the local board.

8. The Panel recommends the following with respect to student deferments:

(a) All student deferments are to be terminated at the student's twenty-fourth birthday, with selection and possible induction to be scheduled and take place by the time the student reaches his twenty-fifth birthday.

(b) All deferred students must be returned to the nineteen-twenty-year-old group for selection and possible induction whenever their formal post-high school student status is terminated for any reason whatsoever. (The exceptions for continued student deferment after the twenty-fourth birthday or securing an undergraduate degree will be for full-time students studying medical, dental, veterinary, or related allied specialty programs in health professions and such limited additional scientific and other essential and critically-needed occupations and professions as may be designated by the National Security Council (see Par. III.L.9.). The deferred status of these groups of students is to extend until they have terminated their studies or received appropriate degrees, at which time they will be eligible for selection and induction.)

(c) Student deferments should be automatically granted by the local boards upon certification by the college or educational institution that the individual is a registered student, pursuing a full-time course of instruction and is meeting the institution's academic and other requirements to continue as a full-time member of its student body.

9. These procedures would result in elimination of the present practice of requiring each educational institution to determine and report each student's "relative class standing," and elimination of the necessity of administering the "Selective Service College Qualification Test" which, in the judgment of the Panel, was of questionable value.

L. OCCUPATIONAL DEFERMENT POLICY

1. On November 30, 1966, there were 236,590 occupational deferments. These included a variety of skills, a number of unskilled, and about 20,000 apprentices. The deferred individuals were involved in industry, science, engineering, and health resources.

2. The United States Department of Commerce maintains the official list of Currently Essential Activities. The Department of Labor maintains the official list of Currently Critical Occupations.

3. The list of Currently Essential Activities relates to aircraft, chemical and allied products, educational services, electronic equipment and electrical communication equipment, health and welfare, missile and space systems, ordnance, precision and scientific instru-

12

ments and apparatus, research and development services, ship and boat engineering and water and sewerage systems.

4. The list of Currently Critical Occupations includes occupational titles which range from physicians and aircraft and engine mechanics, apprentices, astronomers, physicists, and teachers, to tool and die makers and veterinarians, among others.

5. The criterion generally followed in the identification of the Critical Occupation is that persons employed therein are not readily available and are in short supply.

6. It is the understanding of the Panel that in the field of agriculture, due to technical developments, migration of farm workers to other employment in cities, and mechanization of farms, only about 22,000 agricultural workers have been deferred.

7. The administration of the present system of granting occupational deferments appears to be satisfactory and no evidence of abuse was presented. However, there is evidence of lack of uniformity among local boards in the identification and determination of critical skills, occupations and professions. The Panel believes that the determination of those to whom occupational deferments are granted is a matter of highest importance in the proper utilization of our most skilled human resources, especially those in shortest supply.

8. Both our national security and the armed forces require the wise and effective use of our national supply of highly specialized and highly skilled manpower. Decisions concerning the best use of our most skilled manpower should be made where the issues of total national security are the primary consideration—not just the need and demands of the military forces *per se.*

9. Therefore, the Panel recommended that the Congress amend the legislation establishing the National Security Council to provide for establishing a national manpower resources board, reporting to the National Security Council, to determine and promulgate lists of highly essential and critically-needed categories of occupations and professions, and to issue appropriate recommendations to the Director of Selective Service to enable local boards to make necessary judgments regarding deferral of each individual employed in or preparing (see Par. III.K.8.b.) for these critical and essential activities. In this connection, the Panel recommended that final determination and approval of the list of Currently Essential Activities and list of Currently Critical Occupations be vested in the National Security Council (see Par. III.L.2.).

M. CONSCIENTIOUS OBJECTORS

1. The Panel reviewed the provisions of law relating to conscientious objectors to military service along with its administration by the Selective Service System and believes that this section of law requires revision. This belief is largely predicated on two basic considerations:

(a) appeal procedures, with particular reference to the role played by the Department of Justice, have resulted in unusually long and unnecessary delays in the processing of cases involving conscientious objectors, and

(b) that a recent Supreme Court decision as reflected in the so-called Seeger case 380-US 163) unduly expanded the basis upon which individual registrants could claim conscientious objections to military service.

13

2. Information provided the Panel indicated that some appeals by conscientious objectors that had been referred to the Department of Justice for investigation and advisory opinions had resulted in delays in processing exceeding one year. This delay in the processing of conscientious objectors' appeals appears unwarranted and lends itself to possible utilization as a delaying tactic by individuals who desire to evade military service. The Panel, therefore, recommends that the provisions of law which require the referral of these cases to the Department of Justice be modified to provide that action be completed by the Department of Justice within sixty days.

3. The Supreme Court decision in the Seeger case appears to ingore the intent of Congress which, in amending the language of the 1940 Draft Act, attempted to narrow the circumstances and more clearly define the basis for claiming conscientious objection to military service. The interpretation by the Court of the language added by Congress in this regard actually resulted in a significant broadening of the basis on which these claims can be made with the very real possibility that in the future there will be an ever-increasing number of unjustified appeals for exemption from military service.

4. The Panel fully appreciates that this country has a tradition of respecting the conscience of the individual. Many people came to this country seeking freedom to employ this principle, and others came because they wished to avoid military service in their homelands.

5. Our draft law has, therefore, made adequate provision for groups which, for reasons of conscience, deny that war is a legitimate way of achieving objectives. However, there is danger in permitting the individual to be the judge in his own case. If the current interpretation of the draft law as made by the Supreme Court in the Seeger case is permitted to stand unchanged, it will, for practical purposes, permit individual registrants the right to determine for themselves whether or not they wish to bear arms in support of their country. Placed in this context, it is clear that a revision of this provision of law is imperative to ensure that the original intent of Congress in drafting this provision of law will be fulfilled.

6. In view of the foregoing circumstances, the Panel recommended that the Congress restate those provisions of the present statute relating to conscientious objectors so as to eliminate the confusion caused by the Supreme Court decision and thus provide local draft boards with comprehensible criteria for identifying bona fide conscientious objectors. In this connection, the Panel recommended that Congress give consideration to returning to the original language of the 1940 Act.

N. PUBLIC IMAGE OF MILITARY MANPOWER PROCUREMENT

1. In its review of current military manpower procurement regulations and policies and their implementation, the Panel discovered a great deal of public misunderstanding. On scrutiny, the Panel found efficiency, effectiveness, and equity in several areas which are currently the object of apparently sincere public criticism. Panel members highly praised the signal accomplishments of the Selective Service System in providing—without disrupting the economy or discriminating against any group because of race, color, or creed—the drastically varying manpower needs of the armed services through flexible and effective procedures developed over the years.

2. The Panel was disturbed by the disparity between the fairness existing in military manpower procurement practices and the inclination of the public to believe that gross unfairness prevails throughout the draft system. To alleviate this situation and to emphasize that military service is a responsibility of citizenship, it is recommended that the Director of Selective Service and the State Directors endeavor constantly to provide the public with a better understanding of the draft. In this connection, it is hoped that any action taken by the Committees on Armed Services of the Congress in response to Panel recommendations that the draft system be monitored by those Committees (see Par. III.J.) will result in the public being further informed concerning all aspects of the draft and the degree of equity that is achieved.

3. The Panel further recommended that Sec. 10 of the Universal Military Training and Service Act be amended to establish the position of Deputy Director of Selective Service for Public Affairs and that the individual be charged with informing the public concerning Selective Service operations and investigating complaints against the Selective Service System. The Panel felt that public support and acceptance of the Universal Military Training and Service Act would be eroded if action were not taken to counteract the vocal minority, which is making a continually-stronger effort to discredit the act and effect its repeal. Therefore, the Panel considered it advisable for the Deputy Director of Selective Service for Public Affairs to invite mass communications media voluntarily to assist in informing the public about the draft.

O. STATUTORY RESERVE TRAINING OBLIGATIONS

1. Under existing law, individuals who enter active military service acquire a two-fold statutory military obligation:

    (a) entrance upon active duty under the Universal Military Training and Service Act requires the performance of twenty-four months of active military service, and

    (b) concurrently with entrance on active service, the individual acquires a statutory Reserve obligation of four additional years, making him liable for a maximum of six years of Reserve military service.

2. As a consequence of the foregoing statutory requirements, those individuals who, by vitrue of involuntary or voluntary enlistment, enter active military service acquire a liability for military service extending over a six-year period. On the other hand, their civilian contemporaries who do not enter military service, completely escape this statutory requirement, and make no direct contribution in the form of military service.

3. The Reserve military obligation of six years is reduced by the number of years of active military service performed. Therefore, an inductee who performs two years of active military service, has a remaining Reserve obligation of four years' duration. This obligation requires a minimum of three additional years in the Ready Reserve and the fourth year in the Standby Reserve.

4. During the period an individual is assigned to the Ready Reserve he may be required to participate in Reserve training under regulations issued by the Secretary of Defense and implemented by the respective service secretaries. This contemplates weekly drills during

15

the three-year period plus an annual two-week period of summer training.

5. Another consequence of the Ready Reserve categorization is increased liability for recall to active duty. While in a Ready Reserve status, a reservist may be involuntarily ordered to active duty for a period not to exceed twenty-four months during national emergencies declared by the President.

6. As a practical matter, the Army, which is the principal user of Reserve military manpower, does not require three years of involuntary Reserve training. Present policy requires reservists involuntarily assigned to Reserve training units to perform not less than two years of drill participation following completion of two years of active duty along with summer training. However, although in Fiscal Year 1966, more than 141,000 Army inductees completed their two years of active military service and became available for involuntary transfer to Reserve drilling units, less than fourteen per cent of this number (or 19,400) were involuntarily assigned to such Army Reserve drilling units with the net result that the remaining "obligors" were placed in the Ready Reserves pool with, for practical purposes, no further Reserve training requirements (see Par. III.B.).

7. The inequity of this system which selects individuals for involuntary assignments to Reserve training for an additional two years is heightened by the fact that the vast majority of individuals who complete their statutory period of active service escape this additional Reserve training responsibility. The Panel, therefore, believes that some administrative device should be developed which would permit, to the maximum degree possible, a voluntary Reserve program. This would eliminate the inequity of involuntary selection for Reserve training and ensure that Reserve personnel were more receptive to training requirements with a resulting increased combat capability in Reserve units.

8. The panel emphasized that it did not recommend repeal nor modification of existing laws prescribing liability for possible recall to active service; i.e., a five-year Ready Reserve liability, and a one-year Standby Reserve liability. The Panel believed that these statutory periods of liability should continue in order to ensure the availability of a reservoir of trained military manpower to meet national emergencies or wars.

9. Panel did not propose a specific solution to the Reserve training requirements, but suggested that thorough consideration be given to employing a reenlistment bonus which would permit individuals who had completed two or more years of active service to be recruited into the Organized Reserve program on a career basis. The Panel, therefore, recommends that the Committees on Armed Services of the Congress explore this problem with a view to achieving a completely voluntary Reserve training program.

P. ANALYSIS OF THE UNIVERSAL MILITARY TRAINING AND SERVICE ACT

1. After hearing the views of the Chairman of the Committee on Armed Services; the Chief Counsel and Counsel of that Committee; the Director of Selective Service; the Commanding General of the largest Continental United States Army; the Assistant Secretary of Defense (Manpower); other representatives of the Departments of Defense and Army; State Directors of Selective Service; chairmen of

16

local boards; and after reviewing the Hearings before the Committee on Armed Services, House of Representatives, June, 1966; the testimony members of both Houses of Congress presented during those hearings; the conscription practices of several foreign nations; the Defense Department Study of the Draft, July, 1966; and many other primary reference sources; the Panel concluded that fundamentally the Universal Military Training and Service Act is an amazingly utilitarian and democratic law under which military manpower essential to the security of the nation has been consistently provided.

2. Notwithstanding the demonstrated practicality and durability of the Universal Military Training and Service Act, the Panel took notice of the fact that widespread dissatisfaction with the law had been expressed. Exploration of the principal areas of dissatisfaction, corroborated by information from many sources, established conclusively that the major discontents were, in fact, with the operation and administration of the law and policies relating thereto rather than with the law *per se;* and that much of the dissatisfaction stemmed from public misunderstanding.

3. Having accepted that the law is an effective instrument for procuring military manpower to meet the needs of the nation, the Panel turned its attention to particularizing complaints against the existing military manpower procurement mechanism. The Panel considered resentment toward the "draft system" that the Panel members had observed in their communities, expressions of discontent which Members of Congress have made for public record, news media reports of lack of acceptance of various facets of the draft, and shortcomings in the administration of the law which were commented on by experts who appeared before the Panel. The problem areas evolved are treated individually in this Report.

Q. UNIVERSAL MILITARY TRAINING

1. The Panel devoted considerable attention to the feasibility of instituting Universal Military Training as an alternative to the current "selective" system of providing military manpower. Although Universal Military Training offers certain advantages, the Panel found fallacies in the concept that Universal Military Training was a panacea for effecting equitability of opportunity and sacrifice.

2. It was the opinion of the Panel that the term "universal" embodied far-reaching implications that should be faced, and that Universal Military Training envisioned every qualified American male serving actively in the military establishments. The Panel felt that the public would not look with favor on, nor long tolerate maintaining the mammoth training base that Universal Military Training would entail, and that the public would sharply resist maintaining on active duty infinitely more men than were required for all military commitments short of all-out war.

3. The Panel concluded further that Universal Military Training would be inordinately expensive, and reacted negatively to investing a high proportion of the nation's resources in such a concept, particularly under present conditions when only a fraction of our available manpower is needed.

4. The Panel noted that the present Universal Military Training and Service Act can be "triggered" to initiate full mobilization of manpower on what would amount to a "universal" basis in the event of all-out war.

17

R. UNIVERSAL NATIONAL SERVICE

Universal National Service, Universal Government Service, etc., as alternatives to the draft which would require all young men to serve the nation in some capacity whether in military service, in the Peace Corps, in the Volunteers in Service to America (VISTA), in the National Teacher Corps, or in some other capacity, were considered unfavorably by the Panel. The Panel's opinion was that under present conditions no one should be drafted for service other than that essential to the security of the nation, and that it would be impossible to devise an acceptable formula for equating non-military service with military duty, particularly in time of war.

S. A COMPLETELY VOLUNTARY MILITARY ESTABLISHMENT

Manning all United States military organizations with volunteers attracted by massive increases in compensation was studied by the Panel. The Panel rejected this idea as an alternative to the draft on the grounds that in the opinion of the Panel it would:

(1) risk jeopardizing the security of America by depending on an uncertain method of military manpower procurement, while abandoning the invaluable flexibility inherent in current military manpower procurement systems (for example, if we had an all-volunteer military establishment tailored to the war in Vietnam or some other less-than-an-all-out combat requirement, we would need a draft mechanism to provide manpower quickly to meet additional conflicts which could be precipitated by enemy forces at a time and place of their choosing; and there appears to be no logical way of providing this needed flexibility solely through volunteer manpower),

(2) be exorbitantly expensive, and in the final analysis reprehensible to the American psychology in that it would in effect place a monetary value on the lives of citizens, creating the concept of defense of the nation by mercenaries, and

(3) abandon the unifying influences of the nation placing its faith in its own citizenry to rally to its defense when the national security is threatened.

T. STATE QUOTAS

1. The Panel supported the present formula contained in Section 5(b) of the Universal Military Training and Service Act for establishing state quotas for induction.

2. The existing formula for establishing the various state quotas for induction gives equitable and appropriate consideration to differences in population both from the standpoint of numbers and composition. The Panel did not believe that implementation of this formula has resulted in a disproportionate military service burden between the various states and, therefore, recommended against any change in this feature of the law.

U. LOTTERY

1. The Selective Service System has developed orderly procedures as a result of exacting experience over a long period of time. After men of a given age have been registered, there is control of the order in which they are considered, processed, and eventually assigned military service.

18

2. Today after many years of trial and error in the use of various systems and methods, including the lottery, date of birth establishes the sequence for the operation of Selective Service regarding each registrant. That sequence results in greater certainty than would be the case if a haphazard order were arrived at by chance or lot, and yet it does inherently contain some element of chance but with no possibility of fraud or favoritism.

3. Much of the current discussion regarding lottery whether national or local, seems to stem from the notion that such a device for developing sequence of selection is new. Historically, of course, there was in the North and the South in Civil War days the unsatisfactory use of the primitive drawing of names by lottery, accompanied by charges of fraud, manipulation, and favoritism. That experience was followed by the lottery efforts of World War I and the early part of World War II when the lottery foundered on classification. Out of those rather costly experiences grew the present system of sequence by date of birth.

4. Part of the recent agitation in favor of lottery relates to the fact that under present conditions the supply of young men exceeds the needs of the armed forces so that all those available and qualified for military service are not required for active duty (see Par. III.W.). It is largely this point from which arises charges of inequity and uncertainty which some critics believe would be relieved if young men were called for military service by use of a lottery.

5. Ideas regarding a lottery vary from those concerning a pure lottery, eliminating all deferments, to a more limited form of lottery simply to establish the sequence of induction calls for class I–A available men. A pure lottery would thereby negate the objective of Selective Service, because if there were no deferment, there would be no way of allocating and using skilled workers or scientists in essential defense industries, for example, or deferring individuals for other essential purposes.

6. As to a lottery for those registrants classified I–A, the Panel feels that a lottery substituted for date of birth in determining the order of call for induction from among I–A registrants has much less merit than the true lottery. As stated, this would be a change merely for the sake of change as there is as much and even more equity in using date of birth to determine the order as there is in conducting a lottery to make that determination. With hundreds of thousands of classifications being made each month by local boards, the I–A pool fluctuates too rapidly to lend itself to a lottery.

7. There is the argument that with the large increase of men now reaching age eighteen each year, many I–A's will reach twenty-six without having seen military service; that it would be more nearly equitable on that account to select the few who will be inducted by lot rather than by date of birth. This seemed to the Panel a peculiarly fallacious approach. Our Selective Service System must be prepared for all kinds of national emergencies. It must be able to expand or contract swiftly. The present method permits quick action, whereas a cumbersome lottery device would only impede and complicate the task. The essential weakness of the lottery rests in the inability to maintain a basic sequential order under the impact of classification which nullifies the element of pure chance.

8. We agree that the present reliable method of date-of-birth sequence evolved after the bitter experience of two World Wars and

the severe test of the Korean Conflict should remain the System's effective instrument. Thus, the classification process flows from the date-of-birth sequence, and every man is considered available for military service until he has clearly established to the appropriate local board his right to a deferred classification.

9. It is argued by some that young men of military age are entitled to more certainty as to whether they will be inducted before reaching the age of twenty-six (see Par. III.A.). Whatever uncertainty exists is largely a reflection of the overall uncertainties inherent in the international position of the United States. Our country is subject to emergencies of varying degrees. Those such as Korea and Vietnam require military service by only limited age groups. Concentrating on the elimination of all uncertainty for the individual registrant could easily endanger the national interest and security.

10. To enable the Selective Service System to perform its vital mission of procuring the military manpower required by the United States, the present flexible and tested method of date-of-birth sequence should be maintained. The Panel is firmly of the opinion that readoption of a lottery would be unwise and retrogressive.

V. APPLICATION OF ELECTRONIC DATA PROCESSING TO SELECTIVE SERVICE

1. The question has been raised as to whether a more equitable method of selection should be considered in administering the Selective Service System which would be national in scope, uniform, and centralized by the use of automatic data processing equipment.

2. The discussion by the Panel of the advantages of introducing modern office techniques to the Selective Service System was primarily concerned with studies made by knowledgeable representatives from companies in the field of data processing. These companies failed to advance a system that would be useful to the local boards.

3. It was evident to the Panel from testimony received throughout its proceedings that the success of the Selective Service System was based on the autonomy of local boards. Changing to a centralized data processing system located in Washington would lessen the confidence of communities in the draft, as any such non-personalized centralized system would reduce the local boards to reporting agencies.

W. LIMITED USE OF MANPOWER CREATES INEQUITIES

1. The Panel took cognizance of the irony in the fact that much dissatisfaction with the draft results from an overabundance of manpower to meet the limited calls of recent years in that so few are selected from so many. The Panel concluded that most complaints of inequities in the administration of the draft would disappear if all available manpower were being mobilized. It should again be emphasized that objections to the draft relate primarily to the fact that only a small percentage of available men need to be inducted. This necessitates leaving uncalled the preponderance of young American manhood, and observing the great numbers of men who are not inducted creates serious questions of equity on the part of these comparatively few who are called on to serve.

2. It is patent that any "selective" system inherently contains inequities. The Panel, therefore, recognized that inequities would exist as long as some are called while some are deferred. However,

20

the Panel undertook to minimize such inequities by recommending changes in law and procedure that would equalize to the maximum extent possible exposure to call for induction.

IV. RECOMMENDATIONS OF THE PANEL

Based on the foregoing discussion and the various conclusions enunciated earlier in this Report, the Panel submits the following recommendations for appropriate action by the agency indicated below as having cognizance over the matter.

A. RECOMMENDATIONS FOR THE PRESIDENT OF THE UNITED STATES

1. Age (See Par. III.A.)

That the "Modified Young Age Class System" described in Par. III.A.3. be adopted.

2. Six-Month Enlistment—Reserve Enlistment Program (REP) (See Par. III.B.1.)

a. General:

(1) That the secretary of the respective military services order to active duty for twenty-four months, including any period of active duty previously performed, any individual REP who does not participate satisfactorily in a unit of the National Guard or Organized Reserve during the period of his military obligation if at least fifteen months remain to be served on his active duty commitment.

(2) That provision be made for the secretary of the military service concerned to grant an exception to the foregoing policy when circumstances warrant, and that in such cases the individual be discharged from the Reserve component concerned and reported for disposition to the Selective Service System.

b. Professional Athletes (see Par. III.B.2.): That the Department of Defense policy with respect to the Reserve Component Enlistment Standards and Procedures, which was promulgated on December 22, 1966 to become effective prior to February 1, 1967, be altered to provide that, in the case of professional athletes, no exception be made to the provision of the policy which states that "It shall be normal practice to accept the earliest applicant for enlistment who meets the minimum qualifications for a vacancy and whose availability to serve the unit is assured."

3. Utilization of Reserve Forces by Ordering Them to Active Duty During Periods of High Induction Calls (See Par. III.C.3.)

That the President spread the burden of the Vietnam war more equitably between inductees and reservists by ordering some reservists to active duty.

4. Local Board Procedures (See Par. III.D.)

a. That the Director of Selective Service schedule periodic regional meetings of local board members to exchange ideas and discuss common problems, with a representative of the Director of Selective Service present to ensure the effectiveness of such meetings.

b. That the title of the position of Chief Clerk of each local board be changed to "Executive Secretary."

c. That the Director of Selective Service establish in local boards, as a function of the "Executive Secretary," procedures for referring returning veterans to appropriate agencies qualified to assist them in readjusting in their home communities (see Par. III.D.2.).

5. PYHSICAL STANDARDS (SEE PAR. III.E.2.)

That consideration be given to extending the benefits of the Medically-Remedial Enlistment Program to registrants who may desire to qualify to fulfill their military obligation by availing themselves of the corrective medical services of the Program.

6. MORAL STANDARDS (SEE PAR. III.E.4.)

That the Department of Defense review of moral standards applicable to involuntary induction and voluntary enlistment be continued to preclude unnecessary rejection of inductees and enlistees because of minor civil offenses and because of temporary periods of probation or civil restraint.

7. SO-CALLED "DRAFT CARD BURNERS" (SEE PAR. III.F.)

That those who destroy draft cards or certificates be severely and expeditiously punished under authority of law.

8. LEGAL ACTION AGAINST DRAFT EVADERS (SEE PAR. III.G.)

That a vigorous program be undertaken to identify, apprehend, and take punitive action against individuals who:

(a) fail to register within the prescribed time after their eighteenth birthday, and

(b) escape service by leaving the continental limits of the United States, notably by moving to Canada.

9. IMPROVING PUBLIC UNDERSTANDING OF THE DRAFT (SEE PAR. III.N.2.)

That the Director of Selective Service and State Directors endeavor constantly to provide the public with a better understanding of the draft (see related recommendation in Par. IV.B.8.)

B. RECOMMENDATIONS FOR THE CONGRESS OF THE UNITED STATES

1. INDUCTION AUTHORITY (see Par. III.H.)

That the induction authority contained in the Universal Military Training and Service Act be extended.

2. TITLE OF THE LAW (see Par. III.I.)

That the title of the "Universal Military Training and Service Act" be changed to "The Selective Service Act."

3. MONITORING THE SYSTEM (see Par. III.J.2.)

That the Committees on Armed Services of the Congress serve as monitoring agency to maintain surveillance over and close scrutiny of the overall administration of the Universal Military Traning and Service Act with a view to achieving optimum uniformity in the implementation of the law.

4. STUDENT DEFERMENT POLICY (see Par. III.K.)

a. That deferment be granted for bona fide students of institutions of higher learning who request and qualify for such deferment and that this deferment remain in effect until the student terminates his student status, receives his undergraduate degree, or reaches the age of twenty-four, whichever occurs earlier, at which time the individual would revert to the I–A pool for consideration for induction by his local board with equal exposure to the draft as others then in the pool, with the understanding that a student so deferred would waive any possible entitlement to subsequnet deferment based on other than student status (for example, paternity) except in extreme hardship cases as determined by the local board.

b. That student deferment be automatically granted by local boards on certification by an insitution of higher learning that the individual is a registered student, pursuing a full-time course of instruction and meeting the institution's requirements to continue as a full-time member of its student body.

c. That exceptions for continued student deferment after the twenty-fourth birthday or securing an undergraduate degree be granted only for full-time students studying medical, dental, veterinary, or related allied specialty programs in health professions and such limited additional scientific and other essential and critically-needed occupations and professions as may be designated by the National Security Council (see Par. III.K.8.b.).

5. OCCUPATIONAL DEFERMENT POLICY (see Par. III.L.)

a. That legislation establishing the National Security Council be amended to provide for establishing a national manpower resources board, reporting to the National Security Council, to determine and promulgate lists of highly essential and critically-needed categories of occupations and professions, and to issue appropriate recommendations to the Director of Selective Service to enable local boards to make necessary judgments regarding deferral for each individual employed in or preparing (see Par. III.K.8.b.) for these critical and essential activities.

b. That final determination and approval of the List of Currently Essential Activities and List of Currently Critical Occupations be vested in the National Security Council (see Par. III.L.2.).

6. CONSCIENTIOUS OBJECTORS (SEE PAR. III.M.)

a. That the wording of section 6(j) of the Universal Military Training and Service Act with respect to conscientious objectors be changed to provide local draft boards with understandable criteria for identifying bona fide conscientious objectors, and that Congress give consideration to returning to the language that dealt with the subject in the Draft Act of 1940.

b. That provisions of law which require referral of appeals to the Department of Justice in the case of those seeking conscientious objector status be modified to provide that action be completed by the Department of Justice within sixty days.

23

7. Authority To Order Reserve Forces to Active Duty Without Declaring a New National Emergency (see Par. III.C.4.)

That the President be given permanent statutory authority to order Reserve forces to active duty without the necessity of declaring that a new national emergency exists.

8. Deputy Director of Selective Service for Public Affairs (see Par. III.N.3.)

That section 10 of the University Military Training and Service Act be amended to establish the position of Deputy Director of Selective Service for Public Affairs, and that the individual be charged with informing the public concerning Selective Service operations and investigating complaints against the Selective Service System.

9. A Volunttary Reserve Training Program (see Par. III.0.9.)

That consideration be given to employing a reenlistment bonus to induce individuals who have completed two or more years of active service to enlist voluntarily in the Organized Reserve Program on a career basis with a view to achieving a completely voluntary Reserve training program.

10. Tenure of Local Board Members (see Par. III.D.1.)

That the tenure of local draft board members be limited to ten years.

C. OTHER RECOMMENDATIONS WITH RESPECT TO CERTAIN ASPECTS OF MILITARY MANPOWER PROCUREMENT

1. Retention of the Universal Military Training and Service Act (see Par. III.P.)

That the Universal Military Training and Service Act be retained with the modifications herein recommended as the legal basis for insuring the availability of necessary military manpower for the defense of the United States.

2. Universal Military Training (See Par. III.Q.)

That Universal Military Training not be instituted as the means of providing military manpower for the United States under present conditions.

3. Universal National Service (See Par. III.R.)

That no one be drafted for service other than that essential to the security of the nation, and that no effort be made to equate nonmilitary service with military duty.

4. A Completely Voluntary Military Establishment (See Par. III.S.)

That the concern of attempting to satisfy all future military manpower requirements with volunteers attracted by massive increases in compensation be rejected as an alternative to the draft.

24

5. State Quotas (See Par. III.T.)

That no changes be made in the formula currently employed to establish state quotas for induction.

6. Lottery (See Par. III.U.10.)

That a lottery not be adopted to perform any of the functions of the Selective Service System.

7. Limited Trainability (See Par. III.E.1.)

That the military service not be forced to accept inductees and enlistees whose trainability to render effective military service is questionable.

8. Mental Standards (See Par. III.E.3.)

That the Department of Defense make no further attempt to reduce existing mental standards of acceptability for inductees until the long-term implications of present low acceptance standards have been evaluated by the military service.

9. Application of Electronic Data Processing to Selective Service (See Par. III.V.)

That a data processing system centralized in Washington not be adopted as an administrative device of the Selective Service System at this time.

10. Authority of Local Boards (See Par. III.D.4)

That care be exercised to ensure that any effort to establish greater uniformity in local board actions avoids diminishing the discretionary authority of local draft boards.

APPENDIXES

Appendix A

Experts Who Appeared at the Request of the Panel

Mr. John R. Blandford, Chief Counsel, Committee on Armed Services, House of Representatives.
Col. Bernard R. Franck, III, Chief, Legislation and Liaison, Headquarters, Selective Service System.
Hon. Durward G. Hall (R-Mo.), member of House Committee on Armed Services.
Lt. Gen. Lewis B. Hershey, USA, Ret., Director, Selective Service System.
Lt. Col. Maxwell O. Jensen, USAR, Asst. Chief, Legislation and Liaison Hdqs. Selective Service System.
Maj. Gen. Thomas A. Kenan, USA, Deputy Chief, Office of Reserve Components, Department of the Army.
Hon. Thomas D. Morris, Asst. Secretary of Defense (Manpower).
Lt. Gen. Charles W. G. Rich, USA, Chief, Office of Reserve Components, Department of the Army.
The Honorable L. Mendel Rivers, Chairman, Committee on Armed Services, House of Representatives.
Mr. Frank M. Slatinshek, Counsel, Committee on Armed Services, House of Representatives.
Lt. Gen. Louis Truman, Commanding General, Third U.S. Army.
Col. Ralph L. Whitt, USA, Chief, Personnel Division, Office of Reserve Components, Department of the Army.
Dr. Harold Wool, Director for Procurement Policy, Office of the Assistant Secretary of Defense (Manpower).

NOTE.—Although not invited to appear in person before the Panel, the following heads of major veterans' organizations were invited to present to the Panel, in writing, their views on military manpower procurement:

Mr. John E. Davis, National Commander, The American Legion.
Mr. Leslie M. Fry, Commander in Chief, Veterans of Foreign Wars of the U.S.
Mr. A. Leo Anderson, National Commander, American Veterans of World War II and Korea.

A similar invitation was extended to the Executive Director, American Veterans Committee, in response to a letter she addressed to the Chairman of the Panel on December 21, 1966.

Appendix B

Acknowledgments

The Panel acknowledged with gratitude the generous assistance of the following individuals who provided administrative advice and support to the members of the Panel while the Panel was in formal session:

Mr. John R. Blandford, Chief Counsel, Committee on Armed Services.
Mr. Frank M. Slatinshek, Counsel, Committee on Armed Services.
Miss Bernice Kalinowski, Secretary to Mr. Slatinshek, Committee on Armed Services.
Mrs. Cora Lee Bull, Administrative Assistant to the Honorable L. Mendel Rivers (D-S.C.).

In addition to the above, the Panel expressed deep appreciation for all the individuals who appeared before the Panel as experts (see Appendix A).

PANEL PERSONNEL

General Mark W. Clark, U.S. Army (Retired), Chairman. He was graduated from the United States Military Academy in 1917, and holds sixteen honorary degrees. In 1942 he served as Chief of Staff of Army Ground Forces before going to England in June 1942, as Commanding General of the II Corps. He became Deputy Commander-in-Chief of Allied Forces in North Africa in October, 1942, and in January, 1943, was named Commanding General of the Fifth U.S. Army, and in December, 1944, he was placed in command of the 15th Army Group, consisting of the Fifth U.S. Army and the Eighth British Army. On May 2, 1945, General Clark accepted the surrender of all German forces in Italy.

In June, 1945, General Clark was appointed Commander-in-Chief of U.S. Occupation Forces in Austria and U.S. High Commissioner for Austria. In 1947 he was deputy to the U.S. Secretary of State and sat in London and Moscow with the Council of Foreign Ministers negotiating a treaty for Austria.

General Clark was Chief of Army Field Forces from 1949 to 1952 when he was appointed Commander-in-Chief, Far East Command, serving simultaneously as Commander-in-Chief, United Nations Command; Commanding General, U.S. Army Forces, Far East, and Governor of the Ryukyu Islands.

On July 27, 1953, General Clark signed a military armistice agreement between the United Nations Command and the military commanders of the North Korean Army and the Chinese People's Volunteers. The General retired from the Army on October 31, 1953, and accepted the presidency of The Citadel, The Military College of South Carolina. On July 1, 1965, he retired from the presidency of The Citadel and became president emeritus of the college.

General Clark has been awarded the Distinguished Service Cross and many other U.S. and foreign decorations.

Hon. W. Sterling Cole, Vice-Chairman. Mr. Cole was graduated from Colgate University in 1925, and earned his LL.B. degree from Albany Law School of Union University in 1929, and he holds three honorary degrees. He was a Member of the U.S. House of Representatives in the 74th to the 85th Congresses, and previously was a public school teacher in 1925–26.

Mr. Cole was elected by the unanimous vote of the constituent countries and resigned his seat in Congress to become the first Director General of the International Atomic Energy Agency, Vienna, Austria from 1957 to 1961. He also served as a member of the Joint Committee on Atomic Energy of the U.S. Congress from 1947 to 1957 and was Chairman in 1953–54. He was a member of the Armed Services Committee of the House while in Congress. He is a lieutenant commander, U.S. Naval Reserve (Retired) and a Member of Phi Beta Kappa.

Mr. Cole is a member of the Cole and Norris law firm in Washington.

Earl H. Blaik, Member. Mr. Blaik was graduated from Miami University (Ohio) in 1918 and from the U.S. Military Academy in 1920. He holds an honorary LL.D. degree from Miami University.

He resigned from the Army in 1923 to enter the building business, and from 1927 to 1934 was part-time football coach for the U.S. Military Academy. He was head football coach at Dartmouth College from 1934 to 1941 when he became head football coach at the U.S. Military Academy. In 1949 he was named Athletic Director and Chairman of the Athletic Board, in addition to his position as head football coach.

Mr. Blaik served as a lieutenant colonel in the U.S. Army commencing in 1943, and was promoted to colonel of cavalry in 1944. He was named Coach of the Year in 1946. He received the National Football Foundation's Gold Medal award in 1966 for conspicuous service to his country.

He was Vice-president and Director of the Avco Corporation 1959–60, and became Chairman of the Executive Committee of that corporation in 1960.

Dr. Jerome H. Holland, Member. He was graduated from Cornell University in 1939 and received his M.S. degree from that institution in 1941. He received his Ph.D. degree from the University of Pennsylvania in 1950, and he holds four honorary degrees.

Dr. Holland was successively instructor in sociology and physical education and assistant coach at Lincoln University from 1939 to 1942, a personnel director for Sun Shipbuilding and Dry Dock Company from 1942 to 1946, Director of the Division of Political and Social Sciences and football coach at Tennessee Agricultural and Industrial State University from 1947 to 1951. From 1951 to 1953 he conducted social research for the Pew Memorial Foundation. He was Presi-

28

dent of Delaware State College from 1953 until 1960 when he assumed the presidency of Hampton Institute.

Author of several books and articles, Dr. Holland has served on numerous civic and governmental boards.

Dr. Frederick L. Hovde, Member. Dr. Hovde was graduated from the University of Minnesota in 1929, and earned his M.A. degree from Oxford University which he attended as a Rhodes Scholar from 1929 to 1932. He holds thirteen honorary degrees.

From 1932 to 1936 he was Assistant to the Director, General College, University of Minnesota, and from 1936 to 1941 he was Assistant to the President, University of Rochester. In 1941–42 he served as Head, London Mission of the Office of Scientific Research and Development, Washington, D.C. The following year he was Executive Assistant to the Chairman, National Defense Research Commission, and from 1950 to 1952 he was Chairman, Building Research Advisory Committee, National Research Council. He was Chairman, Board of Foreign Scholarships, Department of State from 1951 to 1955, and in 1961 he was Chairman, President's Task Force Commission on Education.

Dr. Hovde has been president of Purdue University since 1946.

Hon. Robert D. Murphy, Member. Mr. Murphy received his undergraduate education at Marquette University and received LL.E. and L.M. degrees from George Washington University in 1920 and 1928, respectively, and he holds fourteen honorary degrees.

After serving briefly in the Post Office and Treasury Departments, Mr. Murphy served in the Diplomatic Corps from 1921 until 1959 when he assumed the presidency of Corning Glass International.

Mr. Murphy was Counselor of Embassy in Paris in 1940 and charge d'affaires, Vichy from July to August of that year. He was sent by President Roosevelt to investigate conditions in French North Africa in 1942 and became the President's personal representative with the rank of Minister.

The rank of Ambassador was bestowed on Mr. Murphy in 1943 for his appointment as United States political adviser Allied Force Headquarters. He was appointed United States political adviser for Germany in 1944, and Director, Office of German and Austrian Affairs, Department of State, in 1949. He was Ambassador to Belgium to 1949 to 1952, and to Japan in 1952. In 1953 he was made Assistant Secretary of State for United Nations Affairs and later Deputy Under Secretary of State. Six years later he was named Under Secrerary of State for Political Affairs. He holds several foreign and United States military awards, and is the author of the book, *Diplomat Among Warriors.*

Rt. Rev. Maurice S. Sheehy, Member. Msgr. Sheehy received his A.B. degree from Loras College and was graduated from St. Paul Seminary in 1922. He received his S.T.B. degree from Catholic University, and holds three honorary degrees.

He was Professor and Athletic Director, Loras College from 1922 to 1927. He was associated with Catholic University from 1927 to 1958, and headed the department of religion there for 20 years.

In 1958 Msgr. Sheehy was promoted to the rank of vice admiral in the U.S. Naval Reserve (Chaplain Corps), with which he served during World War II.

He was domestic prelate to Pope Pius XII and named prothonotary apostalic by Pope John XXIII, and he served as dean of the Cedar Rapids Catholic Church from 1958 until his retirement in 1966.

Msgr. Sheehy is author of several books and articles on religious subjects.

Charles E. Saltzman, Member. Mr. Saltzman attended Cornell University for a year before entering the U.S. Military Academy from which he was graduated in 1925. He received his M.A. degree in 1928 from Oxford University which he attended as a Rhodes scholar.

After five years with the New York Telephone Company with which he began his business career, he became Assistant to the Executive Vice-president of the New York Stock Exchange and was later Secretary and Vice-president of the Exchange. He was Assistant Secretary of State from 1947 to 1949, and a partner in Henry Sears and Co., from 1949 to 1956. In 1954–55 he was Under Secretary of State for Administration. He became a partner in Goldman, Sachs and Co. in 1956.

Saltzman served in the U.S. Army from 1925 to 1930 when he entered the New York National Guard. He returned to active duty with the Army from 1940 to 1946, serving overseas, and is a major general, U.S. Army Reserve (Retired). He holds a number of United States and foreign decorations.

Lt. Col. Dennis D. Nicholson, Jr., U.S. Marine Corps (Retired), Executive Coordinator. Colonel Nicholson, who retired from the Marine Corps in 1958 after more than twenty years' service has been Public Relations Director of The Citadel for the past seven years. Since 1965 he has also served as Executive Assistant to the President of The Citadel.

APPENDIX II

IN PURSUIT OF EQUITY:

WHO SERVES WHEN NOT ALL SERVE?

SUMMARY OF THE REPORT OF THE NATIONAL ADVISORY COMMISSION ON SELECTIVE SERVICE

Sweeping changes have come to our society since the system for selecting men for induction into the Armed Forces was established a quarter of a century ago.

Among them are two which work with opposite effect on the manpower situation: A dramatic population growth has increased the supply of eligible men available for military service. But changes in military technology and transitions in strategic concepts have at the same time modified manpower requirements for national security. Of the nearly 2 million men now reaching draft age each year, our Armed Forces are likely to need only half to one-third of them, varying with the circumstances. And of those, only a portion must be selected for nonvoluntary induction. (The range in recent years has been from 10 to 40 percent, depending on the total size of the force level.) The problem which results, and which confronted this Commission, as one member expressed it for all the others, is: Who serves when not all serve?

It is an enduring problem, but floodlighted today by the war in Vietnam. The echo of American battle fire impels, as it always should, the hard probe for better solutions.

The Commission saw as its overriding obligation the necessity to search for a method of manpower procurement which would assure the Armed Forces' ability to acquire the men they need, under any circumstances, to protect the nation's security and meet its commitments; and at the same time function as uniformly and equitably as possible with due regard for the problems and the rights of the individuals into whose lives it must intrude.

Following the mandate of its charter, the Commission examined proposals ranging from elimination of all compulsory service to compulsion for all.

Aware of the spirit of social concern that animates much of young America today, the Commission considered whether other programs such as the Peace Corps and VISTA, elevating society and benefiting the participants alike, could be developed and serve as substitutes for military service.

It made a thorough study of the Selective Service System as it presently works — the entire system, from the policies that guide its nationwide operation to the actual functioning of its local draft boards; the procedures by which men are examined, classified, and readied for induction; the variety of deferments and exemptions, and the factors which influence them; the appeals machinery; the people's attitude toward the system itself.

It reviewed the administrative procedures governing enlistment into the Army Reserve and National Guard which have subjected those components to wide and often legitimate public criticism.

Its search directed Commission attention to serious defects in our national life. Of each group of men coming to draft age each year, from one-fourth to one-third of those examined are found ineligible for service because of educational or health deficiencies or both; almost 700,000 potential draftees were found unqualified to serve in the last fiscal year. A total of 5 million men between the ages of 18½ and 34 who have been examined for the draft are today considered ineligible to serve. The Commission studied the implication of these figures as they affect the national security and reveal weaknesses in our society.

In pursuit of the answers to all the questions it faced, the Commission sought to hear the nation's voice. It invited the opinions of more than 120 organizations across the country, reflecting every sector of the society; a group of college student leaders; some 250 editors of student newspapers; each of the more than 4,000 local draft boards and the 97 appeal boards; many prominent private citizens; every Governor, the head of every appropriate Federal department and agency, the mayors of a number of cities. Answers came from many of these sources. The Commission had access to and studied the testimony and data provided in Congressional hearings. Members conferred with political leaders and college presidents and representatives of the poor. Observers attended and reported on three national conferences on the draft. The Commission listened to specialists who spoke on particular points of law and military need, management procedures and the values of social programs. And finally it had letters, which it gratefully acknowledges, from people across the land who voiced their suggestions, their convictions, their resentments, and their hopes.

But seeking to know the national mind was not, of course, enough. In the diversity of its interests, the nation does not think with one mind, or speak with one voice. To meet its responsibility, the Commission had to find its own answers, based on its own comprehension of issues that involve both the national welfare and the rights of the individual.

After long and careful deliberation, those answers are presented here in summary form, and discussed in detail in the body of this report.

*　　　*　　　*　　　*　　　*　　　*　　　*

To provide a flexible system of manpower procurement which will assure the Armed Forces' ability to meet their national security commitments under all foreseeable circumstances, the Commission recommends:

1. Continuation of a selective service system.

To make the controlling concept of that system the rule of law, rather than a policy of discretion, so as to assure equal treatment for those in like circumstances, the Commission recommends:

2. A consolidated selective service system under more centralized administration to be organized and operated as follows:

A. National headquarters should formulate and issue clear and binding policies concerning classifications, exemptions, and deferments, to be applied uniformly throughout the country.

B. A structure of eight regional offices (aligned for national security purposes with the eight regions of the Office of Emergency Planning) should be established to administer the policy and monitor its uniform application.

C. An additional structure of area offices should be established on a population basis with at least one in each state. At these offices men would be registered and classified in accordance with the policy directives disseminated from national headquarters. (The Commission sees the possibility of 300-500 of these offices being able to answer the national need.)

(1) The use of modern data-handling equipment, as well as the application of uniform rules, would facilitate processing, registration, and classification.

(2) Under appropriate regulations, registrants would change their registration from one area office to another as they changed their permanent residence.

D. Local boards, composed of volunteer citizens, would operate at the area office level as the registrants' court of first appeal.

E. These changes should be made in the organization of the local boards:

(1) Their composition should represent all elements of the public they serve.

(2) The maximum term of service should be 5 years.

(3) A maximum retirement age should be established.

(4) The President's power to appoint members should not be limited to those nominated by the governors of the states.

(5) Women should be eligible to serve.

F. The entire appeals process should be made uniform and strengthened in the following ways:

(1) The registrant should be able to appeal his classification to his local board within 30 days instead of the 10 days presently stipulated.

(2) Local boards should put their decisions in writing so appeal boards will have the benefit of the record in making their decisions, and the registrant will be able to know the reasons for the decision.

(3) Appeal boards should be colocated with the eight regional offices, although operate independently of them. The National Selective Service (Presidential) Appeal Board would remain as presently constituted.

(4) Appeal agents should be readily available at the area offices to assist registrants in making appeals.

(5) An adequate number of panels should be established, above the local board level, for the specific purpose of hearing conscientious objector cases on an expedited basis.

To remove widespread public ignorance concerning the operations of the Selective Service System, the Commission recommends:

3. Both the registrant and the general public should be made fully acquainted with the workings of the improved system and the registrant's rights under it, in these ways:

A. Easily understandable information should be prepared in written form and made available to all registrants each time they are classified.

B. An adviser to registrants should be readily available at the area office to inform and counsel registrants who need assistance with registration and classification problems.

C. Public information procedures regarding the entire system should be made more effective by national headquarters.

To reduce the uncertainty in personal lives that the draft creates, and to minimize the disruption it often causes in the lives of those men who are called, the Commission recommends:

4. The present "oldest first" order of call should be reversed so that the youngest men, beginning at age 19, are taken first.

To further reduce uncertainty and to insure fairness in the selection of inductees from a large pool of eligible men, when all are not needed, the Commission recommends:

5. Draft-eligible men should be inducted into service as needed according to an order of call which has been impartially and randomly determined. The procedure would be as follows:

A. At age 18, all men would register, and as soon as practicable thereafter would receive the physical, moral, and educational achievement tests and evaluations which determine their eligibility for military service according to Department of Defense standards. (This universal testing would meet social as well as military needs.)

B. Those found to be qualified for service (I—A) who would reach the age of 19 before a designated date would be included in a pool of draft eligibles. Those men reaching 19 after that date would be placed in a later draft-eligible pool.

C. The names of all men in the current draft-eligible pool would be arranged in an order of call for the draft through a system of impartial random selection.

D. For a specified period (a year, or possibly less), men in the pool would undergo their maximum vulnerability to the draft. Induction, according to the needs of the Department of Defense throughout that period, would be in the sequence determined by the impartial and random process.

E. When the specified period of maximum vulnerability had elapsed, an order of call would be determined for a new group of men, and the remaining men in the previous pool would not be called unless military circumstances first required calling all of the men in the new group.

6. No further student or occupational deferments should be granted, with these exceptions:

A. Under appropriate regulations which will safeguard against abuses, students who are in school and men who are in recognized apprentice training when this plan goes into effect will be permitted to complete the degrees or programs for which they are candidates. Upon termination of those deferments they will be entered into the random selection pool with that year's 18-year-olds.

B. Thereafter, men who are already in college when they are randomly selected for service would be permitted to finish their sophomore year before induction.

C. Men who undertake officer training programs in college should be deferred, provided they commit to serve in the Armed Forces as enlisted men if they do not complete their officer programs.

(These represent majority decisions; a minority of the Commission favors continued student deferment.)

D. Hardship deferments, which defy rigid classification but which must be judged realistically on individual merits, would continue to be granted.

7. Study should begin now to determine the feasibility of a plan which would permit all men who are selected at 18 for induction to decide themselves when,

between the ages of 19 and 23, to fulfill that obligation. Inducements would be offered to make earlier choice more attractive, and the option of choice could always be canceled if manpower needs were not met. If the feasibility of this plan is confirmed, the plan should be put into effect as soon as possible.

To broaden the opportunities for those who wish to volunteer for military service, the Commission recommends:

8. Opportunities should be made available for more women to serve in the Armed Forces, thus reducing the numbers of men who must involuntarily be called to duty.

9. The Department of Defense should propose programs to achieve the objective, insofar as it proves practicable, of accepting volunteers who do not meet induction standards but who can be brought up to a level of usefulness as a soldier, even if this requires special educational and training programs to be conducted by the armed services.

To remove the inequities in the enlistment procedures of the Reserve and National Guard programs, the Commission recommends:

10. Direct enlistment into Reserve and National Guard forces should not provide immunity from the draft for those with no prior service except for those who enlist before receiving their I–A classification.

11. If the Reserves and National Guard units are not able to maintain their force levels with volunteers alone, they should be filled by inductions. Inductions would be determined by the same impartial random selection system which determines the order of call for active duty service.

The Commission supports recommendations presented to it by the National Advisory Commission on Health Manpower and the Department of State:

12. A national computer file of draft eligible health professionals should be established to assist selective service area offices to place their calls for doctors and dentists and allied professions so as to cause minimum disruption in the medical needs of the community.

13. Policies governing the drafting of aliens in the United States should be modified in the following ways to make those policies more equitable and bring them into closer conformity with the country's treaty arrangements:

A. All nonimmigrant aliens should be exempt from military service.
B. Resident aliens should not be subject to military service until 1 year after their entry into the United States as immigrants.

C. One year after entry, all resident aliens should be subject to military draft equally with U.S. citizens unless they elect to abandon permanently the status of permanent alien and the prospect of U.S. citizenship.

D. Aliens who have served 12 months or more in the Armed Forces of a country with which the United States is allied in mutual defense activities should be exempted from U.S. military service, and credit toward the U.S. military service obligation should be given for any such service of a shorter period.

*   *   *   *   *   *   *

In arriving at the recommendations presented herein, the Commission considered other propositions which it rejected. Among them were:

1. Elimination of the draft and reliance on an all-volunteer military force.

Although there are many arguments against an exclusively volunteer force, the decisive one, the Commission concluded, was its inflexible nature, allowing no provision for the rapid procurement of larger numbers of men if they were needed in times of crisis.

2. A system of universal training.

In the context in which the Commission studied it, universal training is a program designed by its proponents to offer physical fitness, self-discipline and remedial training to great numbers of young Americans – and not a substitute for the draft. The Commission concluded that:

A. Such a program cannot be justified on the grounds of military need, and

B. Compulsion is not a proper means of accomplishing the worthwhile objectives of rehabilitation.

The problem of men rejected for service for health and educational deficiencies, to which universal training is directed, is one which presents the country with a tragedy of urgent dimensions. Recommendations in this report will, the Commission hopes, help to alleviate this problem. The proposal to examine all 18-year-old men (recommendation 5A, p.6) will help in identifying the problems and obtaining assistant for those rejected. (See ch. VIII.) The proposal to permit men failing to meet induction standards to volunteer for service and receive special training (recommendation 9, p. 7) will also be of value. But the larger part of this problem is imbedded in the conditions of the rejected men's lives, such as discrimination and poverty. It is essential to the future of the country that further steps be taken to correct those conditions before they can grow – as they are growing now – into a national shame and a threat to the nation's security.

3. A system of compulsory national service; and along with that,

4. Volunteer national service as an alternative to military service.

The Commission found first of all that there are difficult questions of public policy – and a lack of constitutional basis – involved in compulsory national service. Second, it concluded that no fair way exists to equate voluntary service programs with military service.

Volunteer national service must, then, be considered on its own merits as a separate program unrelated to military service. That there is a spirited interest in such service today is abundantly clear. But the needs which such service would meet and the way in which programs would be administered and financed are matters which are still inconclusive. The Commission received no clear or precise answers to the questions it raised concerning them. The Commission is sensitive to the spirit which motivates the desire for national service, and it suggests further research to define the issues more clearly, together with public and private experimentation with pilot programs.

5. Recognition as conscientious objectors of those opposed to particular wars (instead of war in any form).

There is support within the Commission for this proposal. However, a majority of the Commission opposes it. The Commission majority believes, moreover, that the recent Supreme Court decision in *U.S. v. Seeger* offers sufficient guidance in defining the standards of the conscientious objector's position. That decision interprets the statute's requirement that conscientious objection be based on religious training and belief, to include "a given belief that is sincere and meaningful [and] occupies a place in the life of its possessor parallel to that filled by the orthodox belief in God of one who clearly qualifies for the exemption."

*   *   *   *   *   *   *

There remains another point to be made in this summary:

The Commission gave careful study to the effect of the draft on and its fairness to the Negro. His position in the military manpower situation is in many ways disproportionate, even though he does not serve in the Armed Forces out of proportion to his percentage of the population. He is underrepresented (1.3 percent) on local draft boards. The number of men rejected for service reflects a much higher percentage (almost 50 percent) of Negro men found disqualified than of whites (25 percent). And yet, recent studies indicate that proportionately more (30 percent) Negroes of the group qualified for service are drafted than whites (18 percent) – primarily because fewer Negroes are admitted into Reserve or officer training programs. Enlistment rates for qualified Negroes and whites are about equal, but reenlistments for Negroes are higher: Department of Defense figures show that the rate of first-term reenlistments is now more than double that of white troops. Negro soldiers have a high record of volunteering for service in elite combat units. This is reflected in, but could not be said to be the sole reason for, the Negro's overrepresentation in combat (in terms of his proportion of the population): Although Negro troops account for only 11 percent of the total U.S. enlisted personnel in Vietnam, Negro soldiers comprise 14.5 percent of all Army units, and in Army combat units the proportion is, according to the Department of Defense, "appreciably higher" than that. During the first 11 months of 1966, Negro soldiers totaled 22.4 percent of all Army troops killed in action.

There are reasons to believe, the Commission finds, that many of the statistics are comparable for some other minority groups, although precise information is not available. Social and economic injustices in the society itself are at the root of inequities which exist. It is the Commission's hope that the recommendations contained in this report will have the effect of helping to correct those inequities.

APPENDIX III

Public Law 90-40
90th Congress, S. 1432
June 30, 1967
81 STAT. 100

An Act to amend the Universal Military Training and Service Act, and for other purposes.

Be it enacted by the Senate and House of Representatives of the United States of America in Congress assembled, That the Universal Military Training and Service Act is amended as follows:

(1) Section 1(a) [(50 App. U.S.C. 451 (a)] is amended to read as follows: "(a) This Act may be cited as the 'Military Selective Service Act of 1967'."

(2) Section 4 (50 App. U.S.C. 454) is amended by:

(a) Inserting after the first proviso of subsection (a) the following: *"provided further,* That, notwithstanding any other provision of law, any registrant who has failed or refused to report for induction shall continue to remain liable for induction and when available shall be immediately inducted.", and

(b) Adding the following new subsection (g) to read as follows:

"(g) The National Security Council shall periodically advise the Director of the Selective Service System and coordinate with him the work of such State and local volunteer advisory committees which the Director of Selective Service may establish, with respect to the identification, selection, and deferment of needed professional and scientific personnel and those engaged in, and preparing for, critical skills and other essential occupations. In the performance of its duties under this subsection the National Security Council shall consider the needs of both the Armed Forces and the civilian segment of the population."

(3) Section 5 (a) (50 App. U.S.C. 455 (a)) is amended by inserting "(1)" immediately after "SEC. 5.(a)"; and by adding at the end thereof a new paragraph as follows:

"(2) Notwithstanding the provisions of paragraph (1) of this subsection, the President in establishing the order of induction for registrants within the various age groups found qualified for induction shall not effect any change in the method of determining the relative order of induction for such registrants within such age groups as has been heretofore established and in effect on the date of enactment of this paragraph, unless authorized by law enacted after the date of enactment of the Military Selective Service Act of 1967."

(4) Section 6 (c) (2) (A) (50 App. U.S.C. 456 (c) (2) (A)), is amended to read as follows:

"(2) (A) Any person, other than a person referred to in subsection (d) of this section, who —

"(i) prior to the issuance of orders for him to report for induction; or

"(ii) prior to the date scheduled for his induction and pursuant to a proclamation by the Governor of a State to the effect that the authorized strength of any organized unit of the National Guard of that State cannot be maintained by the enlistment or appointment of persons who have not been issued orders to report for induction under this title; or

"(iii) prior to the date scheduled for his induction and pursuant to a determination by the President that the strength of the Ready Reserve of the Army Reserve, Naval Reserve, Marine Corps Reserve, Air Force Reserve, or Coast Guard Reserve cannot be maintained by the enlistment or appointment of persons who have not been issued orders to report for induction, under this title;

enlists or accepts appointment, before attaining the age of 26 years, in the Ready Reserve of any Reserve component of the Armed Forces, the Army National Guard, or the Air National Guard, shall be deferred from training and service under this title so long as he serves satisfactorily as a member of an organized unit of such Reserve or National Guard in accordance with section 270 of title 10 or section 502 of title 32, United States Code, as the case may be, or satisfactorily performs such other Ready Reserve service as may be prescribed by the Secretary of Defense. Enlistments or appointments under subparagraphs (ii) and (iii) of this clause may be accepted notwithstanding the provisions of section 15 (d) of this title. Notwithstanding the provisions of subsection (h) of this section, no person deferred under this clause who has completed six years of such satisfactory service as a member of the Ready Reserve or National Guard, and who during such service has performed active duty for training with an armed force for not less than four consecutive months, shall be liable for induction for training and service under this Act, except after a declaration of war or national emergency made by the Congress after August 9, 1955. In no event shall the number of enlistments or appointments made under authority of this paragraph in any fiscal year in any Reserve component of the Armed Forces or in the Army National Guard or the Air National Guard cause the personnel strength of such Reserve component or the Army National Guard or the Air National Guard, as the case may be, to exceed the personnel strength for which funds have been made available by the Congress for such fiscal year."

(5) Section 6 (a) (50 App. U.S.C. 456 (a)) is hereby amended to read as follows:

"SEC. 6. (a) (1) Commissioned officers, warrant officers, pay clerks, enlisted men, and aviation cadets of the Regular Army, the Navy, the Air Force, the Marine Corps, the Coast Guard, and the Environmental Science Services Administration; cadets, United States Military Academy; midshipmen, United States Naval Academy; cadets, United States Air Force Academy; cadets, United States Coast Guard Academy; midshipmen , Merchant Marine Reserve, United States Naval Reserves; students enrolled in an officer procurement program at military colleges the curriculum of which is approved by the Secretary of Defense; members of the reserve components of the Armed Forces, and the Coast Guard, while on active duty; and foreign diplomatic representatives, technical attachés of foreign embassies and legations, consuls general, consuls, vice consuls and other consular agents of foreign countries who are not citizens of the United States, and members of their families, and persons in other categories to be specified by the President who are not citizens of the United States, shall not be required to be registered under section 3 and shall be relieved from liability for training and service under section 4, except that aliens admitted for permanent residence in the United States shall not be so exempted. Any person who subsequent to June 24, 1948, serves on active duty for a period of not less than eighteen months in the armed forces of a nation with which the United States is associated in mutual defense activities as defined by the President, may be exempted from training and service, but not from registration, in accordance with regulations prescribed by the President, except that no such exemption shall be granted to any person who is a national of a country which does not grant reciprocal privileges to citizens of the United States: *Provided,* That any active duty performed prior to June 24, 1948, by a person in the armed forces of a country allied with the United States during World War II and with which the United States is associated in such mutual defense activities, shall be credited in the computation of such eighteen-month period: *Provided further,* That any person who is in a medical, dental, or allied specialist category not otherwise deferred or exempted under this subsection shall be liable for registration and training and service until the thirty-fifth anniversary of the date of his birth.

"(2) Commissioned officers of the Public Health Service and members of the Reserve of the Public Health Service while on active duty and assigned to staff the various offices and bureaus of the Public Health Service, including the

National Institutes of Health, or assigned to the Coast Guard, the Bureau of Prisons, Department of Justice, or the Environmental Science Services Administration, shall not be required to be registered under section 3 and shall be relieved from liability for training and service under section 4. Notwithstanding the preceding sentence, commissioned officers of the Public Health Service and members of the Reserve of the Public Health Service who, prior to the enactment of this paragraph, had been detailed or assigned to duty other than that specified in the preceding sentence shall not be required to be registered under section 3 and shall be relieved from liability for training and service under section 4."

(6) Section 6 (h) (50 App. U.S.C. 456 (h)) is amended to read as follows:

"(h) (1) Except as otherwise provided in this paragraph, the President shall, under such rules and regulations as he may prescribe, provide for the deferment from training and service in the Armed Forces of persons satisfactorily pursuing a full-time course of instruction at a college, university, or similar institution of learning and who request such deferment. A deferment granted to any person under authority of the preceding sentence shall continue until such person completes the requirements for his baccalaureate degree, fails to pursue satisfactorily a full-time course of instruction, or attains the twenty-fourth anniversary of the date of his birth, whichever first occurs. Student deferments provided for under this paragraph may be substantially restricted or terminated by the President only upon finding by him that the needs of the Armed Forces require such action. No person who has received a student deferment under the provisions of this paragraph shall thereafter be granted a deferment under this subsection, nor shall any such person be granted a deferment under subsection (i) of this section if he has been awarded a baccalaureate degree, except for extreme hardship to dependents (under regulations governing hardship deferments), or for graduate study, occupation, or employment necessary to the maintenance of the national health, safety, or interest. Any person who is in a deferred status under the provisions of subsection (i) of this section after attaining the nineteenth anniversary of the date of his birth, or who requests and is granted a student deferment under this paragraph, shall, upon the termination of such deferred status or deferment, and if qualified, be liable for induction as a registrant within the prime age group irrespective of his actual age, unless he is otherwise deferred under one of the exceptions specified in the preceding sentence. As used in this subsection, the term 'prime age group' means the age group which has been designated by the President as the age group from which selections for induction into the Armed Forces are first to be made after delinquents and volunteers.

"(2) Except as otherwise provided in this subsection the President is authorized, under such rules and regulations as he may prescribe, to provide for the deferment from training and service in the Armed Forces of any or all categories of persons whose employment in industry, agriculture, or other occupations or employment, or whose continued service in an Office (other than an Office described in subsection (f)) under the United States or any State. territory, or possession, or the District of Columbia, or whose activity in graduate study, research, or medical, dental, veterinary, optometric, osteopathic, scientific, pharmaceutical, chiropractic, chiropodial, or other endeavors is found to be necessary to the maintenance of the national health, safety, or interest: *Provided,* That no person within any such category shall be deferred except upon the basis of his individual status: *Provided further,* That persons who are or may be deferred under the provisions of this section shall remain liable for training and service in the Armed Forces under the provisions of section 4 (a) of this Act until the thirty-fifth anniversary of the date of their birth. This proviso shall not be construed to prevent the continued deferment of such persons if otherwise deferrable under any other provisions of this Act. The President is also authorized, under such rules and regulations as he may prescribe, to provide for the deferment from training and service in the Armed Forces (1) of any or all categories of persons in a status with respect to persons (other than wives alone, except in cases of extreme hardship) dependent upon them for support which renders their deferment advisable, and (2) of any or all categories of those persons found to be physically, mentally, or morally deficient or defective. For the purpose of determining whether or not the deferment of any person is advisable, because of his status with respect to persons dependent upon him for support, any payments of allowances which are payable by the United States to the dependents of persons serving in the Armed Forces of the United States shall be taken into consideration, but the fact that such payments of allowances are payable shall not be deemed conclusively to remove the grounds for deferment when the dependency is based upon financial considerations and shall not be deemed to remove the ground for deferment when the dependency is based upon other than financial considerations and cannot be eliminated by financial assistance to the dependents. Except as otherwise provided in this subsection, the President is also authorized, under such rules and regulations as he may prescribe, to provide for the deferment from training and service in the Armed Forces of any or all categories of persons who have children, or wives and children, with whom they maintain a bona fide family relationship in their homes. No deferment from such training and service in the Armed Forces shall be made in the case of any individual except upon the basis of the status of such individual. There shall be posted in a conspicuous place at the office of each local board a list setting forth the names and classifications of those persons who have been classified by such local board. The President may, in carrying out the provisions of this title, recommend criteria for the classification of persons subject to induction under this title, and to the extent that such action is determined by the President to be consistent with the national interest, recommend that such criteria be administered uniformly throughout the United States whenever practicable; except that no local board, appeal board, or other agency of appeal of the Selective Service System shall be required to postpone or defer any person by reason of his activity in study, research, or medical, dental, veterinary, optometric, osteopathic, scientific, pharmaceutical, chiropractic, chiropodial, or other endeavors found to be necessary to the maintenance of the national health, safety, or interest solely on the basis of any test, examination, selection system, class standing, or any other means conducted, sponsored, administered, or prepared by any agency or department of the Federal Government, or any private institution, corporation, association, partnership, or individual employed by an agency or department of the Federal Government."

(7) Section 6 (j) (50 App. U.S.C. 456 (j)) is amended to read as follows:

"(j) Nothing contained in this title shall be construed to require any person to be subject to combatant training and service in the armed forces of the United States who, by reason of religious training and belief, is conscientiously opposed to participation in war in any form. As used in this subsection, the term 'religious training and belief' does not include essentially political, sociological, or philosophical views, or a merely personal moral code. Any person claiming exemption from combatant training and service because of such conscientious objections whose claim is sustained by the local board shall, if he is inducted into the armed forces under this title, be assigned to noncombatant service as defined by the President, or shall, if he is found to be conscientiously opposed to participation in such noncombatant service, in lieu of such induction, be ordered by his local board, subject to such regulations as the President may prescribe, to perform for a period equal to the period prescribed in section 4 (b) such civilian work contributing to the maintenance of the national health, safety, or interest as the local board pursuant to Presidential regulations may deem appropriate and any such person who knowingly fails or neglects to obey any such order from his local board shall be deemed, for the purposes of section 12 of this title, to have knowingly failed or neglected to perform a duty required of him under this title."

(8) Section 10 (b) (3) (50 App. U.S.C. 460 (b) (3)) is amended by:

(a) Inserting the following new proviso at the end of the first sentence thereof: "*Provided,* That no person shall be disqualified from serving as a counselor to registrants, including service as Government appeal agent, because of his membership in a Reserve component of the Armed Forces."

(b) Deleting the colon immediately preceding the first proviso, substituting a period therefor and inserting the following: "No member shall serve on any local board or appeal board for more than twenty-five years, or after he has attained the age of seventy-five. No citizen shall be denied membership on any local board or appeal board on account of sex. The requirements outlined in the preceding two sentences shall be fully implemented and effective not later than January 1, 1968."

(c) Inserting immediately before the last sentence thereof the following: "No judicial review shall be made of the classification or processing of any registrant by local boards, appeal boards, or the President, except as a defense to a criminal prosecution instituted under section 12 of this title, after the registrant has responded either affirmatively or negatively to an order to report for induction, or for civilian work in the case of a registrant determined to be opposed to participation in war in any form: *Provided,* That such review shall go to the question of the jurisdiction herein reserved to local boards, appeal boards, and the President only when there is no basis in fact for the classification assigned to such registrant."

(9) Sections 10 (b) (4) (50 App. U.S.C. 460 (b) (4)) is amended by deleting the semicolon at the end of the paragraph, substituting a colon therefor, and adding the following: "*Provided further,* That an employee of a local board having supervisory duties with respect to other employees of one or more local boards shall be designated as the 'executive secretary' of the local board or boards: *And provided further,* That the term of employment of such 'executive secretary' in such position shall in no case exceed ten years except when reappointed;".

(10) Section 10 (g) (50 App. U.S.C. 460 (g)) is amended to read as follows:

"(g) The Director of Selective Service shall submit to the Congress semiannually a written report covering the operation of the Selective Service System and such report shall include, by States, information as to the number of persons registered under this Act; the number of persons inducted into the military service under this Act; the number of deferments granted under this Act and the basis for such deferments; and such other specific kinds of information as the Congress may from time to time request."

(11) Section 12 (50 App. U.S.C. 462) is amended by:

(a) Deleting the last sentence of subsection (a) and substituting the following in lieu thereof: "Precedence shall be given by courts to the trial of cases arising under this title, and such cases shall be advanced on the docket for immediate hearing, and an appeal from the decision or decree of any United States district court or United States court of appeals shall take precedence over all other cases pending before the court to which the case has been referred."

(b) Adding a new subsection (c) as follows:

"(c) The Department of Justice shall proceed as expeditiously as possible with a prosecution under this section, or with an appeal, upon the request of the

Director of Selective Service System or shall advise the House of Representatives and the Senate in writing the reasons for its failure to do so."

(12) Section 17 (c) (50 App. U.S.C. 467 (c)) is amended by striking out "July 1, 1967" and inserting in place thereof "July 1, 1971".

SEC. 2. Section 1 of the Act of August 3, 1950, chapter 537, as amended (77 Stat. 4), is amended by striking out "July 1, 1967" and inserting in place thereof "July 1, 1971".

SEC. 3. Section 16 of the Dependents Assistance Act of 1950, as amended (50 App. U.S.C. 2216), is amended by striking out "July 1, 1967" and inserting in place thereof "July 1, 1971".

SEC. 4. Section 9 of the Act of June 27, 1957, Public Law 85–62, as amended (77 Stat. 4), is amended by striking out "July 1, 1967" and inserting in place thereof "July 1, 1971".

SEC. 4. Sections 302 and 303 of title 37, United States Code, are each amended by striking out "July 1, 1967" whenever that date appears and inserting in place thereof "July 1, 1971".

SEC. 6. Chapter 39 of title 10, United States Code, is amended –

(1) by inserting the following new section after section 673:

"§673a. Ready Reserve: members not assigned to, or participating satisfactorily in, units

"(a) Notwithstanding any other provision of law, the President may order to active duty any member of the Ready Reserve of an armed force who –

"(1) is not assigned to, or participating satisfactorily in, a unit of the Ready Reserve;

"(2) has not fulfilled his statutory reserve obligation; and

"(3) has not served on active duty for a total of 24 months.

"(b) A member who is ordered to active duty under this section may be required to serve on active duty until his total service on active duty equals 24 months. If his enlistment or other period of military service would expire before he has served the required period under this section, it may be extended until he has served the required period.

"(c) To achieve fair treatment among members of the Ready Reserve who are being considered for active duty under this section, appropriate consideration shall be given to –

"(1) family responsibilities; and

"(2) employment necessary to maintain the national health, safety, or interest."; and

(2) by inserting the following item in the analysis:

"673a Ready Reserve: members not assigned to, or participating satisfactorily in, units."

Approved June 30, 1967.

Legislative History:

HOUSE REPORTS: No. 267 (Comm. on Armed Services) and
No. 346 (Comm. of Conference).
SENATE REPORT No. 209 (Comm. on Armed Services).
CONGRESSIONAL RECORD, Vol. 113 (1967):
May 9, 10: Considered in Senate.
May 11: Considered and passed Senate.
May 25: Considered and passed House, amended.
June 12, 14: Senate agreed to conference report.
June 20: House agreed to conference report.

Executive Order

Amending the Selective Service Regulations

By virtue of the authority vested in me by the Military Selective Service Act of 1967 (62 Stat. 604), as amended, I hereby prescribe the following amendments of the Selective Service Regulations prescribed by Executive Orders No. 9979 of July 2, 1948, No. 9988 of August 20, 1948, No. 10008 of October 18, 1948, No. 10001 of September 17, 1948, No. 10202 of January 12, 1951, No. 10292 of September 25, 1951, No. 10363 of June 17, 1952, No. 10366 of June 26, 1952, No. 10469 of July 11, 1953, No. 10562 of September 20, 1954, No. 10659 of February 15, 1956, No. 10714 of June 13, 1957, No. 10735 of October 17, 1957, No. 10809 of March 19, 1959, No. 10984 of January 5, 1962, No. 11098 of March 14, 1963, No. 11188 of November 17, 1964, No. 11241 of August 26, 1965, No. 11266 of January 18, 1966, and No. 11350 of May 3, 1967, and constituting portions of Chapter XVI of Title 32 of the Code of Federal Regulations:

1. The term "Military Selective Service Act of 1967" shall be substituted for "Universal Military Training and Service Act, as amended," wherever the latter appears in the Selective Service Regulations.

2. The term "Environmental Science Services Administration" shall be substituted for "Coast and Geodetic Survey" wherever the latter appears in the Selective Service Regulations.

3. Part 1604, *Selective Service Officers,* is amended as follows:

(a) Section 1604.22, Composition and Appointment, is amended to read as follows:

"For each appeal board area an appeal board, normally of five members, shall be appointed by the President, upon recommendation of the Governor. The members shall be citizens of the United States who are not members of the armed forces or any reserve component thereof; they shall be residents of the area in which their board is appointed; and they shall be at least 30 years of age. No member shall serve on an appeal board for more than twenty-five years, or after he has attained the age of seventy-five years. The appeal board should be a composite board, representative of the activities of its area, and as such should include one member from labor, one member from industry, one physician, one lawyer, and, where applicable, one member from agriculture. If the number of appeals sent to the board becomes too great for the board to handle without undue delay, additional panels of five members similarly constituted shall be appointed to the board by the President, upon recommendation of the Governor. Each such panel shall have full authority to act on all cases assigned to it. Each panel shall act separately. The State Director of Selective Service shall coordinate the work of all the panels to effect an equitable distribution of the workload."

(b) Section 1604.52, Composition and Appointment, is amended by:

(1) Amending paragraph (c) to read as follows:

"(c) The members of local boards shall be citizens of the United States who shall be residents of a county in which their local board has jurisdiction and who shall also, if at all practicable, be residents of the area in which their local board has jurisdiction. No member of a local board shall be a member of the armed forces or any reserve component thereof. Members of local boards shall be at least 30 years of age."

(2) Adding at the end a new paragraph (d) to read as follows:

"(d) No member shall serve on any local board for more than twenty-five years, or after he has attained the age of seventy-five years."

(c) Section 1604.71, Appointment and Duties, is amended as follows:

(1) Paragraph (c) is amended to read as follows:

"(c) Each government appeal agent and associate government appeal agent shall be, whenever possible, a person with legal training and experience."

(2) A new paragraph (e) is added, to read as follows:

"(e) The State Director of Selective Service may authorize any duly appointed government appeal agent or associate government appeal agent to perform such duties for any local board within the state."

4. Part 1611, *Duty and Responsibility to Register,* is amended as follows:

(a) Paragraph (a) of section 1611.2, Persons Not Required to be Registered, is amended to read as follows:

"(a) Under the provisions of section 6 (a) of the Military Selective Service Act of 1967 the following persons are not required to be registered:

"(1) Commissioned officers, warrant officers, pay clerks, enlisted men, and aviation cadets of the Regular Army, the Navy, the Air Force, the Marine Corps, the Coast Guard, the Environmental Science Services Administration, and the Public Health Service;

"(2) cadets, United States Military Academy;

"(3) midshipmen, United States Navy;

"(4) cadets, United States Air Force Academy;

"(5) cadets, United States Coast Guard Academy;

"(6) midshipmen, Merchant Marine Reserve, United States Naval Reserves;

"(7) students enrolled in an officer procurement program at military colleges the curriculum of which is approved by the Secretary of Defense;

"(8) members of the reserve components of the Armed Forces, the Coast Guard, and the Public Health Service, while on active duty, provided that such active duty in the Public Health Service that commences after the enactment of the Military Selective Service Act of 1967 is performed by members of the

Reserve of the Public Health Service while assigned to staff any of the various offices and bureaus of the Public Health Service, including the National Institutes of Health, or while assigned to the Coast Guard, the Bureau of Prisons of the Department of Justice, or the Environmental Science Services Administration; and

"(9) foreign diplomatic representatives, technical attachés of foreign embassies and legations, consuls general, consuls, vice consuls and other consular agents of foreign countries who are not citizens of the United States, and members of their families."

(b) Section 1611.5, Registration of Certain Persons Entering the United States, is amended by striking paragraph (a) and redesignating the provisions of the present paragraph (b) as section 1611.5.

5. Part 1622, *Classification Rules and Principles,* is amended as follows:

(a) Section 1622.1, General Principles of Classification, is amended as follows:

(1) Paragraph (a) is amended to read as follows:

"(a) (1) Primary liability for military training and service provided by the selective service law is placed on those persons in the following categories who are between the ages of 18 years and 6 months and 26 years:

"(i) Every male citizen of the United States;

"(ii) Every male alien admitted to the United States for permanent residence; and

"(iii) Every male alien who has remained in the United States in a status other than that of a permanent resident for a period or periods totaling one year.

"(2) Persons who on June 19, 1951, or thereafter were deferred under the provisions of section 6 (c) (2) (A) of the Act that were in effect prior to September 3 1963 remain liable for training and service until they attain age 28.

"(3) Persons whose liability for training and service is extended by the Act to age 35 are: —

"(i) persons in a medical, dental or allied specialist category, and

"(ii) persons who on June 19, 1951, were, or thereafter are, deferred under any other provisions of section 6 of the Act.

(2) A new paragraph (e) is prescribed, to read as follows:

"(e) Notwithstanding any other provision of law, any registrant who has failed or refused to report for induction shall continue to remain liable for induction, and when available shall be immediately inducted."

(b) Section 1622.11, Class I-A-O: Conscientious Objector Available for Noncombatant Military Service Only, is amended by deleting paragraph (b) thereof, and paragraph (a) is redesignated as section 1622.11.

(c) Paragraph (d) of section 1622.12, Class I-C: Member of the Armed Forces of the United States, the Environmental Science Services Administration, or the Public Health Service, is amended to read as follows:

"(d) Exclusive of periods for training only, every registrant who is a member of a reserve component of the Armed Forces and is on active duty, and every member of the Reserve of the Public Health Service on duty prior to the enactment of the Military Selective Service Act of 1967 or who after such enactment is on active duty and assigned to staff the various offices and bureaus of the Public Health Service including the National Institutes of Health, or assigned to the Coast Guard, or the Bureau of Prisons of the Department of Justice, or the Environmental Science Services Administration."

(d) Paragraph (f) of section 1622.13, Class I-D: Member of Reserve Component or Student Taking Military Training, is amended to read as follows:

"(f) In Class I-D shall be placed any registrant, other than a registrant referred to in paragraph (b) or (g) of this section, who —

"(1) prior to the issuance of orders for him to report for induction; or

"(2) prior to the date scheduled for his induction and pursuant to a proclamation by the Governor of a State to the effect that the authorized strength of any unit of the National Guard of that State cannot be maintained by the enlistment or appointment of persons who have not been issued orders to report for induction; or

"(3) prior to the date scheduled for his induction and pursuant to a determination by the President that the strength of the Ready Reserve of the Army Reserve, Naval Reserve, Marine Corps Reserve, Air Force Reserve, or Coast Guard Reserve cannot be maintained by the enlistment or appointment of persons who have not been issued orders to report for induction; enlists or accepts appointment, before attaining the age of 26 years, in the Ready Reserve of any Reserve component of the Armed Forces, the Army National Guard, or the Air National Guard. Such registrant shall remain eligible for Class I-D so long as he serves satisfactorily as a member of an organized unit of such Ready Reserve or National Guard, or satisfactorily performs such other Ready Reserve service as may be prescribed by the Secretary of Defense, or serves satisfactorily as a member of the Ready Reserve of another reserve component, the Army National Guard, or the Air National Guard, as the case may be."

(e) Paragraph (b) of section 1622.14, Class I-O: Conscientious Objector Available for Civilian Work Contributing to the Maintenance of the National Health, Safety, or Interest, is hereby rescinded, and paragraph (a) is redesignated as section 1622.14.

(f) Paragraph (b) of section 1622.15, Class I-S: Student Deferred by Statute, is amended to read as follows:

"(b) In Class I-S shall be placed any registrant who while satisfactorily pursuing a full-time course of instruction at a college, university or similar institution of learning and during his academic year at such institution is ordered to report for induction, except that no registrant shall be placed in Class I-S under the provisions of this paragraph

"(1) who has previously been placed in Class I-S thereunder or

"(2) who has been deferred as a student in Class II-S and has received his baccalaureate degree. A registrant who is placed in Class I-S under the provision of this paragraph shall be retained in Class I-S

"(1) until the end of his academic year or

"(2) until he ceases satisfactorily to pursue such course of instruction, whichever is the earlier. The date of the classification in Class I-S and the date of its termination shall be entered in the "Remarks" column of the Classification Record (SSS Form 102) and be identified on that record as Class I-S (C)."

(g) Section 1622.22, Class II-A: Registrant Deferred Because of Civilian Occupation (Except Agriculture and Activity in Study), is amended by designating the present provisions thereof as paragraph (a) and by adding thereto a new paragraph (b), to read as follows:

"(b) In Class II-A shall be placed any registrant who is preparing for critical skills and other essential occupations as identified by the Director of Selective Service upon the advice of the National Security Council."

(h) Paragraph (c) of section 1622.23, Necessary Employment Defined, is amended to read as follows: "(c) The Director of Selective Service may from time to time, upon the advice of the National Security Council, identify needed professional and scientific personnel and those engaged in and preparing for critical skills and other essential occupations."

(i) Section 1622.24, Class II-C: Registrant Deferred Because of Agricultural Occupation, is amended by rescinding paragraph (c) thereof.

(j) Section 1622.25, Class II-S: Registrant Deferred Because of Activity in Study, is amended to read as follows:

"(a) In Class II-S shall be placed any registrant who has requested such deferment and who is satisfactorily pursuing a fulltime course of instruction at a college, university, or similar institution of learning, such deferment to continue until such registrant completes the requirement for his baccalaureate degree, fails to pursue satisfactorily a full-time course of instruction, or attains the twenty-fourth anniversary of the date of his birth, whichever occurs first.

"(b) In determining eligibility for deferment in Class II-S, a student's 'academic year' shall include the 12-month period following the beginning of his course of study.

"(c) A student shall be deemed to be 'satisfactorily pursuing a full-time course of instruction' when, during his academic year, he has earned, as a minimum, credits toward his degree which, when added to any credits earned during prior academic years, represent a proportion of the total number required to earn his degree at least equal to the proportion which the number of academic years completed bears to the normal number of years established by the school to obtain such degree. For example, a student pursuing a four-year course should have earned 25% of the credits required for his baccalaureate degree at the end of his first academic year, 50% at the end of his second academic year, and 75% at the end of his third academic year.

"(d) It shall be the registrant's duty to provide the local board each year with evidence that he is satisfactorily pursuing a full-time course of instruction at a college, university, or similar institution of learning."

(k) Section 1622.26, Class II-S: Registrant Deferred Because of Activity in Graduate Study, is hereby prescribed, to read as follows:

"(a) In Class II-S shall be placed any registrant who is satisfactorily pursuing a course of graduate study in medicine, dentistry, veterinary medicine, osteopathy or optometry, or in such other subjects necessary to the maintenance of the national health, safety, or interest as are identified by the Director of Selective Service upon the advice of the National Security Council

"(b) Any registrant who is entering his second or subsequent year of post-baccalaureate study without interruption on October 1, 1967, may be placed in Class II-S if his school certifies that he is satisfactorily pursuing a full-time course of instruction leading to his degree; but such registrant shall not be deferred for a course of study leading to a master's degree or the equivalent for more than one additional year, or for a course of study leading to a doctoral or professional degree or the equivalent (or combination of master's and doctoral degrees) for more than a total of five years, inclusive of the years already used in such course of study, or for one additional year, whichever is greater. Any registrant enrolled for his first year of post-baccalaureate study in a graduate school or a professional school on October 1, 1967, or accepted for admission involving enrolled status on October 1, 1967, may be placed in Class II-S if he has entered the first class commencing after the date he completed the requirements for admission and shall be deferred for one academic year only, or until he ceases satisfactorily to pursue such course of instruction, whichever is the earlier."

(1) Paragraph (a) of section 1622.30, Class III-A: Registrant With a Child or Children; and Registrant Deferred by Reason of Extreme Hardship to Dependents, is amended to read as follows:

"(a) In Class III-A shall be placed any registrant who has a child or children with whom he maintains a bona fide family relationship in their home and who is not a physician, dentist or veterinarian, or who is not in an allied specialist category which may be announced by the Director of Selective Service after being advised by the Secretary of Defense that a special requisition under authority of section 1631.4 of these regulations will be issued by the delivery of registrants in such category, except that a registrant who is classified in Class II-S after the date of enactment of the Military Selective Service Act of 1967 shall not be eligible for classification in Class III-A under the provisions of this paragraph."

(m) Section 1622.40, Class IV-A: Registrant Who Has Completed Service; Sole Surviving Son, is amended by:

(1) Amending subparagraph (3) of paragraph (a) to read as follows:

"(3) A registrant who has served on active duty for a period of not less than twenty-four months as a commissioned officer in the Environmental Science Services Administration or in the Public Health Service, provided that such period of active duty in the Public Health Service as a commissioned reserve officer commencing after the date of enactment of the Military Selective Service Act of 1967 shall have been performed by the registrant while assigned to staff any of the various offices and bureaus of the Public Health Service including the National Institutes of Health, or while assigned to the Coast Guard, or the Bureau of Prisons of the Department of Justice, or the Environmental Science Services Administration."

(2) Amending paragraph (b) by adding at the end thereof a new subparagraph (6), to read as follows:

"(6) Periods of active duty of members of the Reserve of the Public Health Service commencing after the date of enactment of the Military Selective Service Act of 1967 other than when assigned to staff any of the various offices and bureaus of the Public Health Service, including the National Institutes of Health, or the Coast Guard or the Bureau of Prisons of the Department of Justice, or the Environmental Science Services Administration."

(n) Section 1622.42, Class IV-C: Aliens, is amended by adding thereto a new paragraph (d), to read as follows:

"(d) In Class IV-C shall be placed an alien who has registered at a time when he was required by the selective service law to present himself for and submit to registration and thereafter has acquired status within one of the groups of persons exempt from registration."

(o) Paragraph (a) and (b) of section 1622.50, Class V-A: Registrant Over the Age of Liability for Military Service, are amended to read as follows:

"(a) In Class V-A shall be placed every registrant who has attained the twenty-sixth anniversary of the day of his birth except —

"(1) those registrants who are in active military service in the armed forces and are in Class I-C,

"(2) those registrants who are performing civilian work contributing to the maintenance of the national health, safety, or interest in accordance with the order of the local board and are in Class I-W,

"(3) those registrants who have consented to induction,

"(4) those registrants who on June 19, 1951, or at any time thereafter, were deferred under the provisions of section 6 of the Military Selective Service Act of 1967, and

"(5) registrants who are in a medical, dental, or allied specialist category."

"(b) In Class V-A shall be placed every registrant who has attained the twenty-eighth anniversary of the day of his birth except

"(1) those registrants who are in active military service in the armed forces and are in Class I-C,

"(2) those registrants who are performing civilian work contributing to the maintenance of the national health, safety, or interest in accordance with the order of the local board and are in Class I-W,

"(3) those registrants who have consented to induction,

"(4) those registrants who on June 19, 1951, or at any time thereafter, were deferred under any provisions of section 6 of the Military Selective Service Act of 1967 other than the provisions of subsection (c) (2) (A) of such section which were in effect prior to September 3, 1963, and

"(5) those registrants who are in a medical, dental, or allied specialist category."

6. Part 1626, *Appeal to Appeal Board*, is amended as follows:

(a) Subparagraph (3) and (4) of paragraph (b) of section 1626.24, Review by Appeal Board, are rescinded.

(b) Section 1626.25, Special Provisions When Appeal Involves Claim that Registrant Is a Conscientious Objector, is hereby rescinded.

7. Paragraph (a) of section 1630.4, of Part 1630, *Volunteers*, is amended to read as follows:

"(a) Disregarding all other grounds for deferment, he would be classified in Class II-A, Class II-C, or Class III-A;"

8. Part 1631, *Quotas and Calls*, is amended as follows:

(a) Section 1631.4, Calls by the Secretary of Defense, is amended to read as follows:

"(a) The Secretary of Defense may from time to time place with the Director of Selective Service a call or requisition for a specified number of men required for induction into the Armed Forces. The Secretary of Defense may also from time to time place with the Director of Selective Service a call or requisition for a specified number of men in any medical, dental, or allied specialist category required for induction into the Armed Forces.

"(b) When future needs of the Armed Forces may require it, the Secretary of Defense also may from time to time place with the Director of Selective Service a call or requisition for a specified number of men for induction into the Armed Forces, designating the age group or groups from which such men shall be selected.

"(c) All registrants born within any calendar year shall constitute an age group within the meaning of this section.

"(d) The Secretary of Defense shall present such calls or requisition to the Director of Selective Service not less than 60 days prior to the period during which the delivery and induction of such men are to be accomplished."

(b) Paragraph (a) of section 1631.5, Calls by the Director of Selective Service, is amended to read as follows:

"(a) The Director of Selective Service shall, upon receipt of a call or requisition from the Secretary of Defense for a specified number of men to be inducted into the Armed Forces, allocate such call or requisition among the several States."

(c) Section 1631.7, Action by Local Board Upon Receipt of Notice of Call, is amended as follows:

(1) Paragraph (a) is amended by adding the phrase, "When a call is placed without designation of age group or groups," immediately before the phrase "Each local board. . ." at the beginning of the first sentence so that the beginning will read as follows: "When a call is placed without designation of age group or groups, each local board, upon receiving a. . ."; and is further amended by striking from the second proviso thereof the phrase "if an appeal is not pending in his case and the period during which an appeal may be taken has expired," so that the beginning of the second proviso will read as follows: "*And provided further,* That a registrant classified in Class I-A or Class I-A-O who has volunteered for induction may be selected and ordered for induction. ... "

(2) Paragraph (b) is redesignated as paragraph (c) and a new paragraph (b) is prescribed to read as follows:

"(b) When a call is placed with designation of age group or groups, each local board, upon receiving a Notice of Call on Local Board (SSS Form 201) from the State Director of Selective Service for a specified number of men to be delivered for induction, shall select and order to report for induction the number of men required to fill the call from among its registrants who have been classified in Class I-A and Class I-A-O and who have been found acceptable for service in the Armed Forces and to whom the local board has mailed a Statement of Acceptability (DD Form 62) at least 21 days before the date fixed for induction; *Provided,* That a registrant classified in Class I-A or Class I-A-O who is a delinquent may be selected and ordered to report for induction to fill an induction call notwithstanding the fact that he has not been found acceptable for service in the Armed Forces and has not been mailed a Statement of Acceptability (DD Form 62); *And provided further,* That a registrant classified in Class I-A or Class I-A-O who has volunteered for induction may be selected and ordered to report for induction notwithstanding the fact that he has not been found acceptable for service in the Armed Forces and regardless of whether a Statement of Acceptability (DD Form 62) has been mailed to him. Such registrants shall be selected and ordered to report for induction in the following order:

"(1) Delinquents who have attained the age of 19 years in the order of their dates of birth with the oldest being selected first.

"(2) Volunteers who have not attained the age of 26 years in the sequence in which they have volunteered for induction.

"(3) Registrants in the designated age group; and registrants who previously have been deferred in Class I-S-C after attaining the age of 19 years, or who have requested and have been granted a deferment in Class II-S after the enactment of the Military Selective Service Act of 1967, and who are no longer so deferred, shall be considered as being within the age group called regardless of their actual age. These registrants shall be integrated and called according to the month and day of their birth, the oldest first. Registrants who have been deferred in Class I-S-C or Class II-S and have been integrated with a prime age group under the provisions of this paragraph shall, for the purposes of selection and call, thereafter be considered a member of such age group."

(d) Section 1631.8, Registrants Who Shall Be Inducted Without Calls, is amended by adding at the end thereof a new paragraph (c), to read as follows:

"(c) Notwithstanding any other provision of law, any registrant who has failed or refused to report for induction shall continue to remain liable for induction and when available shall be immediately inducted."

9. Subparagraph (3) of paragraph (b) of section 1632.20 of Part 1632, *Delivery and Induction,* is amended to read as follows:

"(3) For each registrant found not qualified for service in the Armed Forces, file the original Record of Induction (DD Form 47), the original Report of Medical Examination (Standard Form 88), the copy of the Report of Medical History (Standard Form 89) and any copy of the Application for Voluntary Induction (SSS Form 254) in the Cover Sheet (SSS Form 101) and forward to the State Director of Selective Service the copy of the Record of Induction (DD Form 47)."

10. Part 1642, *Delinquents,* is amended as follows:

(a) Section 1642.10, Restriction on Classification and Induction of Delinquents, is amended to read as follows:

"No delinquent registrant shall be placed in Class I-A, Class I-A-O, or Class I-O under the provisions of section 1642.12 or shall be ordered to report for induction under the provisions of section 1642.13 or section 1631.7 of this chapter, or, in the case of a conscientious objector opposed to noncombatant training and service, ordered to report for civilian work in lieu of induction, unless the local board has declared him to be a delinquent in accordance with the provisions of section 1642.4 and thereafter has not removed him from such delinquency status."

(b) Section 1642.12, Classification of Delinquent Registrant, is amended to read as follows:

"Any delinquent registrant between the ages of 18 years and 6 months and 26 years and any delinquent registrant between the ages of 26 and 28 who was deferred under the provisions of section 6 (c) (2) (A) of the Military Selective Service Act of 1967 which were in effect prior to September 3, 1963, and any delinquent registrant between the ages of 26 and 35 who on June 19, 1951, was, or thereafter has been or may be, deferred under any other provision of section 6 of such Act, including the provisions of subsection (c) (2) (A) in effect on and after September 3, 1963, may be classified in or reclassified into Class I-A, Class I-A-O or Class I-O, whichever is applicable, regardless of other circumstances: *Provided,* That a delinquent registrant who by reason of his service in the Armed Forces is eligible for classification into Class IV-A may not be classified or reclassified into Class I-A, Class I-A-O or Class I-O under this section unless such action is specifically authorized by the Director of Selective Service."

(c) Section 1642.13, Certain Delinquents to Be Ordered to Report for Induction or for Civilian Work in Lieu of Induction, is amended to read as follows:

"The local board shall order each delinquent registrant between the ages of 18 years and 6 months and 26 years and each delinquent registrant between the ages of 26 and 28 who was deferred under the provisions of section 6 (c) (2) (A) of the Military Selective Service Act of 1967 which were in effect prior to September 3, 1963, and each delinquent registrant between the ages of 26 and 35 who on June 19, 1951, was, or thereafter has been or may be, deferred under any other provisions of section 6 of such Act, including the provisions of subsection (c) (2) (A) in effect on and after September 3, 1963, who is classified in or reclassified into Class I-A or Class I-A-O to report for induction in the manner provided in section 1631.7 of this chapter, or in the case of a delinquent registrant classified or reclassified into Class I-O, the local board shall determine the type of civilian work it is appropriate for him to perform and shall order him to perform such civilian work in lieu of induction in accordance with the provisions of Part 1660 of this chapter, unless in either case (a) it has already issued such order, or (b) pursuant to a written request of the United States Attorney, the local board determines not to order such registrant to report for induction or civilian work."

(d) Section 1642.14, Personal Appearance, Reopening, and Appeal, is amended to read as follows:

"(a) When a delinquent registrant is classified in or reclassified into Class I-A, Class I-A-O or Class I-O under the provisions of this part, a personal appearance may be requested and shall be granted under the same circumstances as in any other case.

"(b) The classification of a delinquent registrant who is classified in or reclassified into Class I-A, Class I-A-O or Class I-O under the provisions of this part may be reopened at any time before induction or before the date he is to report for civilian work in the discretion of the local board without regard to the restrictions against reopening prescribed in section 1625.2 of this chapter.

"(c) When a delinquent registrant is classified in or reclassified into Class I-A, Class I-A-O or Class I-O under the provisions of this part, an appeal may be taken under the same circumstances and by the same persons as in any other case."

(e) Section 1642.15, Continuous Duty of Certain Registrants to Report for Induction or for Civilian Work in Lieu of Induction, is amended to read as follows:

"Regardless of the time when or the circumstances under which a registrant fails or has failed to report for induction pursuant to an Order to Report for Induction (SSS Form 252) or pursuant to an Order for Transferred Man to Report for Induction (SSS Form 253), or fails or has failed to report for civilian work in lieu of induction pursuant to an Order to Report for Civilian Work and Statement of Employer (SSS Form 153), it shall thereafter be his continuing duty from day to day to report for induction or for civilian work in lieu of induction to his own local board, and to each local board whose area he enters or in whose area he remains."

(f) Section 1642.21, Procedure, is amended as follows:

(1) Paragraph (c) is redesignated as paragraph (e).

(2) New paragraph (c) and (d) are prescribed to read as follows:

"(c) If a delinquent registrant who is in Class I-O reports to or is brought before a local board other than his own local board, the local board to which he reports or before which he is brought shall advise his own local board by telegram or other expeditious means that the delinquent has reported to or has been brought before such local board, and that he will be ordered under the provisions of Part 1660 to perform civilian work deemed appropriate by such local board for the registrant to perform in lieu of induction, if it is satisfactory to his own local board. The registrant's own local board shall reply by telegram or other expeditious means.

"(d) If the registrant's own local board advises that the registrant is delinquent because he has failed to respond to an Order to Report for Civilian Work and Statement of Employer (SSS Form 153), the local board at which the registrant appeared or was brought shall issue to him written instructions regarding the date and place he is to report for work and the type of work he is to perform. Whenever necessary, travel, meals and lodging may be furnished the registrant under the provisions of section 1660.21 (b) of this chapter."

(3) Paragraph (c), as redesignated, is amended to read as follows:

"(e) If the registrant's own local board advises that no Order to Report for

Induction (SSS Form 252) or Order for Transferred Man to Report for Induction (SSS Form 253) or Order to Report for Civilian Work and Statement of Employer (SSS Form 153) has been issued to such registrant or that the registrant is no longer a delinquent, it shall advise the local board before which the registrant has appeared or has been brought of the action to be taken with reference to such registrant."

The White House 1967   Lyndon B. Johnson

INDEX

Abele, Representative Homer E., 1
Adams, President John, 56
American Association of Junior Colleges, 159, 160
American Association of University Professors, 77, 162
American Civil Liberties Union, 63
American Council on Education, 22, 41, 159–164
  Commission on Federal Relations, 41
American Economic Association, 62
American Friends Service Committee, 68
American Veterans Committee, Conference of, 22, 40, 60, 77, 99, 139, 148
Appeals Agents, 12, 13
Appeals Boards, 7, 12, 13, 88, 90
Apprenticeship Programs, 103, 126, 127, 128
Arends, Representative Leslie, 132
Armed Services Committee, House, 1, 20, 22, 34, 35, 37, 41, 43, 45, 47, 50, 52, 58, 59, 74–76, 85, 86, 96, 99, 113, 130, 135, 138, 141, 147, 148, 153
Armed Services Committee, Senate, 1, 104, 113, 116, 127, 135, 141
Automation, 81

"Baby boom," 50
Baldwin, Hanson, 2
Bates, Representative William, 132
Blandensburg, Battle of, 56
Booth, Wayne, 82
Bradford, Representative Daniel R., 83
Bramson, Leon, 69
Brewster, Kingman, 19, 41, 90, 149
Brewster, Senator Daniel, 67
Brown, Representative George E. Jr., 1
Brown, H. Rap., 140
Bureau of the Budget, 94, 164
Bureau of the Census, 30, 31, 34, 63

Burke, Senator Edward, 9
Burke-Wadsworth Bill, 9
Byrnes, James, 37

Califano, Joseph, 164
Carmichael, Stokely, 122, 140
Cater, Douglass, 164
Channeling, see Selective Service System
Chapman, Bruce, 59, 60, 63, 80, 81, 82, 85
Chicago Conference on the Draft, 22, 60, 62, 67, 80, 139
Civilian Advisory Panel on Military Manpower Procurement, see Clark Report
Civil Rights Movement, 48, 141
Civil War, 36, 48, 49, 57, 58
  bounties, 6, 55–58
  substitutes, 6, 55, 58
Clark, Grenville, 8, 9
Clark, Senator Joseph S., 96, 97, 136
Clark, Mark, 76, 84, 104–107, 122–127, 145, 165
  Panel Report, 45, 54, 55, 76, 80, 83–88, 92, 94, 95, 100, 105, 106, 113–117, 119, 122–127, 139, 141, 145, 149, 155
Clark, Ramsey, 135, 136
Class rank, 20, 22, 39, 41, 77, 78, 80, 82, 110, 160
Clay, Cassius (Mohammed Ali), 140
Coast Guard, 131
Commerce, Department of, 130, 157, 165, 167
Committee on Physicians and Dentists, 13
Computers, 24–28, 53, 54, 81, 87, 88, 89, 98, 110, 157
Conference bill, 134, 135–138, 146
Conference Committee, 104, 132, 133, 137, 146, 167
Conference Report, 104, 132–139, 144
Conscientious objectors, 61, 80, 87, 91, 97,